PRACTICAL MANAGEMENT OF LIPID DISORDERS

EDITED BY

John C. LaRosa, M.D.

HCC
HEALTH CARE COMMUNICATIONS, INC.   FORT LEE, NEW JERSEY

Library of Congress Catalog Card Number: 92-073553

ISBN: 0-945986-18-1

Cover design by Jill E. Kalish.

Contents

›

Introduction

The relationships between circulating lipids, lipoproteins and coronary atherosclerosis have become clearer in the last decade. There is now widespread consensus that lowering of low-density lipoprotein cholesterol (LDL-C) can provide significant health benefits.

The value of changes in other circulating blood lipid levels, including high-density lipoprotein cholesterol (HDL-C) and triglyceride (TG) is less certain. Epidemiologic and clinical data strongly suggest that increases in HDL-C are of value but less consistently demonstrate benefits in triglyceride-lowering. Therapy of abnormal blood lipids may require diet or drug therapy, or both.

This book is meant to be a practical guide to the use of both diet and drug therapy in clinical practice. Chapters on the selections of patients for therapy, the use of both diet and drug therapies and the effects of commonly used drugs, including lipid-lowering agents, antihypertensive agents and gonadal hormones, are presented. The book is intended to be a text for practitioners to be used in their daily patient encounters. A large number of adult Americans are potentially affected with hyper-cholesterolemia and related lipid abnormalities. Proper clinical use of the guidelines provided in this book can provide an effective tool for the successful treatment of an important coronary risk factor.

John C. LaRosa, M.D.
July, 1992

Contributors

Conrad B. Blum, M.D.
Associate Professor of Clinical Medicine
Columbia University
College of Physicians and Surgeons
New York, New York

William Virgil Brown, M.D.
Professor of Medicine
Emory University School of Medicine
Division of Arteriosclerosis and Lipid Metabolism
Atlanta, Georgia

Henry N. Ginsberg, M.D.
Associate Professor of Medicine
Columbia University
College of Physicians and Surgeons
New York, New York

David J. Gordon, M.D., Ph.D.
Cardiovascular Epidemiologist
Bethesda, Maryland

John T. Gwynne, M.D.
Associate Professor of Medicine
Division of Endocrinology
Department of Medicine
University of North Carolina at Chapel Hill
Chapel Hill, North Carolina

Donald B. Hunninghake, M.D.
Professor of Medicine and Pharmacology
Director, Heart Disease Prevention Clinic
University of Minnesota
Minneapolis, Minnesota

John C. LaRosa, M.D.
Dean for Clinical Affairs
Director, Lipid Research Clinic
George Washington University Medical Center
Washington, D.C.

Valery T. Miller, M.D.
Associate Research Professor of Medicine
Medical Director, Lipid Research Clinic
George Washington University Medical Center
Washington, D.C.

Gustav Schonfeld, M.D.
Kountz Professor of Medicine
Director, Division of Atherosclerosis and Lipid Research
Washington University School of Medicine
St. Louis, Missouri

Neil J. Stone, M.D.
Associate Professor of Medicine
Northwestern University School of Medicine
Chicago, Illinois

Diane B. Stoy, R.N., M.A.
Operations Director, Lipid Research Clinic
George Washington University Medical Center
Washington, D.C.

CHAPTER 1

Guidelines for the Diagnosis and Treatment of Lipid Abnormalities

John C. LaRosa, M.D.
Washington, D.C.

INTRODUCTION

In the last decade the value of lowering elevated blood cholesterol for the prevention of clinical coronary artery disease has become well established. The transfer of that concept to clinical practice, however, involves several discrete steps and a fund of knowledge that may not yet be readily available to all physicians.

In this chapter, the currently recommended approach to identifying and selecting patients who require cholesterol lowering will be reviewed.

SCREENING FOR HIGH BLOOD CHOLESTEROL

Overall Guidelines

As the relationship between high blood cholesterol and coronary heart disease (CHD) has gained widespread public recognition, various screening projects of one kind or another have appeared. These projects range from formal programs sponsored by hospitals and other medical facilities with strong physician support to more commercial enterprises in shopping malls and other public places. The National Cholesterol Education Program (NCEP), in its initial report describing guidelines for identifying and treating adults with hypercholesterolemia,[1] did not endorse such mass screening. Rather, the report emphasized that cholesterol testing should be part of a physician-patient encounter.

Subsequent to the issuance of that report, however, it became clear that mass screenings were going to go on, with or without the endorsement of the NCEP. Therefore, a set of screening guidelines was issued in 1989 by the NCEP.[2] These recent guidelines do not endorse the notion of widespread mass screenings, but suggest that, if such screenings were performed, they be done with:

- properly calibrated instruments;
- trained medical personnel on site to obtain proper specimens and advise individuals about their cholesterol results; and
- the local medical community prepared to accept patients referred with hypercholesterolemia for further evaluation and treatment.

There are now several studies in progress to evaluate the efficacy of such widespread screening and to determine the conditions under which it is most likely to be productive. It is already established that accurate mass screening can be accomplished with newer fingerstick methodologies only as long as careful attention is paid both to the proper training of technical personnel and to the careful maintenance and calibration of the devices used to make measurements.[3] Until requirements for reliable public screening are better defined, the ideal setting for cholesterol "screening" remains the doctor's office, where the results can be discussed and a proper plan designed to deal with the findings.

Adults

Of note, the first report of the NCEP, outlining guidelines for the detection and treatment of hypercholesterolemia in adults, recommended that every adult know his or her cholesterol level. Adults were defined as individuals over 20 years old and included both men and women. Left unresolved were questions about cholesterol screening at the extremes of age, i.e., below age 20 and above age 65.

Children

A separate panel of the NCEP is now considering the issues surrounding cholesterol screening and treatment in children and adolescents. Current screening recommendations, endorsed by both the American Academy of Pediatrics and the American Heart Association, suggest that children from "high-risk" families (defined as those children with a first degree relative with coronary artery disease or dyslipidemia) be screened, but that screening in children not be extended beyond such individuals.[4] Unfortunately, it has been repeatedly demonstrated that no more than half of the children with hypercholesterolemia (defined as total cholesterol above about 200 mg/dl) will be detected by such a strategy.[5] This underdetection is accounted for by a variety of reasons, particularly the fact that many children will not have parents old enough themselves to have manifested overt evidence of coronary disease. Whatever recommendations are finally made by the NCEP, anything short of measuring the cholesterol level of all children at the time of the physician visit may be made functionally irrelevant because of the ease, accuracy and widespread availability of fingerstick methods.

The Elderly

Cholesterol screening in individuals over age 65 is more problematic. As cohorts in Framingham and Honolulu have aged in sufficient numbers to provide reliable data, it has become clear that total cholesterol, as well as lipoprotein cholesterol subfractions, including low-density lipoprotein cholesterol (LDL-C) and high-density lipoprotein cholesterol (HDL-C), are predictive of coronary morbidity and mortality, even in older individuals.[6,7] In fact, the case can be made that since coronary morbidity and mortality are more prevalent in older individuals, the potential benefits of cholesterol lowering are likely to be even greater in this age group. On the other hand, it seems likely that there is an age beyond which attempts to prevent atherosclerosis collide with the law of diminishing returns. There is simply insufficient data to know where to draw the line. However, because older patients are often more concerned with health issues, the physician may be under increased pressure to provide cholesterol measurements and follow-up for these individuals.

Until these issues are clarified it is prudent to treat hypercholesterolemia in older individuals with caution, reassurance and tolerable dietary change. Cholesterol-lowering drugs should probably be reserved for those who already have established atherosclerosis.

Women

Critics of the NCEP have tried to make the case that cholesterol is a less important risk factor in women than in men. It is certainly true that manifestations of coronary morbidity and mortality in women lag about 10 years behind their appearance in men.[8] Nevertheless, it should be remembered that more women die of cardiovascular disease than from all forms of cancer combined, and that even among premenopausal women, the rate of death from myocardial infarction almost equals that of the rate of death of breast cancer.[9] Since total cholesterol, as well as lipoprotein subfractions, are potent predicators of risk in women as well as in men, it is entirely proper and indeed essential that adult women, as well as adult men, be evaluated and treated for hypercholesterolemia.

THE NCEP GUIDELINES FOR DETECTION AND TREATMENT OF HYPERCHOLESTEROLEMIA IN ADULTS

The first major report of the NCEP addressed the issue of the detection and treatment of hypercholesterolemia in adults.[1] These guidelines are anchored on two principles. First, screening for hypercholesterolemia should be accomplished by measuring circulating levels of total cholesterol — remembering that the blood cholesterol level is composed of the sum of cholesterol carried in all lipoprotein fractions, including LDL, HDL, very low-density lipoprotein (VLDL), and in the nonfasting state, chylomicrons. Since the cholesterol in chylomicrons (which are present only 6-8 hours after a meal) accounts for such a very small amount of the total cholesterol, screening for total cholesterol need not be done on a fasting sample. Thus, total cholesterol can be measured during any patient-physician encounter, and indeed, could be done in the context of a mass screening, provided that the previously discussed conditions for successful screening[2] have been met.

TABLE I. Total cholesterol level: relationship to classification of individuals and recommended action (modified from reference 1)

Total Cholesterol Level	Classification	Action
< 200 mg/dl	Desirable	Repeat in 5 years
200-239 mg/dl	Borderline high	IF NO RISK FACTORS* Diet instruction Repeat in 1 year WITH RISK FACTORS* obtain triglycerides, HDL-C and estimated LDL-C
> 240 mg/dl	High	Obtain triglycerides, HDL-C and estimated LDL-C

*See Table II for risk factors.

The guidelines provide specific, numerical cutpoints, which allow individuals to be placed into one of three categories (Table I). Those with cholesterol over 240 mg/dl are said to have a "high" cholesterol level; those with cholesterol less than 200 mg/dl are said to have a "desirable" blood cholesterol level; and those in the 200 mg/dl to 239 mg/dl range are said to have a "borderline high" level. In the U.S. population a cholesterol level of 240 mg/dl defines roughly the 75th percentile for adults. These guidelines were applied to a representative sample of the U.S. population identified in the Health and Nutrition Survey conducted by the Department of Health and Human Services.[10] Approximately 27 percent of the sample (and, by inference, of the population) had a total cholesterol level above 240 mg/dl. Since the mean cholesterol in the United States is about 210 mg/dl, it can be expected that roughly half of the population will have a total cholesterol level in the "borderline high" or "high" range.

An individual with a cholesterol level below 200 mg/dl on the screening sample need only be advised to have it re-measured within the next five years. In the opinion of this author, since the American Heart Association has recommended, for almost 30 years, that all Americans be on lower saturated, lower cholesterol diets, it is prudent to provide dietary information and advice, even to individuals with cholesterol of less than 200 mg/dl. Such individuals do not, however, require intense dietary instruction and follow-up.

Individuals with cholesterol over 240 mg/dl, i.e., in the "high-risk" range, should be asked to return for a fasting blood sample for a second measurement of total cholesterol, as well as measurements of HDL-C and triglycerides (TG). As long as the TG level is below 400 mg/dl, these values can be used to estimate the level of LDL-C by the following formula:

$$\text{LDL-C} = \text{total cholesterol} - (\text{HDL-C} + \text{TG}/5)^{11}$$

The term "TG/5" is roughly equal to the level of VLDL-C. Thus, LDL-C, by this formula, is defined as the total cholesterol minus the sum of cholesterol in the other fasting lipoprotein fractions, i.e., in HDL and VLDL. Further treatment of patients with cholesterol over 240 mg/dl will depend on the level of LDL, a concept that is discussed in detail in this chapter.

For those individuals in the "borderline high" range, i.e., with cholesterol between 200 mg/dl and 239 mg/dl, the decision to go further with evaluation of their cholesterol level will depend on the presence or absence of other risk factors. All individuals who already have manifestations of coronary atherosclerosis should have the same measurement of LDL as outlined for those with cholesterol over 240 mg/dl. In addition, those who have two or more risk factors listed in Table II should also have an LDL-C determination made.

TABLE II. Factors modifying approach to borderline high risk groups* (modified from reference 1)

Documented coronary heart disease (CHD) or two of the following:

- Male sex
- Family history of premature CHD (definite myocardial infarction or sudden death before age 55 in parent or sibling)
- Cigarette smoking (currently more than 10 cigarettes/day)
- Hypertension
- Low HDL-C level (below 35 mg/dl)
- Diabetes mellitus
- History of cerebrovascular or occlusive peripheral vascular disease
- Severe obesity (≥ 30 percent overweight)

*Total cholesterol 200 mg/dl to 239 mg/dl or LDL-C 130 mg/dl to 159 mg/dl

It is important to note that one of the risk factors to be considered is male gender, so that any man with another coronary risk factor is a candidate for an LDL determination if his total cholesterol is in the 200 mg/dl to 239 mg/dl range.

The requirement of two other risk factors for women reflects the lower risk of coronary disease in females, and therefore the higher threshold for the initiation of cholesterol-lowering therapy.

In practice, about 46 percent of adult Americans in the borderline high range will have two or more of these risk factors, and therefore will be candidates for LDL-C determinations. Moreover, when these guidelines are applied to the sample of the U.S. population, about 41 percent of individuals screened will require LDL-C analysis.[10] This includes about 64 million Americans, so the potential burden on the U.S. medical system is substantial.

SELECTING PATIENTS FOR THERAPY

The Use of the LDL-C Level

Measurements of LDL, like total cholesterol measurements, may be used to classify individuals in one of three categories. Those with LDL-C over 160 mg/dl are designated as having a "high risk" LDL-C. Those with LDL-C below 130 mg/dl are classified as being "desirable." Those with LDL-C between 130 mg/dl and 159 mg/dl are in a "borderline high-risk" range (Table III). Those with an LDL-C level below 130 mg/dl are in the same "desirable" category as individuals who had total cholesterol under 200 mg/dl on initial screening. In fact, in population studies, an average cholesterol of 200 mg/dl is almost equivalent to an LDL-C of 130 mg/dl,[12] although this relationship may vary considerably from one individual to another. Individuals with LDL-C below this cutpoint need only repeat measurements within a five-year period of time and should be provided with general diet information. Individuals with LDL-C over 160 mg/dl require therapy to lower the level to at least below 160 mg/dl and preferably below 130 mg/dl (Table IV). In the absence of coronary disease or other coronary artery disease risk factors (outlined in Table II), treatment should consist only of low-saturated, low-cholesterol diets.

TABLE III. LDL-C level: relationship to classification of individuals and recommended action (modified from reference 1)

LDL-C Level	Classification	Action
< 130 mg/dl	Desirable	Repeat in 5 years
130-159 mg/dl	Borderline high risk	IF NO RISK FACTORS* Repeat in 1 year WITH RISK FACTORS* Begin diet therapy
> 160 mg/dl	High risk	See text and Tables IV,V

*See Table II for risk factors.

If other risk factors are present and if diet therapy, after a 3 to 6 month trial period, has failed to lower LDL-C below 160 mg/dl, drug therapy may be considered.

Individuals with LDL-C between 130 mg/dl and 159 mg/dl, but without other risk factors, should be provided diet information and instructed to return in a year for repeat sampling. Those who have other risk factors are candidates for more intensive dietary counseling, with the goal to lower the LDL-C below 130 mg/dl. Whether or not such individuals are ever candidates for drug therapy is a matter of physician judgment. However, drug therapy should not be routinely initiated in those individuals without CHD or other risk factors unless LDL-C cannot be lowered below 160 mg/dl with diet alone.

TABLE IV. Factors warranting initiation of diet therapy (modified from reference 1)

LDL-C Level (Total Cholesterol Level)*	Risk Factors	Action
≥ 160 mg/dl (≥ 270 mg/dl)	No CHD or risk factors (See Table II)	Initiate diet therapy
≥ 130 mg/dl (≥ 240 mg/dl)	CHD or 2 risk factors (See Table II)	Initiate diet therapy

* LDL-C, rather than total cholesterol, should be used to select patients for therapy. Once the relationship of total cholesterol to LDL-C is established in the patient, total cholesterol may be used to *follow* patients.

Individuals with LDL-C above 160 mg/dl, but with no other risk factors, are not considered candidates for drug therapy unless their LDL-C level cannot be lowered below 190 mg/dl on diet alone (Table V). Thus, by making the thresholds for institution of drug therapy 30 mg/dl higher than they are for diet therapy, these guidelines build in a barrier to the initiation of drug therapy. The committee that put together these guidelines provided this barrier to emphasize that drug therapy should be carefully considered and applied sparingly. In the application of all portions of these guidelines, but most particularly here, medical judgment cannot be suspended. Clearly, in some patients who have multiple risk factors or those with documented coronary disease, LDL-C lowering may be considered desirable, even to points below those outlined.

TABLE V. Factors warranting initiation of drug therapy (modified from reference 1)

LDL-C Level (Total Cholesterol Level)*	Risk Factors	Action
≥ 190 mg/dl (≥ 270 mg/dl)	No CHD or risk factors (See Table II)	Initiate drug therapy
≥ 160 mg/dl (≥ 240 mg/dl)	CHD or 2 risk factors (See Table II)	Initiate drug therapy

* LDL-C, rather than total cholesterol, should be used to select patients for therapy. Once the relationship of total cholesterol to LDL-C is established in the patient, total cholesterol may be used to *follow* patients.

In the opinion of this author, an LDL-C level below 130 mg/dl corresponding to a total cholesterol level below 200 mg/dl, is desirable for all patients, with or without risk factors, who can achieve these levels with diet alone. Since the institution of drug therapy introduces potential risk associated with the drug itself, LDL-C lowering to 160 mg/dl or below is sufficient for patients without other coronary risk factors.

When the relationship between total cholesterol and LDL-C has been well established in an individual patient, a total cholesterol level may be used as a surrogate of LDL-C. Since total cholesterol measurements are less expensive, this approach provides some potential savings. LDL-C, however, should still be measured on a yearly basis to be sure that the relationship to total cholesterol has remained constant.

Secondary Dyslipoproteinemia

Often overlooked in evaluations of patients with hypercholesterolemia are other diseases that may themselves result in or aggravate high levels of LDL-C. These include diabetes, chronic renal failure, nephrosis, hypothyroidism and less commonly, dysgammaglobulinemias, various forms of obstructive liver disease, porphyria and other rare causes.[13] Therefore, every patient with an LDL-C over 160 mg/dl should have one set of measurements of renal, hepatic and thyroid function, as well as a fasting blood sugar, to rule out the possibility of secondary causes. A reasonable screening battery includes a complete blood count, urinalysis, circulating total globulin and albumin, T-4, TSH and creatinine.

On occasion hypercholesterolemia may be the first manifestation of one of these secondary disorders. In older individuals, for example, hypothyroidism may not yet be clinically apparent when cholesterol is elevated. Similarly, hypercholesterolemia may precede other clinical signs of nephrosis.

Confirmation of the LDL-C Level

Before any decisions about the institution of therapy are made, an elevated LDL-C should be confirmed by at least one additional measurement performed 1 to 2 weeks after the initial measurement. This repeat testing allows both the patient and physician to take into account normal biological variation, as well as potential error in the measurement. Multiple measurements are particularly important in LDL-C determinations, since LDL-C is a formula-derived measurement,[11] not one directly determined in the laboratory.

In summary, these guidelines provide an approach to the detection of elevations of total cholesterol and LDL-C in adults and for the initiation of diet and drug therapy for individuals in whom the LDL-C level is deemed too high and of potential risk to the patient.

CRITICISMS OF THE ADULT TREATMENT PANEL GUIDELINES

Since the release of the NCEP guidelines, there has been considerable reaction to them, and not all favorable. The emphasis on LDL-C as the major determinant of therapy has been criticized by some as downplaying the importance of HDL-C determinations, as well as the potential importance of TG levels.[14]

The focus of the guidelines on the LDL-C level is based on data from clinical trials that strongly demonstrate the importance of lowering LDL-C in preventing coronary disease.[15-17] Moreover, a strong case has been made that, without an elevated LDL-C level, coronary atherosclerosis is uncommon, even in the presence of other risk factors.[18] Also, it should be noted that HDL-C is taken into account in these guidelines, both as part of the formula used to estimate the LDL-C level and, separately, as a risk factor that determines how vigorously the LDL-C level should be treated.

With publication of the Helsinki study results,[19] it has become apparent that raising the HDL-C level may, indeed, have a separate and additional beneficial effect on coronary risk. While future iterations of these guidelines may place more emphasis on raising the HDL-C level, such emphasis should not be at the expense of the importance of LDL-C lowering, which remains paramount.

Of note, the guidelines did not make detailed recommendations about the treatment of patients with an elevated TG level. Triglycerides have been a risk factor, the importance of which has not been easy to pin down. From the epidemiologist's point of view, the TG level provides little additional information about coronary risk beyond that which is provided by LDL-C and HDL-C determinations.[20] Nevertheless, a patient with a high TG level often has a low HDL-C level and a higher than normal LDL-C level,[21] so that in an individual patient, high TG may, in fact, identify the patient at increased risk of developing coronary and other forms of atherosclerosis. It is likely that some patients with elevated TG are carrying atherogenic lipoproteins. Unfortunately, a simple total TG does not tell which patients are, and which patients are not, carriers of such lipoproteins.

The report of a consensus conference on hypertriglyceridemia in 1984[22] recommended that individuals with TG over 500 mg/dl be considered candidates for both diet and, if necessary, drug therapy to lower those levels, particularly if they had a personal or family history of coronary disease (Table VI). Certainly individuals with TG over 1000 mg/dl, who are candidates for acute pancreatitis,[23] require diet and, if necessary, drug therapy to lower the TG level. On the other hand, individuals with TG between 250 mg/dl and 500 mg/dl, but without elevations of LDL-C or decreases of HDL-C, should be treated with TG-lowering drugs.

TABLE VI. Categorization of TG level (modified from reference 22)

TG Level	Category
< 250 mg/dl	Normal
250 mg/dl to 499 mg/dl	Borderline high
> 500 mg/dl	High*

* Patients with TG > 1000 mg/dl are at especially high risk to develop acute pancreatitis.

Some have criticized the NCEP guidelines for not requiring routine measurements of HDL-C as a screening device.[24] These critics have pointed out that, even among those patients with total cholesterol below 200 mg/dl, there will be a group of individuals whose HDL-C is below 30 mg/dl. Indeed, results of the Lipid Research Clinics Prevalence Study Population Data, indicate that four percent to five percent of men with a total cholesterol level less than 200 mg/dl will have an HDL-C level of less than 30 mg/dl.[12] Such individuals are at risk of developing coronary atherosclerosis, particularly if their LDL-C is above 100 mg/dl.[25] At the time that these guidelines were published, it was felt that the cost of routine HDL-C screening was not justified by the relatively low yield of subjects at risk.[26] As automated fingerstick methodologies, for both total cholesterol and HDL-C, become available and as the cost of such screening is lowered, it will be important to revisit this aspect of the current NCEP recommendations.

In addition, it has been pointed out that since two risk factors are required for intense therapeutic attention in the LDL-C range between 130 mg/dl and 160 mg/dl, women with diabetes may be overlooked. This possible lack of appropriate attention to women is particularly important since women with diabetes lose their relative protection, compared to men, for developing coronary disease and, in fact, may have rates of coronary disease slightly higher than men with diabetes.[27] Thus, it is prudent in women with diabetes to disregard gender and to establish LDL-C lowering goals as if two risk factors were present.

While these criticisms are important and, in fact, may form the basis for future revisions of the NCEP guidelines, they provide additions to the guidelines rather than subtractions from them. Also, the criticisms do not undermine the soundness of the guidelines as they are currently formulated. In fact, the criticisms emphasize the rather conservative nature of the NCEP guidelines. The fact that many millions of Americans will require attention as a result of these guidelines should not be taken as a shortcoming of the guidelines, but rather as a commentary on the high risk of coronary disease as a result of hypercholesterolemia, which still faces the American population and western populations in general.

Given the substantial remaining risk provided by hypercholesterolemia, even in the face of declining rates of coronary heart disease in western populations, it is not surprising that guidelines similar to these have been suggested for the Canadian, Western European and British populations.[28-30]

OTHER MEASUREMENTS OF LIPOPROTEIN METABOLISM

As has been discussed, the current NCEP guidelines for the detection and treatment of hypercholesterolemia emphasize measurements of total cholesterol, HDL-C and total TG, with particular attention to the level of

LDL-C. Many physicians are confused by other measurements that have been suggested as providing additional information concerning coronary risk.

Lipoprotein Electrophoresis

For many years lipoprotein electrophoresis was used as a means of classifying patients for purposes of tailoring diet and drug therapy.[31] However, it has become clear that electrophoresis is a qualitative, not quantitative, technique and cannot be readily applied to the selection of patients for intensive cholesterol-lowering therapy. The phenotyping classification system based on electrophoresis does not, as was once hoped, provide additional information about genetic abnormalities. In fact, current NCEP guidelines for managing adult hypercholesterolemia do not depend on whether a diagnosis of a genetic lipoprotein disorder is made, but rather focus on treating the elevated LDL-C level, regardless of its origin.

For all practical purposes, lipoprotein electrophoresis should be looked upon as a historical technique that had a profound effect on advancing our knowledge of lipoprotein disorders, but which has no current clinical application.

Ratios

Ratios of total cholesterol to HDL-C or ratios of LDL-C to HDL-C have also been emphasized as important measurements, particularly in analysis of the Framingham study data.[25] While such ratios are useful for characterizing population data, they should not be applied without careful attention to individual patients. Two patients with LDL-C to HDL-C ratios may be equivalent candidates for therapeutic interventions. For example, a patient with an LDL-C level of 180 mg/dl and an HDL-C level of 60 mg/dl has an LDL-C/HDL-C ratio of three, as does a patient with an LDL-C level of 120 mg/dl and an HDL-C level of 40 mg/dl. Under current NCEP guidelines, the first patient is a candidate for intense therapeutic intervention, perhaps even including drug therapy. The second patient is not. The current NCEP guidelines focus attention on LDL-C and HDL-C as separate, independent risk factors.

Apolipoproteins

Measurement of apolipoprotein level (the protein that coats the surface of lipoprotein) has been advocated by some. Apolipoprotein AI, an important component of HDL-C and apolipoprotein B, the major protein component of LDL-C, have been suggested as more likely to identify patients at risk of coronary atherosclerosis. Indeed, there is some information to indicate that these measurements may be slightly better predictors of risk than HDL-C and LDL-C.[32,33] Standardization of these measurements, however, has not yet been achieved. In addition, the clinical and epidemiologic base that allows estimation of their value in predicting risk is inadequate. Moreover, there is little clinical information about the value of changing apolipoprotein level beyond that of changing LDL-C and HDL-C. Until measurement differences are resolved and the clinical and epidemiologic base that relates apolipoprotein levels to risk and benefit in coronary atherosclerosis is broadened, there is little reason to recommend their routine measurement in clinical practice.

Lp(a)

More recently it has been noted that a particular circulating lipoprotein, called lipoprotein(a), has been associated with the prediction of increased coronary risk. Lipoprotein(a) or Lp(a) is, in fact, a lipoprotein that combines a plasminogen analog, apoprotein(a) or apo(a), with LDL-C. The function of Lp(a) is currently unknown. About 25 percent of Caucasian adult populations have an elevated Lp(a) level.

In any event, Lp(a) is a good predictor of coronary risk and is independent of LDL, HDL, and other lipoprotein levels.[34] The means by which Lp(a) increases coronary risk, however, is not clear. It has been postulated that it may interfere either with the catabolism of LDL-C or plasminogen itself (thereby inhibiting the dissolution of a clot), or by some other mechanism, as yet not elucidated. Except for niacin, drugs that alter the LDL-C level do not appear to lower the Lp(a) level and may even increase the Lp(a) levels.[35,36] Importantly, there is no proof that changing the Lp(a) level will reduce risk. Therefore, given the lack of information about Lp(a), it is not a useful measurement to be made routinely in clinical practice.

CONCLUSION

This chapter has provided an outline of NCEP guidelines for the selection of individuals for diet and drug therapy for hypercholesterolemia.

Currently recommended guidelines are based on using total blood cholesterol as a screening measurement and LDL-C as measurements for selecting and evaluating therapy.

Both total cholesterol and LDL-C measurements should be confirmed by repeat measurements. Other risk factors, including gender and HDL-C level, are taken into account by these guidelines in reaching decisions concerning when and by what modalities LDL-C lowering should be implemented.

Ideally, screening to identify individuals with hypercholesterolemia should be done in the context of the patient-physician encounter. If mass screenings are to be performed, these should be conducted only with accurate measurements, trained personnel and a medical community prepared to accept and treat those found to be hypercholesterolemic.

Applying these guidelines to the general population will, it is estimated, result in the classification of over 60 million Americans in categories requiring some therapeutic intervention. Most will be treated adequately with diet, some will require intervention with both diet and drug therapy. As in all such guidelines, a selection of patients for therapy depends not only on numerical parameters, but most importantly, on the judgment of physicians about their individual patients.

REFERENCES

1. National Cholesterol Education Program. 1988 report of the expert panel on detection, evaluation, and treatment of high blood cholesterol in adults. Arch Intern Med. 1988;148:36-69.
2. Recommendations regarding public screening for measuring blood cholesterol. Summary of a National Heart, Lung, and Blood Institute Workshop, October 1988. Arch Intern Med. 1989;149:2650-2654.
3. Naughton MJ, Luepker RV, Strickland D. The accuracy of portable cholesterol analyzers in public screening programs. JAMA. 1990;263:1213-1217.
4. American Academy of Pediatrics Committee on Nutrition. Toward a prudent diet for children. Pediatrics. 1983;71(1):78-80.
5. Garcia RE, Moodie DS. Routine cholesterol surveillance in childhood. Pediatrics. 1989;84:751-755.
6. Kannel WB. Nutrition and the occurrence and prevention of cardiovascular disease in the elderly. Nutrition Reviews. 1988;46:68-78.
7. Benfante R, Reed D. Is elevated serum cholesterol level a risk factor for coronary heart disease in the elderly? JAMA. 1990;263:393-396.
8. Lerner DJ, Kannel WB. Patterns of coronary heart disease morbidity and mortality in the sexes: a 26-year follow-up of the Framingham population. Am Heart J. 1986;111:383-390.
9. Grimes DA. Prevention of cardiovascular disease in women: role of the obstetrician-gynecologist. Am J Obstet Gynecol. 1988;158(pt 2):1662-1668.
10. Sempos C, Robinson F, Haines C, et al. The prevalence of high blood cholesterol levels among adults in the United States. JAMA. 1989;262:45-52.
11. Friedewald WT, Levy RI, Fredrickson PS. Estimation of the concentration of low-density lipoprotein cholesterol in plasma, without use of preparative ultracentrifuge. Clin Chem. 1972;18:499-502.
12. LaRosa JC, Chambless LE, Criqui MH, et al. Patterns of dyslipoproteinemia in selected North American populations. Circulation. 1986;73:(suppl 1):12-29.
13. LaRosa JC. Secondary hyperlipoproteinemia. In: Rifkind BM, Levy RI, eds. Hyperlipidemia: Diagnosis and Therapy. New York, NY: Grune & Stratton; 1977:205-216.
14. Castelli WP. The triglyceride issue: A view from Framingham. Am Heart J. 1986;112:432-437.
15. Lipid Research Clinics Program. The Lipid Research Clinics Coronary Primary Prevention Trial Results. I. Reduction in incidence of coronary heart disease. JAMA. 1984;251:351-364.
16. Lipid Research Clinics Program. The Lipid Research Clinics Coronary Primary Prevention Trial Results. II. The relationship of reduction in incidence of coronary heart disease to cholesterol lowering. JAMA. 1984;251:365-374.

17. Blankenhorn DH, Nessim SA, Johnson RL, et al. Beneficial effects of combined colestipol-niacin therapy on coronary atherosclerosis and coronary venous bypass grafts. JAMA. 1987;257:3233-3240.
18. Roberts WC. Atherosclerotic risk factors. Are there ten or is there only one? Am J Cardiol. 1989;64:552-554.
19. Frick MH, Elo O, Haapa K, et al. Helsinki Heart Study: primary-prevention trial with gemfibrozil in middle-aged men with dyslipidemia. N Engl J Med. 1987;317(20):1237-1245.
20. Hulley SB, Rosenman RH, Bawol RD, et al. Epidemiology as a guide to clinical decisions: the association between triglyceride and coronary heart disease. N Engl J Med. 1980;302:1383-1389.
21. Davis CE, Gordon D, LaRosa JC, et al. Correlations of plasma high-density lipoprotein cholesterol levels with other plasma lipid and lipoprotein concentrations: the Lipid Research Clinics Program Prevalence Study. Circulation. 1980;62:(suppl 4):24-30.
22. Consensus Conference. Treatment of hypertriglyceridemia. JAMA. 1984;251:1196-1200.
23. Farmer RG, Winkelman EI, Brown MB, et al. Hyperlipoproteinemia and pancreatitis. Am J Med. 1973;54:161-165.
24. Abbott RD, Wilson PWF, Kannel WB, et al. High density lipoprotein cholesterol, total cholesterol screening, and myocardial infarction. The Framingham Study. Arteriosclerosis. 1988;8(3):207-211.
25. Castelli WP, Garrison RJ, Wilson PWF, et al. Incidence of coronary heart disease and lipoprotein cholesterol levels. The Framingham Study. JAMA. 1986;256(20):2835-2838.
26. Grundy SM, Goodman DS, Rifkind BM, et al. The place of HDL in cholesterol management. Arch Intern Med. 1989;149:505-510.
27. Kannel WB. Lipids, diabetes and coronary heart disease: insights from the Framingham study. Am Heart J. 1985;110:1100-1107.
28. The Canadian Consensus Conference on the prevention of heart and vascular disease by altering serum cholesterol and lipoprotein risk factors. Proceedings of the Canadian consensus conference on cholesterol. CMAJ. 1988;(suppl)139:2-8.
29. British Cardiac Society Working Group on Coronary Disease Prevention. London, England: British Cardiac Society; 1987.
30. European Atherosclerosis Society Study Group. Strategies for the prevention of coronary heart disease: a policy statement of the European Atherosclerosis Society. Eur Heart J. 1987;8:77-88.
31. Fredrickson DS, Levy RI, Lees RS. Fat transport in lipoproteins: an integrated approach to mechanisms and disorders. N Engl J Med. 1967;276:34-44,94-103,148-156,215-225,273-281.
32. Schmidt SB, Wasserman AG, Muesling RA, et al. Lipoprotein and apolipoprotein levels in angiographically defined coronary atherosclerosis. Am J Cardiol. 1985;55:1459-1462.
33. Rifai N, Chapman JF, Silverman LM, Gwynne JT. Review of serum lipids and apolipoproteins in risk-assessment of coronary heart disease. Ann Clin Lab Sci. 1988;18:429-439.
34. Utermann G. The mysteries of lipoprotein(a). Science. 1989;246:904-910.
35. Carlson LA, Hamsten A, Asplund A. Pronounced lowering of serum levels of lipoprotein Lp(a) in hyperlipidaemic subjects treated with nicotinic acid. J Intern Med. 1989;226:271-276.
36. Kostner GM, Gavish D, Leopold B, et al. HMG CoA reductase inhibitors lower LDL cholesterol without reducing Lp(a) levels. Circulation. 1989;80:1313-1319.

CHAPTER 2

Diet, Lipids and Coronary Heart Disease

Neil J. Stone, M.D.
Chicago, Illinois

INTRODUCTION

There are now a number of risk factors — genetic traits and life style behaviors — known to increase the prevalence of coronary heart disease (CHD). Because it has been shown to be efficacious against many of the major risk factors for CHD, diet should be considered as a prime therapy for the prevention and progression of cardiovascular illness. In fact, diet is intimately involved with low-density lipoprotein cholesterol (LDL-C) levels, high-density lipoprotein cholesterol (HDL-C) levels, hypertension, diabetes and obesity — all known risk factors for CHD.

However, the relationship between diet and risk reduction for CHD is complex. For example, cigarette smoking is a known risk factor for CHD and cigarette smokers appear to ingest less polyunsaturated fats, fiber and fish, as well as more sodium than nonsmokers.[1] Not surprisingly, the lipid profiles of smokers are adversely affected compared to nonsmokers. Another example of the complex relationship between diet and risk reduction for CHD is the observation that a higher calorie intake and a greater intake of fat and sodium often accompany those with a life style characterized by increased psychosocial stress or sedentary behavior. Moreover, it has been shown that risk factors may affect dietary changes. For example, in the Multiple Risk Factor Intervention Trial (MRFIT), men who continued to smoke after being placed on a weight reduction diet had smaller responses to the diet than those who stopped smoking.[2]

Two recent major reports indicate a pivotal role for diet in the prevention of cardiovascular disease. The Surgeon General's Report on Nutrition and Health urged Americans to reduce high fat foods and replace them with complex carbohydrates and fiber.[3] The National Research Council's exhaustively researched report on Diet and Health summarized the current knowledge base by noting "there is a direct relationship between dietary fat and the risk of both coronary heart disease (CHD) and certain kinds of cancer, and possibly also obesity. The evidence is extremely powerful for CHD and is somewhat more limited for cancer."[4]

However, important questions concerning diet and cardiovascular disease/health remain. This chapter will discuss the evidence linking diet to CHD in animals and humans, as well as the intervention trial data showing the benefit of diet, and the effect of dietary cholesterol, fat, fiber and alcohol on lipids and lipoproteins. The chapter concludes with a practical approach to dietary therapy based on the recent guidelines from the Adult Treatment Panel of the National Cholesterol Education Program (NCEP).[5]

RELATIONSHIP OF DIET TO CHD

Experimental Studies

Studies of experimental atherosclerosis in various non-human species have fostered important insights into the pathogenesis of atherosclerosis. Careful review of the data suggests that the degree of atherosclerosis seen is clearly a function of the severity of the hypercholesterolemia that develops from the dietary regimen employed.[6] For regression to occur, it appears that the serum cholesterol level must be lowered to 200 mg/dl or less as a minimum. Armstrong and co-workers showed that regression of dietary-induced atherosclerotic lesions could be obtained in non-human primates who had lipoprotein profiles similar to humans.[7] Although these studies showed regression of advanced lesions, with depletion of the raised cholesterol arterial content by either low fat or modified diets, the atherosclerosis induced was caused by severe hypercholesterolemia more reminiscent of that seen with severe familial hypercholesterolemia. However, while animal data must be viewed cautiously, taken as a whole, the vast array of animal atherosclerosis data suggest that human atherosclerosis may be susceptible to cholesterol-lowering diets.

Population Studies

Autopsy reports. Controlled laboratory experiments permit specific hypotheses about diet and CHD to be answered in careful fashion. However, epidemiologic observations allow unique insights into the relationship between diet and CHD, which are not possible to obtain in animal or human intervention trials owing to the large numbers and prolonged experience of various groups with diet.

An important clue to the diet-heart relationship was seen from the autopsy studies of young Americans killed during the Korean war reported by Enos and colleagues in *JAMA* in 1953.[8] This landmark article documented that atherosclerotic lesions occurred in coronary arteries decades before CHD was clinically recognized. In a more recently reported study,[9] when young children from Muscatine, Iowa, were re-examined as young adults, it was shown that elevated levels of cholesterol during childhood were associated with elevations in young adulthood. Moreover, in this study, obesity, oral contraceptive use and cigarette smoking beginning during adolescence had negative effects on their lipid profiles that were measured in the young adult years.

Autopsy studies reveal that the link between diet and CHD is a worldwide phenomenon. Overall, the data show that geographic differences in the extent of atherosclerosis can be at least partially explained by differences in fat consumption and serum cholesterol values of the populations studied.[10] In fact, recent studies show that American men had approximately three times the amount of atherosclerotic involvement of their aorta and coronary vessels as did their Japanese counterparts, and that the observed differences were related to the fact that the native American diet is proportionately higher in fat and cholesterol.[11]

Multiple population studies. The Seven Countries Study, reported by Ancel Keys in 1980, was a landmark investigation that showed a clear relationship between diet and CHD.[12] A multivariate analysis of carefully obtained dietary data on over 12,000 men aged 40 to 59 years from 18 diverse population groups showed strong correlations among percentage of calories from dietary saturated fat intake, serum cholesterol and CHD. Surprisingly, the researchers did not look at dietary cholesterol intake. When contrasted to the men studied from southern European countries and Japan, the men studied from Finland, the Netherlands and the United States had the highest intakes of saturated fat intake. The contrast between the effect of diet and exercise on CHD was highlighted by the experience of the Finns, who although they were the least sedentary of the groups studied, were also the most hypercholesterolemic and had the highest rates of CHD. On the other hand, although the men of Crete had a high fat intake (about 40 percent of energy) similar to that enjoyed by the Finns and Americans, the rate of CHD for the men of Crete was strikingly lower. The lower rate of CHD in the men of Crete has been attributed to the replacement of saturated fat in the diet by monounsaturated fat in the olive oil-based diet typically used in Crete.

However, when epidemiologists looked within the populations, the results were much less striking. The reasons for these differences between multipopulation and single population study results have been carefully studied and it appears that several problems confound the results.[13] It appears that, unlike the situation in the Seven Countries Study where groups with differing genetics and dietary habits were compared, in individual population studies the small interpersonal diet variability compared with large intrapersonal diet variability,[14] and the inadequacy of the quality and number of dietary measurements and the biologic variability of cholesterol measurements did not permit a relationship to be seen even if one existed.

Migrant population studies. However, studies of migrant populations permitted a way to separate genetic factors from environmental influences. One of the most highly regarded studies evaluated the effects on serum cholesterol and CHD on three groups: Japanese in Japan; Japanese who migrated to Hawaii; and Japanese who migrated to the mainland United States.[15,16] Although genetic background was the same in each of the three groups, the dietary intakes varied considerably. The American cohorts were heavier and consumed diets higher in calories, saturated fats and dietary cholesterol. Rates of CHD were correspondingly higher in this group. Thus, dietary composition leading to hypercholesterolemia, rather than genetic makeup, seemed to explain the increase in CHD observed with the migration to mainland United States.

These results were in contrast to another migration study which looked at 1,001 middle-aged men who were born in Ireland and either lived in Ireland or had migrated to Boston. A third group consisted of unrelated first generation Irishmen who grew up in Boston.[17] Serum cholesterol values for the three groups were similar and there was no difference in CHD rates. However, further analyses showed that those with an increased dietary cholesterol and saturated fat intake had an increased risk of CHD, whereas those with a higher carbohydrate and fiber intake carried a decreased risk.

Relationship of dietary cholesterol and CHD. While the effect of saturated fat on serum cholesterol and CHD seems unquestioned, controversy still rages about the nature of the relationship between dietary cholesterol and CHD. One of the most carefully performed prospective evaluations of diet and its relationship to CHD was the Western Electric Study of 1,900 employees.[18] Diet histories were obtained at baseline and one year later. Dietary cholesterol was found to be significantly associated with CHD risk. Also, 25-year follow-up data showed that dietary cholesterol was associated with the risk of CHD independent of the serum cholesterol level.

Data from three other prospective studies that also show the dietary cholesterol intake of individuals to be significantly related to the long-term risk have been reviewed by Stamler and Shekelle.[19] Their analyses documented that a 200 mg/1,000 kcal higher intake of cholesterol at baseline was associated with a 30 percent higher rate of CHD. Keys reanalyzed a large Israeli survey which initially failed to show a correlation between dietary intake and serum cholesterol and showed that by grouping the participants by birth place a consistent relationship was seen.[21]

Effect of polyunsaturated fat on CHD. Lately there has been great interest in the effect of polyunsaturated fat on CHD incidence. Oliver[1] has reviewed the data suggesting that selective reduction of linoleic acid, an essential polyunsaturated fatty acid, could influence the effect of smoking on atherosclerosis. He cites the example of the southern French in which CHD rates are lower than expected despite predisposing factors such as cigarette smoking, a high fat intake and a high serum cholesterol level that would suggest otherwise. Oliver further notes that populations with high rates of CHD, such as the Scots and Finns, have low concentrations of linoleic acid in their adipose tissue. He compares this to men in Stockholm with high linoleic acid in adipose tissue and a low rate of CHD.

Another group of polyunsaturated fats, the omega-3 fatty acids, also appear to affect the incidence of CHD.[22] The Greenland Eskimos consume 5 to 10 grams of long chain omega-3 fatty acids daily.

The observed effect of the omega-3 fatty acids, derived from the diet by the Eskimos from fish oil, has prompted widespread discussion on how much fish is needed for a protective effect against CHD. Eskimos consume amounts that most patients in the United States would not find practical. Of interest, a protective influence on CHD incidence was seen in Zutphen, Netherlands, where men consumed an average of only 20 grams of fish per day.[23] The effect was seen for lean fish as well as fatty fish. The salutary effect of fish consumption was not mediated by an improvement in serum lipids. Hence, antiplatelet actions may be important in this regard.

Although Eskimos and Japanese fishermen had high enough intakes of fish to decrease their thrombotic tendency by reducing platelet aggregation and increasing their bleeding time, it was not clear whether this could be the case in those with smaller fish intakes. Yet, when patients post-myocardial infarction (MI) were randomized to either a low fat, high fiber diet or added fish intake, the only diet which was associated with increased survival was the added fish diet. Since only a small fraction of these patients were taking aspirin,[24] it suggests that the benefits of fish oil may be due to antiplatelet effects and less coronary thrombosis.

Vegetarians. Vegetarians typically consume a diet high in carbohydrates and low in fat and, not unexpectedly, have lower values for cholesterol and LDL-C than do non-vegetarians.[25] Also, in vegetarians HDL-C/LDL-C ratios to LDL-C are elevated, indicating a favorable risk profile.[26] Lacto-ovovegetarians have 24 percent higher LDL-C and 7 percent higher HDL-C than strict vegetarians owing to ingestion of fatty dairy products.[27] Of note, 250 grams of beef, isocalorically added to the strict daily vegetarian diet, raised plasma cholesterol by 19 percent without changing HDL-C.[29] Also, the added beef was associated with a 3 percent rise in systolic blood pressure.[28]

The effects of a lacto-ovovegetarian life style on CHD mortality was carefully studied among Seventh Day Adventists (SDA) in California.[29] There was a reduced risk of CHD mortality for SDA whom were lacto-ovovegetarians as compared to the general Californian population. However, the observed reduced risk of CHD was likely not a pure effect of diet alone, because the SDA community did not smoke cigarettes. Also, vegetarian status appeared to reduce the risk of fatal CHD among males under 64 years of age, but not among females and males over 65 years old. Overall, however, a vegetarian life style most likely reduces the risk of premature CHD.

Intervention Studies

Large population studies. Early clinical trials of diet and CHD were criticized for numerous problems with design. Small sample size, lack of randomization and mixing of cases with and without CHD in the same trial limited the usefulness of these earlier studies. Yet the results obtained in two of the earlier trials[31,32] had a striking resemblance to those seen in the more recent Lipid Research Clinics Primary Prevention Trial.[30] Both the Oslo Diet-Heart Study,[31] which followed men after a first MI, and the Los Angeles Veterans Administration Domiciliary Study,[32] which followed both men with and without clinical CHD, showed that diets high in polyunsaturated fat and low in saturated fat caused approximately 1 percent lowering of serum cholesterol that was associated with an approximate 2 percent lowering of CHD rates.[31,32]

In the Oslo Dietary and Smoking Intervention Trial, the incidence of CHD in symptomless men 40 to 49 years of age was studied. Those men who were randomized to receive intervention (a diet low in saturated fat and increased in polyunsaturated fat and counseling to reduce smoking) had a 47 percent lower incidence of sudden death and heart attack than a nonintervention control group.[33] Further analysis showed that the net difference of 10 percent in serum cholesterol between intervention and control groups was the main cause for the 47 percent reduction in first CHD events.[34] The antismoking factor, due to a small net difference in quit rates (17 percent vs. 24 percent), contributed to a lesser degree. At five years after initiation of the study, the difference between the two groups in total mortality was quite significant with a 33 percent lower mortality in the intervention group as compared to the control group.[35]

Because of convincing data from the two Oslo studies and the Los Angeles Veterans Administration Study (all long-term trials), the initial results from the MRFIT were difficult to understand. This ambitious undertaking followed 12,866 high risk men 35 to 57 years of age who were hypercholesterolemic, hypertensive and/or smokers. A nonstatistically significant difference in mortality of 7.1 percent between special intervention and usual care groups was reported after eight years.[36] Although quit rates for cigarette smokers were clearly improved in the trial and dietary change was evident, the mean net differences between special intervention and usual care for diastolic blood pressure was only 4 percent and for serum cholesterol was only 2 percent. A possibly unfavorable response to high-dose diuretic antihypertensive medication in the treated group, especially those with ECG abnormalities at baseline, may well explain the lack of a more pronounced effect of intervention.

Of note, the results of the MRFIT underscores the fact that in intervention trials, improvement in CHD seems to be related to the magnitude of the improvement in lipid lowering and/or degree of improvement in other risk factors.

Angiography studies. An advantage of studies employing serial angiography is that there is a more direct look at the primary endpoint — the atherosclerotic plaque — and fewer patients are needed along with a shorter time frame of observation. The Leiden Intervention Trial[37] evaluated the effects of a vegetarian diet in 39 men with angina pectoris who were studied by coronary angiography before diet and two years later. The effectiveness of diet was seen in lower body weights and systolic blood pressure along with lower values for total cholesterol and the cholesterol/HDL-C ratio. Disease progression was significant in those with total cholesterol/HDL-C ratios greater than 6.9. Those with improvement in the total cholesterol/HDL-C ratio had the least progression. The Cholesterol Lowering Atherosclerosis Study, a randomized, placebo-controlled trial of aggressive lipid lowering with niacin and colestipol in coronary bypass patients, demonstrated that low fat dietary habits characterized those in the placebo group in whom new lesions did not develop at a follow-up angiography two years later.[38] The subjects on diet and placebo who did not show coronary progression had a lower saturated fat and total fat intake than those who had progression on the angiogram. They increased their dietary protein to compensate for reduced intake of fat by substituting low fat meats and dairy products for high fat products.

Calculating dietary recommendations from existing data. It is quite likely that the projected large expense will prevent a future, major diet-heart trial from being conducted. Thus, a decision about dietary recommendations must be made from available data. Of interest, Taylor and colleagues[39] recently developed a theoretical model to calculate the benefits of a cholesterol-lowering diet for the general population. Their statistical model suggests that a low risk individual who adheres lifelong to a low cholesterol diet would gain just three days to three months in life expectancy. For persons at high risk, they calculated a range from 18 days to 13 months. The authors acknowledged that their analysis did not consider the benefits of diet that may delay or prevent angina or nonfatal MI. Also, their calculations did not consider the beneficial effects of diet on obesity, hypertension, diabetes and, in certain cases, cancer. These latter points are hardly trivial.

DIET AND ITS EFFECT ON CIRCULATING LIPOPROTEINS

The components of the diet that elevate serum cholesterol are saturated fats (quantitatively the most important), dietary cholesterol and caloric excess. Polyunsaturated fats, monounsaturated fats, fiber and complex carbohydrates, when substituted for saturated fats, lower cholesterol. Alcohol causes triglycerides (TG) to rise along with HDL-C.

TABLE I.   Factors that elevate and lower blood cholesterol

Factors That Elevate Cholesterol	Factors That Lower Cholesterol
1. Saturated fats	1. Polyunsaturated fats
2. Dietary cholesterol	2. Monounsaturated fats
3. Caloric excess	3. Fiber
	4. Complex carbohydrates

Dietary Cholesterol

Dietary cholesterol is found as an integral component of the cell membranes of all mammals, birds and fish, but is essentially not seen in plants, nuts and seeds. In other words, if it doesn't have a liver, it doesn't have cholesterol in it! Sources of increased dietary cholesterol include fatty cuts of beef at about 95 mg/100 gm, egg yolks at about 225 mg to 275 mg per egg yolk and liver at about 450 mg/100 gm.[40] The cholesterol content of meat is dependent on the number of animal cells and not directly on the fat content of the meat.

There is still great controversy as to the relationship of dietary cholesterol to serum cholesterol. Dietary cholesterol appears to increase plasma cholesterol primarily by increasing LDL-C. Sacks and associates[41] evaluated effects of a small increase in dietary cholesterol in a randomized, double-blind, crossover trial of lacto-vegetarian college students. The effect of increasing dietary cholesterol intake from 97 mg/day to 481 mg/day was to cause a 12 percent elevation in LDL-C and a 9 percent elevation in apolipoprotein B level. Since there is one apolipoprotein B molecule per cholesterol molecule, it appears cholesterol feeding affected the number, rather than the composition of circulating LDL particles. Yet, careful metabolic studies have shown that there is considerable variability in the response of blood cholesterol to cholesterol feeding. McNamara and colleagues[42] showed that in 31 percent of selected subjects there was failure to suppress endogenous cholesterol synthesis with a resultant increase in the plasma cholesterol level. To highlight the striking differences in responsiveness to dietary cholesterol, there is the report of an 88-year-old man who ate 25 eggs per day and had a normal cholesterol level because of a marked reduction in cholesterol absorption and conversion of cholesterol to bile acids.[43]

The lack of uniform responsiveness to dietary cholesterol is due, in part, to genetic reasons. In a study performed by Tikkanen and colleagues,[44] it was found that individuals with apolipoprotein E_4/E_4 phenotype had the highest level of cholesterol during high fat feeding and the greatest reduction during low fat feeding as compared to individuals with other apolipoprotein E phenotypes.[44] Dietschy and colleagues,[45] in a series of elegant experiments, have shown that the most significant quantitative response to dietary cholesterol is the suppression of hepatic cholesterol synthesis. Moreover, they found that the effect of dietary cholesterol on the apolipoprotein E/apolipoprotein B receptor-mediated LDL clearance is strikingly affected by the proportion of saturated fat fed. Moreover, in a carefully conducted study of healthy medical students, saturated fat did appear to affect the serum cholesterol response to high cholesterol feeding.[46]

However, the relationship between dietary cholesterol and serum cholesterol is not entirely settled. In a study conducted by Edington and co-workers,[47] normolipidemic subjects who had demonstrated a hyper-response to dietary cholesterol, did not show this same response when placed on a low fat diet and were subsequently rechallenged with dietary cholesterol. On the other hand, Katan and co-workers[20,49] have done numerous studies to establish that the responsiveness to dietary cholesterol among human subjects is quite reproducible and constant over time. Furthermore, the subjects studied by these investigators invariably increased the plasma cholesterol when the number of compounds with double bonds in the diet was reduced. (See the following section for elaboration on double-bonded compounds.) Taken as a whole, the studies of Katan and co-workers show a congruence between responsiveness to dietary cholesterol and saturated fat, although it is not an absolute relationship. Thus, subjects who respond to dietary cholesterol with an increase in serum cholesterol have similar changes when saturated fat is given.

Dietary Fats

Saturated fatty acids raise serum cholesterol. Cholesterol-lowering diets often use varying amounts of unsaturated fats to replace saturated fats. The unsaturated fatty acids are separated into families characterized by the number of double bonds and the site of the first double bond. The omega-6 and omega-3 fatty acids refer to two types of polyunsaturated fats, whereas omega-9 fatty acids characterize the monounsaturated fats. Traditional nomenclature designates a particular fatty acid as [C:D, omega-y] where C is the number of carbon atoms, D is the number of double bonds, and if unsaturated, y is the position of the first double bond counting from the methyl position. Thus, oleic acid is designated [18:1, omega-9] indicating that it has 18 carbon atoms, one double bond and is a member of the omega-9 family.

Saturated Fat

Saturated fatty acids vary in chain length from 4 to 18 carbon atoms. The principal dietary saturated fatty acids are lauric acid [12:0], myristic acid [14:0], palmitic acid [16:0] and stearic acid [18:0]. As noted previously, saturated fats suppress LDL-receptor activity and raise LDL-C.[46] Saturated fats are found typically in animal products such as beef, pork and lamb, and in dairy products such as milk, butter and cheeses. Saturated fats are also found as invisible fats in baked goods and foods rich in coconut, palm and palm kernel oil, and as hard fats used in cooking such as lard and butter.

Formulas and ratios. Keys qualified the observation that, in man, serum cholesterol and LDL-C are more sensitive to the effect of saturated fat in raising cholesterol than in polyunsaturated fat in lowering it.[50] His formula expressing this observation is:

$$Chol = 2.74 \ (S) - 1.31 \ (P)$$

where *Chol* = change in serum cholesterol in mg/dl, *S* is change in dietary saturated fat, and *P* is change in dietary polyunsaturated fat. In other words, serum cholesterol is raised 2.7 percent for every 1 percent of total calories derived from saturated fats. This increase is in relation to carbohydrates, which are considered neutral.

Connor and colleagues[51] have popularized the Cholesterol/Saturated Fat Index (CSI) which is used to compare foods according to their cholesterol raising ability. They noted that:

$$CSI = (1.01 \ x \ gm \ saturated \ fat) + (0.05 \ x \ mg \ cholesterol)$$

They found that in men 55 to 64 years old from 40 countries, CSI per 1,000 kcal correlated well with mortality from CHD, with the largest effect coming from saturated fat. Using the CSI makes it easy to see why poultry and shellfish raise the serum cholesterol less, on average, than portions of red meat with similar dietary cholesterol, but much more saturated fat.

The Polyunsaturated/Saturated Fat (P/S) Ratio is a convenient shorthand convention that has been used in the dietary literature. Diets with high P/S ratios (< 1.0) have been felt to be cholesterol lowering, while diets with low P/S ratios (> 1.0) are believed to cause the opposite response. Unfortunately, ratios tend to hide more than they reveal. Since all saturated fats do not raise serum cholesterol in an identical fashion and since the P/S ratio does not take into account monounsaturated fats, this ratio has given way to a more complete description of the diet.

Also, despite early reports suggesting that different types of saturated fats affect serum cholesterol in variable fashions, a recent report by Grundy and associates[52] showed that when it replaces palmitic acid (a saturated fat) in the diet, stearic acid appears to be as effective as oleic acid (a monounsaturated fatty acid) in lowering plasma cholesterol and LDL-C. The significance of this finding is that the P/S ratio cannot be used as an accurate summary statistic for how a food will lower or raise cholesterol, since not all saturated fats act the same.

Monounsaturated Fats

This class is represented by oleic acid [18:1] which is found in olive oil, rapeseed oil and beef. The human body synthesizes monounsaturates from saturated fatty acids. Olive oil is a staple of the Mediterranean diet and is a rich source of oleic acid. Mensink and Katan[53] evaluated 57 outpatient volunteers who were using olive oil-enriched foods. The olive oil-enriched diet caused a specific fall in non-HDL-C, while leaving TG unchanged. Further studies showed that a diet rich in monounsaturated fats was as effective as a diet rich in polyunsaturated fats in lowering LDL-C. Both diets lowered HDL-C slightly in men, but not in women.[54] Indeed, recent studies have shown that when monounsaturated fat is added to a 30 percent fat-10 percent saturated fat-250 mg cholesterol diet, the beneficial effects of such a diet on LDL-C are not altered.[55] Despite the appealing nature of high monounsaturated fat diets, there are negative aspects to any diet high in fat. The risk of obesity (due to 9 kcal/gm of fat as compared to 4 kcal/gm with carbohydrate) and a possible risk of promoting cancer of the breast and colon should put physicians on guard from recommending any diet too high in fat.

Polyunsaturated Fats

Polyunsaturated fats are divided into the omega-6 and omega-3 fatty acids. The key omega-6 fatty acid is linoleic acid [18:2, omega-6] which is an essential fatty acid because it cannot be synthesized in man. Arachidonic acid [20:4, omega-6] is synthesized in the liver from linoleic acid and is the precursor in man for the synthesis of prostaglandins and leukotrienes. Seeds and leaves are the sources of oils rich in omega-6 polyunsaturated fats such as corn, cottonseed, safflower, soybean and sunflower oil. Cottonseed oil is not as desirable for cholesterol-lowering diets because it has significantly more palmitic acid (a saturated fatty acid) than the other oils.

As noted previously, the polyunsaturates have been considered cholesterol-lowering fatty acids, as the Keys equation suggests that for every one percent of calories of polyunsaturated fat ingested, the serum cholesterol should fall about 1.35 mg/dl.[51] Notably, despite extensive studies, there is not wide acceptance of an explanation for the cholesterol-lowering action of the polyunsaturated fats. A comprehensive review of the omega-6 polyunsaturated fats noted that many of the observed effects may, in fact, be interrelated.[56]

Many studies have shown that polyunsaturated fats lower total cholesterol, TG and LDL-C. In patients with a high TG level, neither a high polyunsaturated fat diet or monounsaturated fat diet had striking effects on the lipoprotein level.[57] In summary, omega-6 vegetable oils reduce serum cholesterol and LDL-C when they replace saturated fats in the diet. In equivalent amounts they are not very different from monounsaturated fats and there are variable effects seen depending on the initial lipid level and genotypes with respect to TG and HDL-C.

As mentioned previously, there are interesting data suggesting an important role for linoleic acid, an essential omega-6 polyunsaturated fat, in providing protection against CHD. Three major intervention trials have shown beneficial effects on CHD for diets rich in omega-6 polyunsaturated fats and low in saturated fats.[31-33] Despite these studies, a polyunsaturated fat intake greater than 10 percent is not recommended based on worries regarding obesity, gallstones and lack of long-term follow-up of populations on such a diet. It appears, though, that diets with only 10 percent of calories from polyunsaturated fats are as effective in lowering cholesterol as diets rich in polyunsaturated fats.[58]

Fish Oils

The fat of the Arctic marine animals is the most unsaturated of all animal fats and is particularly rich in omega-3 fatty acids.[57] The major marine lipids which are derived from marine life who ingest phytoplankton are eicosapentaenic (EPA) acid [20:5, omega-3] and docosahexaenic acid [22:6, omega-3]. Like the omega-6 fatty acids, the body is unable to synthesize them for its use. Land sources abundant in omega-3 fatty acids include plant food, leafy vegetables and certain vegetable oils such as linseed oil, rapeseed oil and soybean oil. Marine sources rich in omega-3 fatty acids include fatty fish such as mackerel, salmon, trout and albacore tuna as well as cod liver oil and salmon oil.

The omega-3 fatty acids of fish oils lower the TG level in human subjects. The effects of this reduction of TG are most marked in individuals with moderate or severe elevations of the TG level and to a lesser extent in normals.[59] The degree of lowering seems dose dependent and caused by a decrease in TG production from the liver. Fish oil supplements should not be thought of as cholesterol-lowering agents. Cholesterol values fall secondarily to the fall in the TG level. In fact, effects on LDL-C have been variable with paradoxic elevation of LDL-C seen in cases where TG are high and cholesterol values are normal. When saturated fat intake is held constant, the LDL-C level does not change or increase in response to fish oil.

What makes the omega-3 fatty acids of special interest are their antithrombotic and anti-inflammatory effects.[22] Aspirin inhibits cyclo-oxygenase, an enzyme which is needed to regulate platelet reactivity at vessel wall sites where thrombosis could occur. Dyerberg and colleagues[60] demonstrated that unlike Western diet rich in arachidonic acid (AA) which favored formation in platelets of the proaggregating thromboxane A_2, diets rich in fish oil-derived EPA did not induce platelet aggregation because its use favored formation of platelet thromboxane A_3. Moreover, on the vessel wall side, diets rich in EPA favor formation of PGI_3, which like the prostacyclin formed from diets rich in AA, is anti-aggregating. This explains the tendency of Eskimos to have nosebleeds and bruise easily.

The safety of chronic ingestion of fish oil concentrates is still a concern. Environmental contamination of fish sources with mercury or pesticides, easy bruising or bleeding with increased ingestion of fish oil supplements, and fat soluble vitamin toxicity if cod liver oil is taken in high doses, must be considered before a physician suggests dietary implementation with fish oils. However, the physician can recommend increased fish intake, which has had some success in the clinical and epidemiologic studies mentioned earlier.[23,24]

Nonfat foods can affect the lipid level and CHD. Outpatient management of the lipid level requires a knowledge of the effects of fiber, complex carbohydrates and alcohol. In fact, many of the questions that patients have regarding diet involve these dietary elements.

Fiber

Fiber is a nondigestible carbohydrate from the cell walls of plant foods. It is, therefore, present in abundant quantities in the unprocessed (or minimally so) plant foods that we eat. It is widely recommended as an important dietary therapy for constipation, diverticulitis and hemorrhoids. Fiber is particularly useful in replacing saturated fat in the diet and to provide a feeling of satiety. Insoluble fibers such as cellulose, hemi-cellulose and lignin do not have the mild hypocholesterolemic effect that is seen with soluble or gel-forming fibers such as gums, pectins and mucilages. Good sources of soluble fibers include citrus fruits, barley, oats, guar gum, dry beans and peas.

Oat bran, in particular, has become a popular source of soluble fiber. There has been debate concerning whether its effects are solely because of the replacement of saturated fat with fiber[61] or because of a small, yet significant, independent effect.[62] A recent study in men with elevated LDL-C values showed a dose-dependent reduction in LDL-C attributable to the hypocholesterolemic effects of the β-glucan in the oatmeal. Psyllium, likewise, is gaining acceptance not only as a useful dietary supplement to help control constipation, but as an aid to cholesterol control. A carefully controlled, double-blind, randomized trial using psyllium hydrophilic mucillioid at a dosage of 3.4 gm daily (one teaspoon three times a day) lowered LDL-C 8.2 percent.[64]

Patients can be advised that cholesterol lowering with fiber is affected by the total dose of the fiber and the baseline lipid level. Also, patients with a higher cholesterol value respond more than those with a lower baseline level. Moreover, the total dietary pattern producing the greatest effect is seen when a lipid-lowering diet is combined with a higher intake of soluble fiber. Do not forget that if the dosage of fiber is increased too rapidly, there is a disturbing excess of eructation, abdominal bloating and flatus. Large amounts of fiber may be tolerated eventually, but the key to success is to "start low and go slow!" Because commercial muffins, even if made with oat bran, may be high in total fat content, such items are not recommended. Sources other than muffins that will increase fiber in a very acceptable manner include whole baked potatoes with skins, pectin-rich fruits, beans with soups, stews and casseroles, dark green vegetables and brown rice. A high fiber diet should be relatively inexpensive to maintain. Extremely high doses of fiber are not recommended because possible interference with vitamin-mineral absorption and gastrointestinal cramping and bloating are possible sequelae.

Alcohol

Chronic, excess ingestion of alcohol is harmful to the cardiovascular system.[65] It is a risk factor for hypertension, atrial arrhythmias, cardiomyopathy and stroke. It is a common cause of secondary hypertriglyceridemia.[66] Patients with a TG value above 800 mg/dl are at risk for pancreatitis and restriction of alcohol is an important therapeutic measure. Also, calories from alcohol can displace other nutrients. Whereas epidemiologic studies have implicated saturated fat and dietary cholesterol as causative of CHD, it is also appreciated that studies suggest a protective effect against CHD from alcohol. Hegsted looked at diet and alcohol consumption data from 18 countries and found that alcohol consumption is negatively correlated with CHD mortality.[67] The mechanism is unclear. When moderate drinkers abstain, the decrease in HDL-C seen is in the HDL_3 fraction and not in the less dense HDL_2 fraction, which is usually associated with decreased CHD and found to be raised in women and marathon runners.[68] One answer to this paradox may be that alcohol and mortality relationships are biased; in one study men who were nondrinkers had pre-existing cardiac disease.[69] Also, while protection against CHD morbidity and mortality occurs at a daily intake of one to two drinks, physicians should not counsel patients to drink more, because of the known risks associated with increased alcohol intake.[70] A far better alternative to improving HDL-C and cardiovascular health is regular exercise.[71]

Dietary Guidelines

The first phase in generating the dietary prescription is to take an accurate dietary history (Table II). The next phase is to set reasonable goals. The NCEP panel has outlined minimal goals of therapy for individuals with elevated LDL-C (Table III).[5] For individuals not at high risk (no CHD or less than two risk factors for CHD), the goal is to lower LDL-C below 160 mg/dl. For those at high risk (definite CHD or two or more risk factors for CHD), the LDL-C goals are lower because the MRFIT data showed clearly that individuals with increased risk factor profiles had a higher CHD incidence at equivalent cholesterol values than those with lower risk profiles. To simplify monitoring during dietary therapy, if HDL-C values are 35 mg/dl to 45 mg/dl, the physician can substitute a total cholesterol goal of 240 mg/dl for an LDL-C goal of 160 mg/dl, and a total cholesterol goal of 200 mg/dl for an LDL-C goal of 130 mg/dl.

TABLE II. The MEDICS diet questionnaire (adapted from reference 72)

Meats:	Fatty meats → leaner, lesser cuts
Eggs:	Egg yolks → whites, egg substitutes
Dairy:	Milk, cream, cheese → low fat
Invisible Fats:	Baked goods, commercial products → bagels, whole wheat products
Cooking/Table Fats:	Lard, butter → unsaturated fats, margarine, oils
Snacks:	Candy bars, nuts, chips → fruits, vegetables, whole grain Alcohol → moderation
Other Considerations:	
Meal Frequency:	How many meals? Does the patient know how to select low fat meals when out?
Spirits:	How many drinks per week (one drink = 1 oz of liquor, 1 can of beer or 4 oz of table wine)?
Salt:	Added at the table? Salty foods like commercial soups, cheese, chips, convenience foods, carry out, or cold cuts?

TABLE III. Risk category and dietary LDL-C goals (from reference 5)

Risk Category	LDL-C Goals
Low risk: No CHD or < 2 Risk Factors	LDL-C < 160 mg/dl
High risk: CHD or > 2 Risk Factors	LDL-C < 130 mg/dl

The NCEP recommended a low fat (less than 30 percent), low saturated fat (less than 10 percent) and low dietary cholesterol (less than 300 mg per day) diet to help achieve these goals. It is called the *Step One Diet* and since the usual American diet contains 35 percent to 40 percent of its calories as fat, this translates to reducing total fat in the diet by 14 percent to 25 percent. Of note, the *Step One Diet* is strikingly similar to the American Heart Association Phase I Diet.

If dietary goals are not met, the NCEP panel recommended that calories from saturated fat should be decreased to less than seven percent of daily intake and dietary cholesterol intake restricted to less than 200 mg per day. This strict dietary plan requires good patient motivation and the help of a registered dietician. Recommendation to reduce total fat intake was not made because a diet with much lower fat is often less filling, which reduces the likelihood of good adherence.

Frequent feedback is another important part of the physician's role in carrying out dietary therapy to reduce a high cholesterol level. During dietary therapy the blood cholesterol level is checked at six weeks after initiation and then again at three months to see if the goal level is attained. If the goal level is attained, LDL-C is checked the following week to 10 days to confirm achievement of the goal LDL-C level and long-term monitoring begun. Initially, patients are monitored more frequently. The intervals can then be increased as patient adherence improves.

To improve chances of success with diet, external resources such as registered dieticians should be used. However, lack of third-party payment for certain ancillary services has greatly diminished the usefulness of recommending a dietician. Since a lower fat diet should be less expensive, it should be explained to the patient that the instruction gained is likely worth the cost even if the cost of the instruction is not reimbursed. A frequent pitfall is to be reassured that the diet is followed to the letter at home and then to learn that the patient has most meals prepared away from home.

Therapy with cholesterol-lowering medication is considered if the benefits are judged to outweigh negative aspects or risks. Because medications are not curative, in most patients, a minimum of six months of diet therapy and counseling is required before initiation of drug therapy. Patients in whom a prolonged attempt at diet makes little sense include those with LDL-C greater than 225 mg/dl in whom genetic, diet-resistant hypercholesterolemia is likely present, and those with active CHD in whom diet alone may prove to be inadequate to achieve the LDL-C goals required to reduce risk of angiographic proven progression of CHD.

Many patients have marked psychosocial tensions that contribute to their poor dietary habits. They require more intensive dietary counseling and if asymptomatic, often do best with a longer period of time on diet and with an emphasis on gradual change. Many patients mistakenly feel that they can abandon diet once medication is started. Patients should be warned that the results with medication will be better if dietary adherence is unchanged. The NCEP report emphasized that "drug therapy should be added to dietary therapy, and not substituted for it."

How likely is a physician to have success with urging patients to stick with diet? A physician survey conducted in 1983 and again in 1986 showed that only 12 percent and 15 percent of physicians polled, respectively, felt that they were successful in helping patients achieve cholesterol change through diet.[72] Several behavioral strategies appear to be useful in counseling patients to reduce lipid values.[73] These include:

- setting realistic goals with an emphasis on the need for gradual change;

- involving the patient in the dietary evaluation process such as diet diaries;

- using external resources, such as registered dieticians (the importance of which cannot be emphasized enough), the family (everyone - except for children under age two should be on the same diet), many of the excellent books on diet that are now available, group meetings such as those given by rehabilitation programs and materials from the NCEP or the American Heart Association; and

- providing regular feedback to the patient as to what kind of progress is being made.

TABLE IV. Seven methods for physicians to improve dietary adherence (adapted from reference 71)

1. Set reasonable goals
2. Understand obstacles: audit what and where the patient eats
3. Improve the patient's understanding of what is needed
4. Make dietary change part of a shift to an overall more healthful life style
5. Emphasize family involvement
6. Provide frequent and positive feedback
7. Use resources wisely (dieticians, health care materials)

Most important to convince a patient to continue with a diet, however, is the physician's endorsement of the benefit of diet in the control of cardiovascular disease. This endorsement need not be time consuming. When given in the wider context of prescribing a more healthful life style and an increased change for better health, a more positive doctor-patient interaction would seem to result.

REFERENCES

1. Oliver MF. Cigarette smoking, polyunsaturated fats, linoleic acid, and coronary heart disease. Lancet. 1989;1:1241-1243.
2. Caggiula AW, Christakis G, Fabrand M, et al. The Multiple Risk Factor Intervention Trial (MRFIT). IV. Intervention on blood lipids. Prev Med. 1981:443-475.
3. The Surgeon General's Report on Nutrition and Health. Washington, DC: US Government Printing Office; 1988. US Department of Health and Human Services 017-001-00465-1.
4. National Research Council. Diet and Health: implications for reducing chronic disease risk. Washington, DC: National Academy Press; 1989:227.
5. Adult Treatment Panel. Report of the National Cholesterol Education Program Expert Panel on the detection, evaluation, and treatment of high blood cholesterol in adults. Arch Intern Med. 1988;148:36-69.

6. St. Clair RW. Atherosclerosis regression in animal models: current concepts of cellular and biochemical mechanisms. Progr Cardiovasc Dis. 1983;36:109-132.

7. Armstrong ML, Megan MB. Lipid depletion in atheromatous coronary arteries in rhesus monkeys after regression diets. Circ Res. 1972;30:675-680.

8. Enos WF, Holmes RH, Beyer J. Coronary disease among United States soldiers killed in action in Korea. JAMA. 1953;152:1090-1093.

9. Lauer RM, Lee J, Clarke WR. Factors affecting the relationship between childhood and adult cholesterol levels: The Muscatine Study. Pediatrics. 1988;82:309-318.

10. Solberg LA, Strong JP. Risk factors and atherosclerotic lesions: a review of autopsy studies. Arteriosclerosis. 1983;3:178-198.

11. Ishii T, Newman WP III, Guzman MA, et al. Coronary and aortic atherosclerosis in young men from Tokyo and New Orleans. Lab Invest. 1986;54:561-565.

12. Keys A, ed. Seven Countries: A Multivariate Analysis of Death and Coronary Heart Disease. Cambridge, Ma: Harvard University Press; 1980.

13. Blackburn H, Jacobs D. Sources of the diet-heart controversy: confusion over population versus individual correlations. Circulation. 1984;70:775-780.

14. Stamler J. Life styles, major risk factors, proof and public policy. Circulation. 1978;58:3-19.

15. Kato H, Tillotson J, Nichaman MZ, et al. Epidemiologic studies of coronary heart disease and stroke in Japanese men living in Japan, Hawaii and California. Am J Epidemiol. 1973;97:372-385.

16. Robertson TI, Kato H, Rhoads GG, et al. Epidemiology studies of coronary heart disease and stroke in Japanese men living in Japan, Hawaii, and California. Am J Cardiol. 1977;39:239-243.

17. Kushi LH, Lew RA, Stare FJ, et al. Diet and 20-year mortality from coronary heart disease: the Ireland-Boston diet heart study. N Engl J Med. 1985;312:811-818.

18. Shekelle RB, Shryock AM, Paul O, et al. Diet, serum cholesterol, and death from coronary heart disease: The Western Electric Study. N Engl J Med. 1981;304;65-70.

19. Stamler J, Shekelle R. Dietary cholesterol and human coronary heart disease. Arch Pathol Lab Med. 1988;112:1032-1040.

20. Katan MB, Beynen AC, deBries JH, et al. Existence of consistent hypo- and hyperresponders to dietary cholesterol in man. Am J Epidemiol. 1986;123:221-234.

21. Keys A. Diet and blood cholesterol in population surveys lessons from analysis of the data from a major survey in Israel. Am J Clin Nutr. 1988;48:1161-1165.

22. Leaf A, Weber PC. Cardiovascular effects of n-3 fatty acids. N Engl J Med. 1988;318:549-557.

23. Kromhout D, Bosschieter EB, de Lezzane Coulander C. The inverse relation between fish consumption and twenty-year mortality from coronary heart disease. N Engl J Med. 1985;312:1205-1209.

24. Burr ML, Gilbert JF, Holiday RM, et al. Effects of changes in fat, fish and fiber intakes on death and myocardial reinfarction: Diet And Reinfarction Trial (DART). Lancet. 1989;11:757-761.

25. Fisher M, Levine PH, Weiner B, et al. The effect of vegetarian diets on plasma lipid and platelet levels. Arch Intern Med. 1986;146:1193-1197.

26. Sacks FM, Ornish D, Rosner B, et al. Plasma lipoprotein levels in vegetarians the effect of ingestion of fats from dairy products. JAMA. 1985;254:1337-1341.

27. Burslem J, Schonfeld G, Howald MA, et al. Plasma apoprotein and lipoprotein lipid levels in vegetarians. Metabolism. 1978;27:711-719.

28. Sacks FM, Donner A, Castelli WP, et al. Effect of ingestion of meat on plasma cholesterol of vegetarians. JAMA. 1981;246:640-644.

29. Phillips RL, Lemon FR, Beeson L, et al. Coronary heart disease mortality among Seventh-Day Adventists with differing dietary habits: a preliminary report. Am J Clin Nutr. 1978;31:S191-S198.

30. Lipid Research Clinics Program. The Lipid Research Clinics Coronary Primary Prevention Trial Results. I. Reduction in incidence of coronary heart disease. JAMA. 1984;351-364.

31. Leren P. The Oslo Diet-Heart Study eleven-year report. Circulation. 1970;42:835-942.

32. Dayton S, Pearce ML, Hashimoto S, et al. A controlled clinical trial of diet high in unsaturated fat in preventing complications of atherosclerosis. Circulation. 1969;II(suppl 20):1-63.

33. Hjermann I, Holme I, Velve Byre K, et al. Effect of diet and smoking intervention on the incidence of coronary heart disease. Lancet. 1981;2:1303-1310.

34. Holme I, Hjermann I, Helgeland A, et al. The Oslo Study: diet and antismoking advice: additional results from a 5-year primary prevention trial in middle-aged men. Prev Med. 1985;14:279-292.

35. Hjermann I, Holme I, Leren P. The Oslo Study: diet and antismoking trial results after 102 months. Am J Med. 1986;80:(suppl 2A)7-12.

36. Multiple Risk Factor Intervention Trial Research Group. Multiple Risk Factor Intervention Trial, risk factor changes and mortality results. JAMA. 1982;248:1465-1477.

37. Arntzenius AC, Kromhout D, Barth JD, et al. Diet, lipoproteins, and the progression of coronary atherosclerosis. The Leiden Intervention Trial. N Engl J Med. 1985;312:805-811.

38. Blankenhorn DH, Johnson RL, Mack WJ, et al. The influence of diet on the appearance of new lesions in the human coronary arteries. JAMA. 1990;263:1646-1652.

39. Taylor WC, Pass TM, Shepard DL, et al. Cholesterol reduction and life expectancy. Ann Intern Med. 1987;106:605-614.

40. Illingworth DR. Cholesterol content of game meat. JAMA. 1987;258:1532.

41. Sacks FM, Salazar J, Miller L, et al. Ingestion of egg raises plasma low-density lipoprotein in free-living subjects. Lancet. 1984;1:647-649.

42. McNamara DJ, Kolb R, Parker TS, et al. Heterogeneity of cholesterol homeostasis in man. Response to changes in dietary fat quality and cholesterol quantity. J Clin Invest. 1987;79:1729-1739.

43. Kern F. Normal plasma cholesterol in an 88-year-old man who eats 25 eggs a day. N Eng J Med. 1991;324:896-899.

44. Tikkanen MJ, Huttunen JK, Ehnholm C, Pietinen P. Apolipoprotein E_4 homozygosity predisposes to serum cholesterol elevation during high fat diet. Arteriosclerosis. 1990;10:285-288.

45. Woolett LA, Spady DK, Dietschy JM. Mechanisms by which saturated triacylglycerols elevate the plasma low-density lipoprotein-cholesterol concentration in hamsters. Differential effects of fatty acid chain length. J Clin Invest. 1989;84:119-128.

46. Schonfeld G, Patsch W, Rudel LL, et al. Effects of dietary cholesterol and fatty acids on plasma lipoproteins. J Clin Invest. 1982;69:1072-1080.

47. Grundy SM, Barrett-Connor E, Rudel LL, et al. Workshop on the impact of dietary cholesterol on plasma lipoproteins and atherogenesis. Arteriosclerosis. 1988;8:95-101.

48. Edington J, Geekie M, Carter R, et al. Effect of dietary cholesterol on plasma cholesterol concentration in subjects following reduced fat, high fibre diet. Br Med J. 1987;294:333-336.

49. Katan MB, Berns MAM, Glatz JFC, et al. Congruence of individual responsiveness to dietary cholesterol and to saturated fat in humans. J Lipid Res. 1988;29:888-892.

50. Keys A, Anderson JT, Grande F. Serum cholesterol response to dietary fat. Lancet. 1957;1:787.

51. Connor SL, Artaud W, Classick-Kohn CJ, et al. The Cholesterol/Saturated Fat Index: an indication of the hypercholesterolemic and atherogenic potential of food. Lancet. 1986;1:1229-1232.

52. Bonanome A, Grundy· SM. Effect of dietary stearic acid on plasma cholesterol and lipoprotein levels. N Engl J Med. 1988;318:1244-1248.

53. Mensink RP, Katan MB. Effect of monounsaturated fatty acids versus complex carbohydrates on high-density lipoproteins in healthy men and women. Lancet. 1987;1:125.

54. Mensink RP, Latan MB. Effect of a diet enriched with monounsaturated or polyunsaturated fatty acids on levels of low-density and high-density lipoprotein cholesterol in healthy women and men. N Engl J Med. 1989;321:436-441.

55. Ginsberg HN, Barr SL, Gilbert A, et al. Reduction of plasma cholesterol levels in normal men on an American Heart Association Step I Diet or a Step I Diet with added monounsaturated fat. N Engl J Med. 1990;332:574-579.

56. Goodnight SH, Harris WS, Connor WE, et al. Polyunsaturated fatty acids, hyperlipidemia, and thrombosis. Arteriosclerosis. 1982;2:87-113.

57. Mattson FH, Grundy SM. Comparison of effects of dietary saturated, monounsaturated, and polyunsaturated fatty acids on plasma lipids and lipoproteins in man. J Lipid Res. 1985;26:194-202.

58. Grundy SM, Nix D, Whelan MF, et al. Comparison of three cholesterol-lowering diets in normolipidemic men. JAMA. 1986;256:2351-2355.

59. Harris WS. Fish oils and plasma lipid and lipoprotein metabolism in humans: a critical review. J Lipid Res. 1989;30:785-807.

60. Dyerberg J, Bang HO, Stoffersen E, et al. Eicosapentaenoic acid and prevention of thrombosis and atherosclerosis? Lancet. 1978;2:117-119.

61. Swain JF, Rouse IL, Curley CB, Sacks FM. Comparison of the effects of oat bran and low-fiber wheat on serum lipoprotein levels and blood pressure. N Engl J Med. 1990;322:147-152.

62. Van Horn LV, Liu K, Parker D, et al. Serum lipid response to oat product intake with a fat-modified diet. JAMA. 1986;86:759-764.

63. Davidson MH, Dugan LD, Burns JH, et al. The hypocholesterolemic effects of β-glucan in oatmeal and oat bran: a dose-controlled study. JAMA. 1991;265:1833-1839.

64. Bell LP, Hectome K, Reynolds H, et al. Cholesterol-lowering effects of psyllium hydrophilic mucilloid. Adjunct therapy to a prudent diet for patients with mild to moderate hypercholesterolemia. JAMA. 1989;261:3419-3423.

65. Davidson DM. Cardiovascular effects of alcohol. West J Med. 1989;151:430-439.

66. Chait A, Mancini M, February AW, et al. Clinical and metabolic study of alcoholic hyperlipidemia. Lancet. 1972;2:62-64.

67. Hegsted DM, Ausman LM. Diet, alcohol, and coronary heart disease in men. J Nutr. 1988;118:1184-1189.

68. Haskell WL, Camargo C, Williams PT, et al. The effect of cessation and resumption of moderate alcohol intake on serum high-density lipoprotein subfractions. N Engl J Med. 1984;310:805-810.

69. Shaper AG, Wannamethee G, Walker M. Alcohol and mortality in British men: explaining the U-shaped curve. Lancet. 1988;2:1267-1273.

70. Klatsky AL, Armstrong MA, Friedman GD. Relations of alcoholic beverage use to subsequent coronary artery disease hospitalization. Am J Cardiol. 1986;58:710-714.

71. Eichner ER. Alcohol versus exercise for coronary protection. Am J Med. 1985;79:231-240.

72. Stone N. Working with your patients to accomplish dietary therapy. Cholesterol and Coronary Disease...Reducing the Risk. 1989;2:1-4.

73. Schucker B, Wittes JT, Cutler JA, et al. Change in physician perspective on cholesterol and heart disease: results from two national surveys. JAMA. 1987;258:3521-3526.

CHAPTER 3

Bile Acid Sequestrants

David J. Gordon, M.D., Ph.D.
Bethesda, Maryland

INTRODUCTION

The bile acid sequestrants, cholestyramine (Questran®) and colestipol (Colestid®), are among the oldest antihyperlipidemic agents currently in use. These agents were first introduced for this purpose in the early 1960s and they are still regarded as first-line drugs in the treatment of patients with a high blood cholesterol level.[1] Of note, many patients regard these agents as inconvenient and/or unpleasant. However, the acceptance and longstanding continued use of these drugs can be attributed to the fact that the actions produced are confined to the gut lumen and therefore, these drugs offer therapy that is relatively free from systemic side effects.

ADMINISTRATION AND DOSAGE

The bile acid sequestrants are traditionally dispensed as powders, mixed with sugar and flavoring, to be drunk in a slurry with water or juice. The dosage unit is 4 gm for cholestyramine or 5 gm for colestipol, mixed in 2 to 6 ounces of liquid. A typical patient might be required to ingest 4 to 6 of these dosage units per day, usually divided equally between morning and evening administrations. Both agents can be purchased in premeasured packets, each corresponding to a single dosage unit, although they are more economically purchased in bulk form with a measuring scoop. Recently, a candy bar form of cholestyramine (Cholebar®) was introduced as an alternative for patients who find the resin powders inconvenient or unpalatable. Although some patients may prefer the taste or consistency of one or another resin preparation, or experience less gastrointestinal upset with one or the other preparation, all forms of cholestyramine and colestipol have essentially the same pharmacologic action and the same constellation of positive and adverse effects.

STRUCTURE AND MECHANISM OF ACTION

The bile acid sequestrants are polycationic resins (Figure 1), which, as their name implies, act by binding bile acids and other anions in the lumen of the small intestine. This binding prevents reabsorption of the bile acids and other anions in the terminal ileum.[1] While under normal circumstances the bile acids are normally recycled and thereby conserved, the fecal excretion of the bile acids increases as much as 30-fold when their enterohepatic circulation is disrupted by one of these agents. Since cholesterol is needed as a precursor for hepatic synthesis of bile acids to replace the amount of bile acid lost in the stool through the action of bile acid sequestrants, cholesterol catabolism increases.

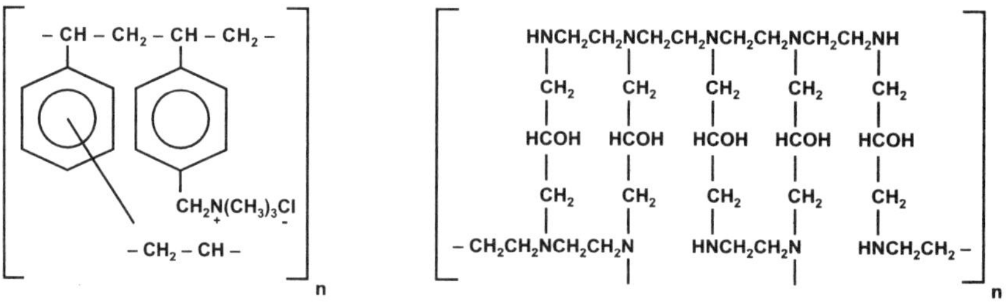

Figure 1. Chemical structures of the repeating monomeric units of the bile acid sequestrant resins

However, the mechanism by which the circulating cholesterol level is reduced is more complex and subtle than as a catabolic response to reduced bile acids. With the use of bile acid sequestrants, increased demand on hepatic cholesterol stores to replace sequestered bile acids elicits two compensatory responses by the liver, one response desirable, the other not desired. The *desired response* is the synthesis of additional low-density lipoprotein (LDL) receptors, which take up and initiate the intracellular catabolism of circulating LDL, the main atherogenic cholesterol-carrying plasma lipoprotein.[2] The *undesired response* is an increase in hepatic cholesterol synthesis. The extent to which one or the other of these responses predominates determines the degree to which circulating LDL and total cholesterol levels will fall as a result of bile acid sequestrant therapy, and varies considerably from one patient to another. The balance between the two responses may also be favorably influenced by concomitant therapy with diet (the first-line treatment in primary hypercholesterolemia) and with drugs that interfere with cholesterol synthesis.

EFFICACY

On average, the cholesterol level of patients receiving the full dose of cholestyramine (24 gm) or colestipol (30 gm) falls by approximately 20 percent to 25 percent. The plasma LDL level typically falls by 30 percent to 35 percent, while the plasma level of high-density lipoprotein (HDL) and very low-density lipoprotein (VLDL), the two other significant circulating carriers of cholesterol, shows little change or a slight increase. Because the dose-response curves for the bile acid sequestrants are not linear and show a saturation effect with increasing dosage, patients with only moderate elevations, i.e., 130 mg/dl to 190 mg/dl in plasma LDL-cholesterol (LDL-C) can often be treated adequately with smaller dosages, i.e., 8 gm to 16 gm of cholestyramine per day, in combination with diet.

In addition to establishing the efficacy of the bile acid sequestrants in lowering plasma total cholesterol and LDL-C levels, clinical trials have now provided solid evidence that this efficacy translates into reduced morbidity and mortality from atherosclerotic coronary heart disease (CHD). Cholestyramine was the drug used in the Lipid Research Clinics Coronary Primary Prevention Trial (CPPT), a multicenter, double-blind, randomized, placebo-controlled clinical trial conducted in 3,806 men, aged 35 years to 59 years, with an LDL-C level above 190 mg/dl at entry.[3] After a mean of 7.4 years of treatment with a moderate cholesterol-lowering diet and cholestyramine (prescribed at a dosage of 24 gm per day) or placebo, the incidence of definite myocardial infarction and/or CHD death (the predetermined primary end-point of the trial) was 19 percent lower in the cholestyramine group (155 events in 1,907 men) than in the placebo group (187 events in 1,899 men). In the group treated with cholestyramine, there were proportionate reductions in fatal and nonfatal CHD events, including angina pectoris and conversion from a negative to a positive exercise electrocardiogram. Also, there was a decrease in coronary revascularization procedures performed in men who received cholestyramine. Altogether, 27 percent of participants assigned to receive cholestyramine versus 33 percent of those assigned to receive placebo suffered one or more of these CHD events at some time during the CPPT.[4]

The reductions in CHD incidence observed in the CPPT were attained despite considerable problems with drug compliance. Many CPPT participants found it difficult to remain on cholestyramine; by the end of the study, only half reported taking the full 24 gm daily dose, while 27 percent of participants reported taking essentially no drug (2 gm or less per day). These numbers probably overestimate actual drug intake since the packet count method used to assess compliance in the CPPT was occasionally foiled by participants who artificially inflated their packet count by disposing of medication they did not actually ingest in order to avoid disappointing their caretakers. Thus, the mean plasma cholesterol reduction associated with assignment to cholestyramine treatment in the CPPT was only 8.5 percent for total cholesterol and 12.6 percent for the LDL-C level. When the CPPT data were analyzed, taking drug compliance and actual reductions in plasma cholesterol level into account, CHD incidence rates were reduced by 0.8 percent for every 1 mg/dl reduction in total cholesterol or LDL-C level, or about 2 percent for every 1 percent reduction in total cholesterol level.[5] Rates of incidence of CHD were reduced by nearly half in good compliers to cholestyramine treatment, with mean reductions of 25 percent in total cholesterol and 35 percent in LDL-C level.

Although there have been no long-term randomized clinical trials of colestipol treatment comparable to the CPPT, the similarity of the two bile acid sequestrant resins is so great that few would dispute a direct extrapolation. Two recent studies designed to determine the effect of plasma lipid modification on the progression of coronary atherosclerosis, as assessed by angiography in patients with established CHD, have used colestipol in combination with other drugs. The Cholesterol Lowering Atherosclerosis Study (CLAS) assessed the effect of combined colestipol-nicotinic acid-diet therapy in nonsmoking patients who had undergone coronary bypass surgery; no restrictions were placed on plasma lipid or lipoprotein levels at entry.[6] After only two years, a highly significant reduction in the mean progression of atherosclerotic lesions (as determined by a semiquantitative "global score") was observed in treated men as compared to those assigned to placebo. Moreover, 16 percent of treated men as compared to only 2 percent of placebo controls showed discernible evidence of *regression* of pre-existing atherosclerotic plaques. Angiograms taken after an additional two years of treatment showed continued divergence of the treated and control groups. Of note, compliance was considerably better in this study than in the CPPT and the inclusion of nicotinic acid in the treatment regimen resulted in substantial rises in plasma HDL-cholesterol (HDL-C) and falls in plasma VLDL-cholesterol (VLDL-C), as well as enhancing the colestipol-associated reduction in the plasma LDL-C level. Similar favorable results were obtained in the Familial Atherosclerosis Treatment Study (FATS), which used colestipol in combination with nicotinic acid or lovastatin in CHD patients with an elevated plasma level of apolipoprotein B (the main protein component of LDL and VLDL).[7]

SIDE EFFECTS

Because the bile acid sequestrants are physically confined within the gut lumen, the side effects of the compounds are mainly referable to the gastrointestinal tract and are generally not associated with medically serious consequences. Because cholesterol-lowering treatment is a lifelong proposition, this relatively low potential for systemic side effects is a major advantage over a number of other currently available drugs used for this purpose. Nevertheless, as might be inferred from the CPPT experience described previously, the gastrointestinal side effects of these drugs are serious enough to limit compliance with (and therefore the real-life efficacy of) prescribed treatment regimens, unless potential problems are anticipated and dealt with effectively.

Constipation

The most frequent complaint from patients taking bile acid sequestrants is constipation. In the CPPT, 39 percent of participants receiving cholestyramine complained of moderate to severe constipation during the first year of the trial versus complaints in 10 percent of participants receiving placebo.[3] In many instances, constipation can be alleviated by a combination of adequate fluid intake (both resins are quite hygroscopic) and increased intake of foods rich in dietary fiber, i.e., dried fruits, cereal brans, etc. In more resistant cases, psyllium, fiber supplements or stool softeners can be prescribed. Some patients who are initially unable to tolerate the full daily dose of cholestyramine or colestipol will tolerate and obtain a worthwhile therapeutic effect from a reduced dose of resin, which if necessary, can be increased in gradual increments until a limit of tolerance is reached. Alternatively, a low dose of a second cholesterol-lowering drug can be added to obtain the desired degree of plasma cholesterol reduction. In the CPPT, where management options were limited by the study protocol, only 8 percent of men in the cholestyramine group, versus 4 percent in the placebo group, were still complaining of moderate to severe constipation during the seventh and last year of the study. This low rate of constipation can probably be explained by a combination of successful management of some affected participants and discontinuation of the study medication by others.

Other Gastrointestinal Side Effects

A number of other moderate to severe gastrointestinal side effects, such as gas, heartburn, belching or bloating, nausea and abdominal pain were reported by 15 percent to 32 percent of cholestyramine-treated CPPT participants during the first year of the trial.[3] Many of these symptoms were almost as frequent in the placebo group as in the cholestyramine group. In fact, only heartburn and bloating/belching were clearly drug-related, with 27 percent of cholestyramine-treated patients versus 10 percent of the placebo group experiencing heartburn and 27 percent of treated patients versus 16 percent of placebo patients having belching/bloating symptomatology. However, symptoms such as gas and nausea that were common in both groups may represent aversive reactions to the taste and consistency of the resin or placebo slurry and may present significant impediments to adherence even if these symptoms are not strictly "drug-related."

Carcinoma

A more serious concern regarding the gastrointestinal effects of bile acid sequestrant therapy relates to the long-term effect of exposure of the gastrointestinal epithelium to the resins and the bile acids that are bound to them. Because bile acids have been suspected as possible carcinogens and/or co-carcinogens, and since cholestyramine has been implicated as a co-carcinogen with 1,2-dimethylhydrazine in germ-free rats,[8] there was some concern that long-term exposure to either cholestyramine or colestipol might lead to an increased incidence of carcinoma of the colon and rectum. In the CPPT, *no such increase* was observed over the 7.4 year mean duration of treatment.[3] The results of 6 additional years of follow-up will soon be reported.

Unexpectedly, a nominally significant drug-placebo difference was observed in the CPPT among cancers of the mouth and pharynx, with six cases observed in the cholestyramine group and none in the placebo group.[3] These cases, none of which were fatal during the study, all occurred in current or former smokers, and one was the recurrence of a lesion that predated cholestyramine treatment. Moreover, the incidence of six such cancers in the cholestyramine group, representing a variety of sites and tissue types, was only slightly higher than the number of cases (4.5) that would have been expected among 1,907 U.S. males in this age group who were followed over this period of time. However, although the possibility of a contributory effect of chronic exposure of the oral and pharyngeal mucosa to cholestyramine resin cannot be entirely ruled out, this adverse trend in incidence of oral and pharyngeal cancers should be put in perspective by noting that the CPPT cholestyramine group showed reductions in the incidence of lung and prostate cancers relative to the placebo group, and that the overall incidence of malignant neoplasia was virtually identical in the two groups.

Hyperlipidemia

Although the bile acid sequestrants are not absorbed, those agents do have some indirect, potentially adverse, systemic effects in addition to their beneficial effect on the plasma cholesterol level.[1] These drugs tend to raise plasma triglyceride and VLDL-C levels, especially in those individuals with a pre-existing propensity to hypertriglyceridemia. These agents are often ineffective in patients who have combined hyperlipidemia, in whom nicotinic acid and the fibrates are the preferred agents. Also, the bile acid sequestrants are contraindicated in patients with Type III dysbetalipoproteinemia. Of note, overindulgence in alcoholic beverage intake may further exacerbate the tendency toward a hypertriglyceridemic response to the bile acid sequestrants.

Interactions With Other Drugs

The nonspecificity of the affinity of the bile acid sequestrant resins for anions in the gastrointestinal tract is also a potential source of difficulty. Patients taking anionic drugs such as cardiac glycosides, coumarin derivatives, beta-adrenergic blockers, thiazide diuretics, and thyroxine should be advised to allow at least two hours between the time they take these drugs and the time they take their dose of resin. Dosages of drugs like warfarin and digoxin, for which fluctuations in blood level can be dangerous, must be titrated carefully while the patient is taking a fixed regimen of a bile acid sequestrant; and the patient must be cautioned against missed doses and sudden changes in dosage schedule. This potential for serious drug interactions may greatly complicate the use of the resins in elderly patients taking multiple drugs and may virtually preclude the use of these agents in those individuals who are forgetful or unreliable.

Malabsorption and Hyperabsorption

Cholestyramine and colestipol may also cause malabsorption of fat and fat-soluble vitamins due to decreased intestinal availability of bile acids.[1] Malabsorption of the anionic vitamin folic acid has also been reported. Since both resins are administered as chloride salts, hyperchloremic acidosis is another potential side effect, especially in children with familial hypercholesterolemia who are exposed to very high doses of the resin. In general, however, clinically significant malabsorption of fats or anions or hyperabsorption of chloride is rarely seen in patients with intact gastrointestinal tracts who receive the usual doses of these drugs.

Blood Chemistry Changes

Treatment with bile acid sequestrant resins is also associated with changes in blood chemistry of uncertain physiologic significance. Typically, the serum alkaline phosphatase level remained within the normal range but increased slightly and the serum carotene level decreased in CPPT participants who received cholestyramine.[3] As is typical of virtually all cholesterol-lowering drugs, a small percentage of resin recipients will show more significant spikes in serum transaminase and/or alkaline phosphatase levels that resolve when the drug is withdrawn and reappear when the drug is reinitiated. A liver biopsy in one such CPPT patient failed to reveal any specific abnormality.

Gallstones

While some cholesterol-lowering agents, particularly the fibric acid derivatives, have a known lithogenic effect on bile composition and are associated with increased incidence of gallstones, the bile acid sequestrants do not appear to alter bile composition unfavorably. In the

CPPT, however, gallstones and gallbladder surgery were more common among men receiving cholestyramine than among those receiving placebo, although the differences were not statistically significant.

LONG-TERM MORTALITY FACTORS

An additional set of concerns related to cholesterol-lowering in general rather than to any particular class of drug should be mentioned. There has not been a randomized trial clearly demonstrating that cholesterol-lowering prolongs life. In the CPPT, there were only three fewer deaths in 7.4 years among men (68 versus 71).[3] The cholestyramine-associated reduction in CHD mortality of 32 CHD-related deaths of men on cholestyramine, as compared to 44 deaths in the placebo group (including "suspect" as well as "definite" cases), was mostly offset by an excess in accidental and violent deaths (11 such deaths of men on cholestyramine as compared to 4 such deaths of men on placebo). Since there was no clear explanation of these excess accidental/violent deaths, most of which bore no apparent relationship to any reckless or violent tendencies of the victims and some of which occurred long after the participant had stopped taking cholestyramine, they were attributed to chance. However, a similar phenomenon was observed in the Helsinki Heart Study[9] which used an entirely different drug (gemfibrozil). Other noncardiovascular causes of death have been increased in those receiving active treatment in other cholesterol-lowering trials, although no clear pattern is evident. A significant reduction in all-cause mortality via cholesterol lowering has been observed in the 9-year post-trial follow-up of the nicotinic acid treatment arm of the Coronary Drug Project,[10] a secondary intervention trial in postmyocardial infarction patients initiated in the late 1960s. However, it is likely that the cholesterol-lowering interventions tested in most clinical trials have been too brief and possibly included too few patients to address the question of cholesterol lowering and longevity.

INDICATIONS FOR BILE ACID SEQUESTRANT THERAPY

In 1987, the National Cholesterol Education Program (NCEP), a cooperative endeavor of governmental agencies and private organizations coordinated by the National Heart, Lung, and Blood Institute, issued guidelines for the Detection, Evaluation, and Treatment of High Blood Cholesterol in Adults.[11] These guidelines were the product of an expert panel of lipid specialists, nutritionists, clinical cardiologists and epidemiologists appointed by the NCEP for the express purpose of developing such guidelines. Similar panels have issued reports on laboratory methods to be used for measurment of lipid parameters, standardization of these methods, population approaches to cholesterol lowering, and detection and treatment of high blood cholesterol in children.

The NCEP report recommends that all adults above 20 years of age have a serum or plasma total cholesterol determination at least once every five years. The report recommends further evaluation for those whose cholesterol level, based on the average of at least two values, exceeds 240 mg/dl. Additional evaluation is also recommended for those individuals who have a total cholesterol level > 200 mg/dl and have pre-existing CHD or have two or more of the following "background" risk factors: male gender; family history of "premature" CHD; cigarette smoking; hypertension; an HDL-C level below 35 mg/dl; diabetes mellitus; pre-existing cerebrovascular or occlusive peripheral vascular disease; and severe obesity.

Decisions as to whether or how to treat patients are made on the basis of the LDL-C level. For an LDL-C level above 160 mg/dl, based on the average of at least two values, treatment should be initiated; however, a level below 130 mg/dl does not require therapy. Between these two LDL-C cutpoints, treatment is required only for those with pre-existing CHD or two or more of the background risk factors listed previously.

The initial mode of treatment should always be diet. In the Step One Diet, total fat intake is reduced to no more than 30 percent of total caloric intake. (Of note, typically, Americans derive 35 to 40 percent of their calories from fat.) Saturated fat intake is reduced to less than 10 percent of total calories, and dietary cholesterol intake is reduced to less than 300 mg daily. If after three months the LDL-C level remains above the aforementioned cutpoints (160 mg/dl for those without and 130 mg/dl for those with CHD or multiple background risk factors), the Step Two Diet should be tried. In the Step Two Diet, intake of saturated fat and cholesterol is further reduced to less than 7 percent of total calories and less than 200 mg daily, respectively. Drug treatment should be considered only in those individuals who fail to respond adequately after a full 6-month trial of dietary therapy. Exceptions are unusual cases (especially patients with familial hypercholesterolemia) that are judged unlikely to be controlled by diet alone and where delay is considered inadvisable.

After an adequate trial of dietary therapy, drug treatment is recommended for patients whose serum or plasma LDL-C levels remain above 190 mg/dl (160 mg/dl for those with CHD or multiple background risk factors). Of note, these cutpoints were set 30 mg/dl higher than those used for dietary treatment to avoid the unnecessary introduction of drugs in patients who are approaching adequate control by diet alone. However, in patients with pre-existing CHD, it may be advisable to introduce drug therapy earlier and at lower LDL-C levels than recommended by the NCEP guideline for the usual asymptomatic patient. Based on the results of randomized clinical trials that had established long-term safety and efficacy in reducing CHD events, the bile acid sequestrants and nicotinic acid are identified in the NCEP guidelines as first-line drugs in the treatment of high blood cholesterol. Also, based on the results of the Helsinki Heart Study,[9] the results of which were announced just prior to publication of the NCEP report, the possible elevation of gemfibrozil to "first-line" status (as a potential alternative to nicotinic acid) received a footnote in the NCEP report.

The choice between a bile acid sequestrant resin versus nicotinic acid in the treatment of high blood cholesterol is governed by considerations both of efficacy and toxicity. When an elevated LDL-C level is the sole or predominant abnormality, a resin will probably provide the greater LDL-C reduction and would, therefore, constitute the treatment of choice. In patients with combined lipid disorders, who often show an inadequate or mixed response to cholestyramine or colestipol, a better choice might be nicotinic acid, which lowers VLDL-C as well as LDL-C levels and raises a low HDL-C level. However, the selection of a drug will often come down to a question of which agent the patient will tolerate. The problems associated with bile acid sequestrants have been described previously in this chapter. Nicotinic acid is associated with a variety of adverse systemic effects, such as vasomotor flushing, hyperglycemia, hyperuricemia and hepatotoxemia, that may preclude its use in 20 percent of potential patients. Sometimes patients who will not tolerate an adequate therapeutic dose of either drug alone will achieve a good therapeutic response from lower doses of nicotinic acid and a bile acid sequestrant resin when given in combination. The pharmacologic action of nicotinic acid, which slows LDL synthesis, complements that of the resins, which increase its catabolism.

The recent advent of the 3-hydroxy-3-methylglutaryl coenzyme A (HMG CoA) reductase inhibitors, the first of which (lovastatin) was released just before the NCEP guidelines were announced, has provided an attractive alternative to the resins for lowering a high LDL-C level.[12] These drugs act by competitively inhibiting HMG CoA reductase, the rate-limiting enzyme for cholesterol synthesis. The physiologic translation of this primary effect of HMG CoA reductase inhibition into a compensatory increase in hepatic LDL receptors and a consequent increase in LDL catabolism (analogous to that produced by the bile and sequestrant resins) is responsible for the fall in the circulating total LDL-C level. (Without the stimulation of receptors, the liver simply manufactures more HMG CoA reductase to overcome the drug's inhibitory effect.)

However, while the HMG CoA reductase inhibitors outperform the resins in lowering the LDL-C level and being well-tolerated by the great majority of patients,[13] these agents have not yet made the resins obsolete. Unlike the resins, the HMG CoA reductase inhibitors act systemically, and the long-term safety and efficacy for these agents in reducing clinical events have not yet been established by clinical trials. Several such trials, involving pravastatin and simvastatin as well as lovastatin, are now in progress. Of note, regimens combining the HMG CoA reductase inhibitors with a bile acid sequestrant resin and/or nicotinic acid are particularly potent in normalizing the circulating lipid and lipoprotein levels of all but the most severely hypercholesterolemic patients.[14]

CONCLUSIONS

The bile acid sequestrant resins, cholestyramine and colestipol, are safe and effective cholesterol-lowering drugs. The chief advantage of these agents is their confinement to the gut lumen, which limits their potential for systemic toxicity. The chief disadvantages of these drugs are their physical characteristics (bulk, taste and consistency) and propensity to cause gastrointestinal side effects, which though minor physiologically, may be major impediments to drug compliance. Therefore, despite the advent of newer, more effective and better tolerated drugs, the resins remain first-line drugs in the clinical management of hypercholesterolemia.

REFERENCES

1. Hunninghake DB, Gordon DJ, Tamir I, et al. Management of hyperlipoproteinemia. In: Pradhan SN, Maickel RP, Dutta SN, eds. Pharmacology in Medicine. Bethesda, MD: SP Press International Inc.; 1986;617-633.
2. Brown MS, Goldstein JL. A receptor-mediated pathway for cholesterol homeostasis. Science. 1986;232:34-47.
3. Lipid Research Clinics Program. The Lipid Research Clinics Coronary Primary Prevention Trial Results. I. Reduction in incidence of coronary heart disease. JAMA. 1984;251:351-364.
4. Gordon DJ, Knoke J, Probstfield JL, et al. High-density lipoprotein cholesterol and coronary heart disease in hypercholesterolemic men: the Lipid Research Clinics Coronary Primary Prevention Trial. Circulation. 1986;74:1217-1225.
5. Lipid Research Clinics Program. The Lipid Research Clinics Coronary Primary Prevention Trial Results. II. The relationship of reduction in incidence of coronary heart disease to cholesterol lowering. JAMA. 1984;251:365-374.
6. Blankenhorn DH, Nessim SA, Johnson RL, et al. Beneficial effects of combined colestipol-niacin therapy on coronary atherosclerosis and coronary venous bypass grafts. JAMA. 1987;257:3233-3240.
7. Brown BG, Lin JT, Schaefer SM, et al. Niacin or lovastatin, combined with colestipol regress coronary atherosclerosis and prevent clinical events in men with elevated apolipoprotein B. Circulation. 1989;80(4)(suppl II):266. Abstract.
8. Asano T, Pollard M, Madsen DC. Effects of cholestyramine on 1,2-dimethylhydrazine induced enteric carcinoma in germ-free rats. Proc Soc Exp Biol Med. 1975;150:780-785.
9. Frick MH, Elo O, Haapa K, et al. Helsinki Heart Study: Primary-Prevention Trial with gemfibrozil in middle-aged men with dyslipidemia. Safety of treatment, changes in risk factors, and incidence of coronary heart disease. N Engl J Med. 1987;317:1237-1245.
10. Canner PL, Berge KG, Wenger NK, et al. Fifteen year mortality in coronary drug project patients: long-term benefit with niacin. J Am Coll Cardiol. 1986;8:1245-1255.

11. Report of the National Cholesterol Education Program Expert Panel on Detection, Evaluation, and Treatment of High Blood Cholesterol in Adults. Arch Intern Med. 1988;148:36-69.

12. Gordon DJ, Rifkind BM. 3-Hydroxy-3-methylglutaryl coenzyme A (HMG-CoA) reductase inhibitors: a new class of cholesterol-lowering agents. Ann Intern Med. 1987;107:759-761.

13. Hoeg JM, Brewer HB. 3-Hydroxy-3-methylglutaryl coenzyme A reductase inhibitors in the treatment of hypercholesterolemia. JAMA. 1987;258:3532-3536.

14. Vega GL, Grundy SN. Treatment of primary moderate hypercholesterolemia with lovastatin (mevinolin) and colestipol. JAMA. 1987;257:33-38.

CHAPTER 4

Nicotinic Acid

Henry N. Ginsberg M.D.
New York, New York

INTRODUCTION

Niacin (nicotinic acid) is a water-soluble vitamin that is very effective as a lipid-altering medication when used in pharmacologic doses. Niacin (Figure 1), has been used for over three decades in the treatment of subjects with hyperlipidemia. More recently, niacin has become a primary agent in the treatment of dyslipidemias characterized by a reduced level of high-density lipoprotein cholesterol (HDL-C) in the presence or absence of elevated levels of plasma low-density lipoprotein cholesterol (LDL-C) and total triglycerides (TG). Niacin therapy reduces plasma levels of total cholesterol and LDL-C, reduces total plasma TG concentrations and significantly, often dramatically, increases the plasma HDL-C level. Long-term effects of treatment with niacin have been well described and documented.[1-3] The use of niacin in the Coronary Drug Project (CDP) to treat middle-aged men with a pre-existing history of coronary heart disease (CHD) was associated with a reduction in nonfatal coronary events.[4] A subsequent, long-term follow-up study of the men involved in this study showed, furthermore, that the niacin-treated group had increased longevity.[5] The use of niacin, though safe, is not without several practical problems and potential adverse outcomes.[6] In the following discussion, an attempt will be made to review the existing knowledge concerning the mechanism of action of niacin as a lipid-altering agent, demonstrate its efficacy and lay the groundwork for the successful use of this agent in clinical practice.

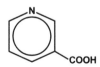

Figure 1. Chemical structure of niacin

PHARMACOLOGY AND METABOLISM

Niacin or nicotinic acid is readily, and nearly completely, absorbed from the gastrointestinal tract, reaching peak blood levels within 60 minutes after ingestion. Absorption from the small intestine is more rapid than absorption from the stomach, which probably accounts for the reduced incidence and severity of cutaneous signs such as flushing and itching when niacin is ingested with a meal.[7] Much of the dose is removed via the liver, before it reaches the circulation, and 88 percent of an oral dose can be recovered in the urine either as nicotinic acid or as one or more metabolites.[8] This high first-pass effect on the liver may be responsible for much of the drug's mechanism of action, although niacin also has important effects on peripheral tissues. Niacin does not bind significantly to plasma proteins and does not appear to interact with other drugs.

MECHANISM OF ACTION

Although the lipid-lowering effects of pharmacologic doses of niacin were first recognized 35 years ago by Altschul,[9] its exact mechanism of action is not yet known. Niacin therapy significantly affects concentrations of all the major classes of plasma lipoproteins. Marked reductions occur in plasma very low-density lipoprotein (VLDL) concentrations as reflected by decreases in the plasma TG level. The TG content, and therefore, the size of the VLDL particles, as well as the number of VLDL particles in the circulation, decrease during niacin therapy. The LDL-C level is also reduced, while an increase is observed in the level of HDL-C, the putative anti-atherogenic lipoprotein.

As noted previously, no specific mechanism of action has been identified for niacin's lipid-lowering effects. One possible site of action is in adipose tissue, where niacin inhibits the action of hormone sensitive lipase.[10] Because of reduced intracellular lipolysis and release of fatty acid from adipose tissue, niacin therapy decreases circulating levels of free fatty acids.[10] This, in turn, reduces fatty acid uptake by the liver and may, in part, be responsible for decreased hepatic VLDL production. Recent studies indicate that fatty acids can increase the assembly and secretion of apolipoprotein B containing lipoproteins, such as VLDL, from the liver.[11-12] In any event, it has been demonstrated in humans that niacin administration is associated with reduced secretion from the liver of both VLDL-TG and VLDL-apolipoprotein B (a measure of the number of VLDL particles).[13]

Reductions in plasma LDL-C levels result from either decreased synthesis of VLDL particles or reduced conversion of precursor VLDL to LDL.[14] Another possible basis for niacin's effect on plasma LDL concentrations is decreased production of LDL directly by the liver. It does not appear that niacin affects LDL-receptor function or removal of LDL from the plasma.

Limited data is available concerning the mechanism responsible for the increase in HDL. Both HDL-C and apolipoprotein AI levels increase during niacin therapy, suggesting that more HDL particles may be in the circulation during treatment. Niacin appears to increase the plasma HDL level by decreasing HDL fractional catabolism, rather than increasing production of HDL.[15] Hypertriglyceridemia is associated with increased fractional catabolism of HDL,[16] and niacin's ability to normalize HDL catabolism may derive from its action to decrease plasma TG concentrations.

Additional actions of niacin have been described which may relate to its beneficial effects in preventing coronary events. Niacin therapy is associated with release of large amounts of prostaglandins,[17] some of which may be associated with the decreased platelet aggregability seen with this drug. Niacin may also decrease the circulating level of fibrinogen and increase the level of tissue plasminogen activator.[18]

CLINICAL USE

Available Forms

Niacin is unique when compared to the other lipid-lowering drugs in that it is a naturally occurring vitamin that is found in small quantities in both foods and multivitamins. Therefore, unlike other lipid-lowering medications, niacin is available as a non-prescription tablet which can be purchased in most pharmacies or health food stores in 50 mg and 500 mg tablets. This also means that niacin is significantly less costly than any of the other lipid-lowering agents. Together with its wide range of effectiveness in reducing plasma concentrations of atherogenic forms of lipoproteins (VLDL and LDL) while increasing the level of the "protective" lipoprotein (HDL) the low cost of niacin makes it a potentially outstanding agent.

Unfortunately, in the doses used to alter plasma lipid and lipoprotein levels, niacin is not without toxicity, and its use should be under the direction of a physician. The fact that it is a naturally occurring vitamin also means that it is not under the control of the U.S. Food and Drug Administration and this has lead to its unmonitored use by many individuals who are attempting to reduce their risk for CHD. Such self-treatment with pharmacologic doses of niacin is potentially dangerous.

An alternative vitamin form of this compound, niacinamide, is not effective for lipid reduction. Slow-release forms of niacin are available, but often at a significantly increased cost. Although some patients prefer the slow-release forms because they tend to be associated with less flushing, the slow-release forms may cause more gastrointestinal problems. Also, while there are limited data relative to the clinical efficacy of the slow release forms, the data available suggest the slow-release forms are less effective than the short-acting agents.[19] The rare instances of severe gastrointestinal side effects (anorexia, vomiting, dehydration) and severe hepatic dysfunction (5-fold to 10-fold increases in liver function tests with symptoms of hepatic dysfunction), occur more frequently with slow-release forms of niacin. Interestingly, an occasional patient will have more severe, prolonged flushing with the slow-release niacin. This response is probably a blood-level related phenomena in very sensitive individuals.

Side Effects

The most troubling side effect associated with niacin administration is a benign vasodilatation of peripheral capillary beds. This side effect is probably related to prostaglandin release by endothelial cells which results, in turn, in peripheral vasodilation. Flushing most commonly involves the face and neck areas, but can be more diffuse. Flushing can be associated with itching, and both flushing and itching, when it does occur, usually begin between 15 minutes and two hours after taking a dose of the drug. These two symptoms can last up to one hour. In association with the peripheral vasodilation, orthostatic hypotension can occasionally occur. Orthostatic hypotension may be more likely to occur if niacin is started at a large dose (500 mg bid or tid) initially, rather than with a slowly increasing dose schedule.

Dosing Schedule

To avoid or minimize this "flush," it is recommended that small amounts of niacin be administered initially (e.g., 100 mg to 250 mg) and that the dose be gradually increased by 250 mg every 3 to 5 days until the dosage level of 1 gram, 2 or 3 times a day is attained (Table I). A good approach is to start with 100 mg bid and increase the dose to 200 mg bid after 4 to 5 days, then to 500 mg bid after an additional four to five days. I keep the patient on 500 mg bid for 1 week, or more if necessary, before increasing to either 750 mg bid or 1,000 mg bid. Further increases in amount and/or frequency of use depends on the clinical response of the individual patient. The response to niacin is variable with good cholesterol lowering occurring in some cases at less than 1 gm/day. Occasionally patients require up to 9 gm/day. Since the flush and pruritus appear to be prostaglandin-induced, use of aspirin in as low a dose as 250 mg may be successful. Non-steroidal anti-inflammatory drugs (NSAIDs) like ibuprofen (400 mg) along with each niacin dose may significantly alleviate these symptoms. Initiation of either aspirin or an NSAID for 3 to 4 days prior to the start of niacin treatment may minimize any subsequent cutaneous signs. Use of either aspirin or ibuprofen with only the morning dose may also be adequate. The niacin should also be taken with meals to decrease flushing and to avoid gastrointestinal irritation.

TABLE I. Schedule for increasing the dose of niacin

Dose (mg bid)	Days of Administration
100	4 - 5
200	4 - 5
500	6 - 7
750	6 - 7
1,000	—

Aspirin or an NSAID before or with each dose (or simply the morning dose) will relieve early flushing.

An alternative approach would be to use bid dosage from the start, using 50 mg bid, 100 mg bid, etc. This may result in lessened flushing.

Another alternative approach is to give aspirin or a NSAID for 3 to 4 days prior to starting the niacin, and then begin niacin at 500 mg bid or even 1000 mg bid. There is some suggestion that little or no flushing will occur with this approach.

Precaution: Initial large doses of niacin may cause symptomatic orthostatic hypotension.

Expected Response to Therapy

Although response to therapy is somewhat variable, reductions of approximately 15 percent to 30 percent in total plasma cholesterol and LDL-C can be expected in most patients.[1-4] HDL-C increases from 15 percent to 25 percent have been reported.[1-4] In patients with hypertriglyceridemia, niacin therapy may be associated with 30 percent to 40 percent decreases in plasma TG concentrations, and dramatic reductions in circulating TG to a normal level may be achieved in some patients. The doses required to achieve these results vary widely. Many patients can be successfully treated with doses in the range of 2 to 3 grams of niacin daily, while others, particularly those with familial hypercholesterolemia (FH), may require as much as 7 to 9 gm/day.[2] However, it should be kept in mind that the various potential toxicities associated with niacin treatment will have an increased incidence at these higher doses. Also, rather than continuing to increase the dose of niacin above the 2 to 3 gm/day range that many physicians use, I recommend that other drugs be added to niacin if adequate results have not been achieved.

Combination Therapy

With bile acid binding resins. Niacin has been used very successfully in combination with bile acid binding resins in the treatment of severely affected subjects with FH, where this combination has reduced LDL-C concentrations by 30 percent to 50 percent.[20,21] The bile acid binding resins, which act to lower LDL-C by increasing LDL-receptor mediated clearance of plasma LDL, may also increase the VLDL level when used alone. Hence, the combination of niacin and a bile acid sequestrant will achieve dramatic reduction of LDL-C (via a combination of two physiologic mechanisms), while still inducing a drop in VLDL-TG because the niacin TG-reducing effect is more potent than the resin TG-increasing effect. An additional benefit to be gained from use of a bile acid binding resin with niacin is a concomitant reduction in peptic ulcer-like signs secondary to proton binding by the resin.

With an HMG CoA reductase inhibitor. An alternative to the combination of niacin and a bile acid sequestrant could be niacin and an HMG CoA reductase inhibitor. This combination has the possibility of reducing LDL-C concentrations more dramatically while achieving at least similar, if not better, reductions in VLDL-TG and increases in HDL-C. Unfortunately, the combination of niacin and lovastatin has been associated with several cases of severe myositis, including clinical signs of muscle pain and weakness. Of note, plasma levels of creatinine phosphokinase (CPK) have been markedly elevated to several thousand units in such patients. The prevalence of this complication has been estimated at 3 percent to 5 percent of patients on such combination regime, but these numbers may change with more experience. Although this reaction may suggest a more generalized potential for myositis associated with HMG CoA reductase inhibitors, it does, in any event, make the combined use of niacin and a reductase inhibitor suspect.

With gemfibrozil. Recently, niacin has also been used with gemfibrozil, particularly in patients with severe combined hyperlipidemia. This severe disorder, which is characterized by increased VLDL and LDL concentrations in plasma, and which frequently also includes a reduced plasma HDL-C level, may not respond adequately to either drug alone. Hence, if gemfibrozil is used alone, LDL-C may not be adequately reduced, or may even increase. On the other hand, if niacin is administered as the sole lipid-lowering agent for such patients, adequate reduction of VLDL-TG may not be achieved. No increased toxicity has been reported as yet for the combination of niacin and gemfibrozil, but since the two drugs have both been associated with myositis when used in combination with lovastatin, the possibility exists that niacin plus gemfibrozil might also have the potential to cause myositis. In addition, since these two drugs have similar lipid-altering characteristics, their combined use should be reserved for severe cases.

ADVERSE REACTIONS

Niacin therapy is associated with two categories of adverse reactions (Table II). The first group, described earlier in this chapter, is related to peripheral vasodilatation and is mainly a nuisance, with the individual manifestations often self-limiting. The second group, related mainly to the gastrointestinal tract, to metabolic alterations and to the musculoskelatal system, can be both chronic and debilitating.

Cutaneous

The cutaneous group of adverse reactions includes the "flush." This "flush" sensation, like a mild sunburn, occurs 15 to 120 minutes after a dose and lasts 30 to 60 minutes. Occasional patients will complain of lightheadedness probably due to postural hypotension, also secondary to peripheral vasodilatation. The postural hypotension may be clinically significant if niacin therapy is initiated at full dose. Pruritus may accompany the flushing. Patients usually develop tachyphylaxis to these cutaneous effects of niacin and, therefore, should be told that the worst flushing will occur upon initiating the therapy or when increasing the dose. Flushing will also occur whenever the patient has omitted several doses of niacin and then restarts medication. Patients should be cautioned about drinking hot liquids and ethanol when they take their niacin dose because these liquids may exacerbate cutaneous symptoms. The flushing and the pruritus are both thought to be prostaglandin-mediated and can

TABLE II.   **Side effects associated with niacin**

Type	Symptom	Occurrence	Measures to Prevent Occurrence
Cutaneous			
	Flushing	15 to 120 minutes after dose	Use aspirin or NSAID and administer niacin with meals; avoid hot beverages and ethanol
	Itching	Lasts 30 to 60 minutes; usually disappears within first few weeks	
	Dry Skin	May disappear after a few weeks but can be chronic	Use skin creams and other local measures
Gastrointestinal			
	Peptic ulcer signs	May occur at any time, particularly whenever other factors increase gastric acid secretion	Take medication with meals and/or antacids
	Hepatic	Increased transaminases may occur at any time; symptomatic hepatitis-like syndrome is rare; may be more common with slow-release forms of niacin	No particular preventive measures can be taken; monitoring of liver function tests must be done regularly
Metabolic			
	Hyperuricemia	Common, especially in predisposed subjects with hypertriglyceridemia	Monitoring of uric acid level on a regular basis; treatment is symptomatic
	Hyperglycemia	Commonly seen when there is a pre-existing history of diabetes or impaired glucose tolerance	Monitoring blood sugar, especially high-risk subjects; may have to alter diabetic treatment or stop niacin

be reduced or sometimes totally eliminated by prior ingestion of aspirin or ibuprofen. Niacin should also be administered with food so that its absorption is slowed.

The slow-release forms of niacin, which are now available in both "brand" names and generics, are usually associated with decreased incidence and severity of flushing. This is probably related to the more slowly changing plasma concentrations of niacin after ingestion of slow-release forms. The reduced cutaneous effects of slow-release niacin are not, however, always achieved. In fact, an occasional patient will have prolonged, sometimes continuous flushing after taking the slow-release form. There is also evidence that gastrointestinal side effects may be more common and/or more severe with the slow-release niacin forms. Dry skin and dry mucous membranes, also can occur and may be quite troublesome for patients who have dermatologic disorders.

Gastrointestinal

Peptic ulcer signs. Niacin is a gastric irritant and its use in predisposed individuals can initiate symptoms of peptic ulcer disease. Existing gastric or duodenal disease may be worsened, and acute exacerbation of peptic ulcer disease may occur upon initiation of niacin therapy. Because of this possibility, we consider the presence of peptic ulcer disease to be an absolute contraindication to the use of niacin. However, ingestion of niacin with an antacid may be protective against these problems.

Hepatic. Increases in liver transaminase levels are common with niacin treatment, and up to a three-fold increase in the blood levels of these enzymes, in the absence of symptoms, is not considered an indication to stop therapy. The elevations in liver transaminases may stabilize or even resolve with stabilization of the drug dose. An occasional patient will, however, develop a clinical picture compatible with acute hepatitis with fever, fatigue, right upper quadrant pain and marked elevations of liver function tests. Liver biopsies usually show prominent cholestasis, hepatocellular damage and nodular formation. These "acute hepatitis-like" effects are dose-related and resolve after discontinuation of therapy. For this reason, liver function tests should be obtained several weeks after the patient has been placed on niacin and after increasing the dose.

Metabolic

Hyperuricemia. Blood uric acid levels invariably increase during niacin treatment because of decreased renal clearance. In predisposed individuals, acute gouty attacks may be precipitated. This gouty arthritis can be a particularly troubling side effect since hyperuricemia is already a common concomitant of hypertriglyceridemia.

Hyperglycemia. Niacin therapy may also be associated with either reduced glucose tolerance, or actual hyperglycemia, as an initial sign of diabetes mellitus, or as an exacerbation of existing diabetes. Although much caution must be used in the treatment of diabetics with niacin, presence of diabetes is not an absolute contraindication to its use.

Other Adverse Reactions

Additional adverse reactions include toxic amblyopia and worsening of existing glaucoma. Niacin may also cause supraventricular tachycardias. Therefore, it may be difficult to use niacin in some patients with pre-existing coronary artery disease. On the other hand, several studies have demonstrated that CHD is reduced by niacin therapy.

Moreover, as noted previously, the combination of niacin therapy with lovastatin appears to raise the risk for development of myositis, including severe elevations of CPK (several thousand units), and both muscle pain and weakness. The biochemical basis for this association is unknown. Because the combination of gemfibrozil and lovastatin has also been associated with myositis, the possibility exists that the combination of niacin and gemfibrozil might be linked to this adverse outcome as well.

EFFECT ON ATHEROSCLEROSIS

Niacin alone or in combination with resins has been used in two important secondary prevention studies: the Coronary Drug Project (CDP) and the Cholesterol Lowering Atherosclerosis Study (CLAS). In the CDP, men who have survived an acute myocardial infarction were entered into a multi-armed trial in which several drugs were compared to placebo. Endpoints included CHD events and mortality. In the initial analysis of that study, niacin treatment was shown to reduce the incidence of second, nonfatal myocardial infarctions.[4] There was no effect of niacin administration on cardiovascular mortality, however. In contrast, the Coronary Drug Project Follow-Up Study[5] demonstrated that 15 years after initiation of the study, niacin treatment during the seven-year period of study was associated with a statistically significant decrease in total and coronary deaths.

The CLAS attempted to demonstrate that aggressive therapy to reduce total cholesterol, LDL-C and TG, while raising HDL-C, would be associated with regression of coronary lesions.[22] Following coronary artery bypass graft surgery, men were entered into the study and placed on either diet plus placebo, or diet plus niacin and colestipol. Combined with colestipol, niacin treatment of patients in CLAS was associated with an angiographically proven decrease in CHD progression, and in 16 percent of cases regression of coronary lesions was demonstrated. These findings were associated with dramatic alterations in plasma lipids and lipoproteins in the treatment group.

CONCLUSION

Niacin, a natural vitamin, when used in pharmacologic doses, can significantly improve the overall lipid profile by reducing total plasma TG and cholesterol levels, decreasing LDL-C level and increasing HDL-C concentrations. Niacin is inexpensive and its overall long-term toxicity profile is good. Its use has been associated with reduced progression of coronary lesions and improved total and cardiovascular mortality. It is not, however, without problems. Several side effects related to peripheral vasodilatation can be very upsetting to patients and can result in poor compliance. Gastrointestinal and metabolic disturbances can also reduce long-term compliance or actually result in discontinuation of the drug. Because of these side effects, niacin should not be used without continuous patient monitoring by a physician for adverse outcomes. This monitoring should include ongoing evaluation of liver transaminases. With careful monitoring by the physician, niacin can be a very economical and efficacious lipid-modifying agent that can significantly reduce an individual's risk for CHD.

REFERENCES

1. Parsons WB, Flinn JH. Reduction in elevated blood cholesterol levels by large doses of nicotinic acid: preliminary report. JAMA. 1957;165:234-238.
2. Nessim SA, Chin HP, Alaupovic P, et al. Combined therapy of niacin, colestipol and fat-controlled diet on men with coronary bypass: effect on blood lipids and apolipoproteins. Arteriosclerosis. 1983;3:568-573.
3. Hoeg JM, Maher MB, Bailey KR, et al. Comparison of six pharmacological regimens for hypercholesterolemia. Am J Cardiol. 1987;59:812-815.
4. Coronary Drug Project Research Group. Clofibrate and niacin in coronary heart disease. JAMA. 1975;231:360-381.
5. Canner PL, Berge KG, Wenger NK, et al. Fifteen-year mortality in coronary drug project patients: long-term benefit with niacin. J Am Coll Cardiol. 1986;8:1254-1255.
6. Figge HL, Figge J, Souney PF, et al. Nicotinic acid: a review of its clinical use in the treatment of lipid disorders. Pharmacotherapy. 1988;8(5):287-294.
7. Bechgaard H, Jespersen S. GI absorption of niacin in humans. J Pharm Sci. 1977;66:871-872.
8. Miller ON, Hamilton JG, Goldsmith GA. Investigation of the mechanism of action of nicotinic acid on serum lipid levels in man. Am J Clin Nutr. 1960;8:480-490.
9. Altschul R. Inhibition of experimental cholesterol arteriosclerosis by ultraviolet irradiation. N Engl J Med. 1953;249:96-99.
10. Carlson LA. Studies on the effect of nicotinic acid on catecholamine-stimulated lipolysis in adipose tissue *in vitro*. Acta Med Scand. 1963;173:719-722.
11. Erickson SK, Fielding PE. Parameters of cholesterol metabolism in the human hepatoma cell line, Hep-G2. J Lipid Res. 1986;27:875-883.
12. Moberly JB, Cole TG, Alpers DH, et al. Oleic acid stimulation of apolipoprotein B secretion from HepG2 and Caco-2 cells occurs post-transcriptionally. Biochem Biophys Acta. 1990;1042:70-80.
13. Grundy SM, Mok HYI, Zech L, et al. Influence of nicotinic acid on metabolism of cholesterol and triglycerides in man. J Lipid Res. 1981;22:24-36.
14. Langer T, Levy RI. The effect of nicotinic acid on the turnover of low-density lipoproteins in type II hyperlipoproteinemia. In: Gey KF, Carlson LA, eds. Metabolic Effects of Nicotinic Acid and its Derivatives. Berne, Switz; Hans Huber; 1971:641-647.

15. Shepard J, Packard CJ, Patsch JR, et al. Effects of nicotinic acid therapy on plasma high-density subfraction and composition and on apolipoprotein A metabolic. J Clin Invest. 1979;63:858-867.

16. Magill P, Rao SN, Miller NE, et al. Relationships between the metabolism of high-density and very low-density lipoproteins in man: studies of apolipoprotein kinetics and adipose tissue lipoprotein lipase activity. Eur J Clin Invest. 1982;12:113-120.

17. Olsson AG, Carlson LA, Anggard E, et al. Prostaglandin production augmented in the short-term by nicotinic acid. Lancet. 1983;2:565-567.

18. Kane JP, Malloy MJ. When to treat hyperlipidemia. In: Siperstein MD, ed. Advances in Internal Medicine. Vol. 33. St. Louis, Mo: Mosby Year Book; 1988;143-164.

19. Knopp RH, Ginsberg J, Albers JJ, et al. Contrasting effects of unmodified and timed-release forms of niacin on lipoproteins in hyperlipidemic subjects: clue to mechanism of action of niacin. Metabolism. 1985;34:642-650.

20. Kane JP, Malloy MJ, Tun P, et al. Normalization of low-density lipoprotein levels in heterozygous familial hypercholesterolemia with combined drug regimen. N Engl J Med. 1981;304:251-258.

21. Illingworth DR, Phillipson BE, Rapp JH, et al. Colestipol plus nicotinic acid in the treatment of heterozygous familial hypercholesterolemia. Lancet. 1981;1:296-298.

22. Blankenhorn DH, Nessim SA, Johnson RL, et al. Beneficial effects of combined colestipol-niacin therapy on coronary atherosclerosis and coronary venous bypass grafts. JAMA. 1987;257:3233-3240.

CHAPTER 5

The Fibric Acid Derivatives

W. Virgil Brown, M.D.
Washington, D.C.

INTRODUCTION

Almost 30 years ago, a group of aryloxyisobutyric acid derivatives was found to reduce cholesterol and triglycerides in laboratory animals.[1] The least toxic of these, chlorophenoxy-isobutyrate (clofibrate) was subsequently shown to lower triglycerides (TG) and cholesterol in man.[2] This drug became one of the most commonly used lipid-lowering drugs during the 1970s and was the prototype for a series of so-called fibric acid derivatives which are now commonly prescribed for hyperlipidemia in many parts of the world. Recent reviews provide in-depth information about some of these agents.[3,4] In the early experiments[1] it was noted that rats with relatively high plasma content of very low-density lipoprotein (VLDL) and low content of low-density lipoprotein (LDL) had a more dramatic reduction of plasma lipids than did animals, such as monkeys, with higher proportions of plasma total cholesterol and LDL.

In retrospect, this early data is consistent with our current extensive knowledge of the efficacy of fibric acid derivatives with regard to lipid lowering in humans. The major effect of the fibric acid derivatives in most patients is to reduce TG-carrying lipoproteins (chylomicrons, VLDL and intermediate-density lipoproteins [IDL]) with lesser effects on LDL. HDL-cholesterol (HDL-C) on the other hand is usually elevated by these compounds. Consequently, the lipid disorders which have been most commonly responsive to fibric acid treatment are those involving elevated plasma TG.

STRUCTURE METABOLISM AND EXCRETION

There are six fibric acid compounds currently in clinical use in various parts of the world: clofibrate; gemfibrozil; fenofibrate; bezafibrate; ciprofibrate; and etofibrate. Only two of these, clofibrate and gemfibrozil are available in the United States, while fenofibrate and bezafibrate are the most commonly used agents in Europe. Ciprofibrate, the most potent on a weight basis, has been recently released for use in the Mediterranean region and Europe. Etofibrate is not simply a fibric acid derivative, but the clofibrate diester of nicotinic acid and is a dual pharmacologic agent. This last compound is hydrolyzed in the tissues of the body and has some properties of both lipid-lowering categories of drugs, i.e., fibric acid derivatives and nicotinic acid.

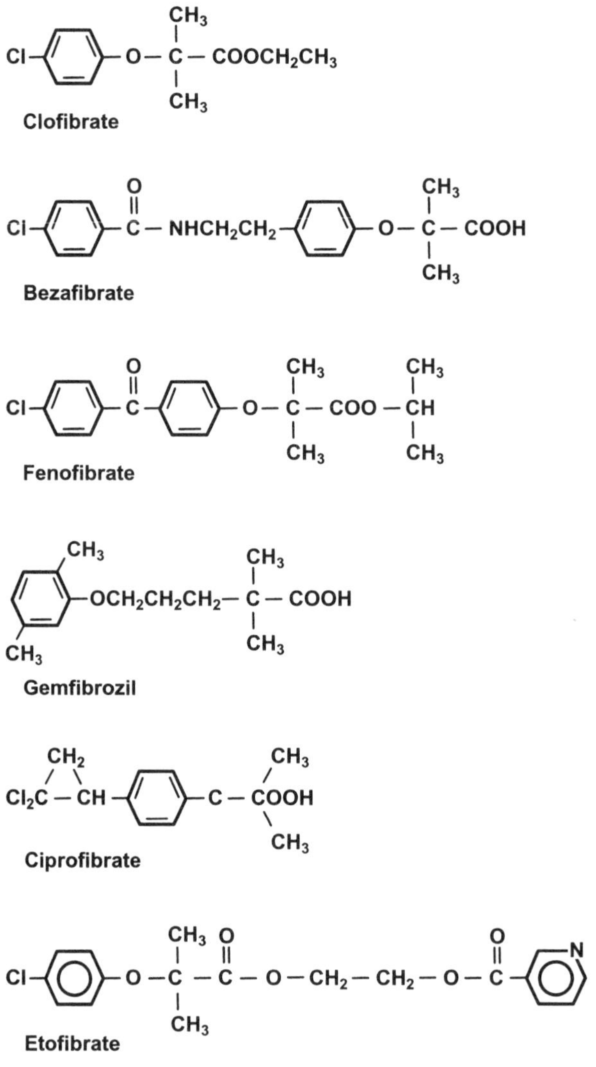

FIGURE 1. Chemical structure of clofibrate and other fibric acid derivatives

The structural features of the fibric acid derivative group of compounds have in common an isobutyric acid moiety linked at the second carbon to a phenoxy ring containing additional chemical substitutions for the hydrogen atoms (Figure 1).

Fibric acid derivatives are tightly bound to albumin and are avidly taken up by most tissues of the body with the highest concentrations achieved in the liver and kidney — the organs of excretion.[4,5] Oxidation and reduction reactions produce multiple metabolites with these agents, but the dominant alteration is usually glucuronide conjugation in the liver. These compounds are then excreted through the biliary route with a significant but variable enterohepatic recirculation. Some of the compounds such as fenofibrate are highly dependent on adequate kidney function for excretion primarily of the glucuronide derivative but also for other derivatives. Impairment of hepatic or renal function can markedly prolong the tissue and plasma half-life of these drugs and their metabolic products. Therefore, the dose of fibrates should be reduced when there is liver or kidney dysfunction and fenofibrate is contraindicated in kidney failure. Dialysis does not remove these agents to a significant degree.[6]

EFFECTS ON PLASMA LIPOPROTEIN CONCENTRATIONS

The dose response effect of the fibric acid derivatives is unusual. Although not completely described in detail in man, the response in plasma lipid reduction appears somewhat sigmoidal with only modest changes at lower dose levels followed by significant but limited response at the maximal levels used. For example, using gemfibrozil at 300 mg twice daily or clofibrate at 500 mg twice daily may produce a response that is hardly detectable in the TG or cholesterol level. Whereas at twice this dose, TG may be reduced by 50 percent. Raising the dose further may produce little or no further reduction in these lipids. As a result, most patients are treated with the full recommended dose of the agents as shown in Table I. An important exception to the use of these doses is the presence of kidney or hepatic dysfunction, conditions in which lower doses must be considered.

TABLE I. Commonly used dosage regimens for fibric acid derivatives currently in clinical use worldwide

Fibrate Derivative	Dosing Schedule	Total Daily Dose
Bezafibrate	Twice daily	600 mg
Ciprofibrate	Once daily	100 mg
Clofibrate	Twice daily	2000 mg
Etofibrate	Once or twice*	1000 mg
Fenofibrate	Once*	300 mg
Gemfibrozil	Twice daily	1200 mg

* Most studies conducted with two or three times daily dosing, but once daily appears to be equally efficacious.

Reductions in plasma TG of 20 percent to 70 percent are common with these agents and all are approximately equal in producing this effect when maximal doses are used.[7,8] The higher the initial plasma level of TG, the greater the reduction.[9] Chylomicrons, VLDL and IDL are diminished. Only in patients whose hyperchylomicronemia is caused by familial lipoprotein lipase deficiency is there little or no response. Other forms of hypertriglyceridemia are usually effectively treated including Type III (dysbetalipoproteinemia), Type IV and Type V (hyperlipoproteinemias) whether inherited as familial hypertriglyceridemia or familial combined hyperlipidemia.[10,11]

Elevated LDL is less responsive to the fibrate, but 10 percent to 25 percent reductions are observed in most patients.[9] The greatest response is usually found in patients with a higher LDL level but with normal TG concentrations (Type IIA hyperlipoproteinemia).[12] However, many patients with elevated VLDL and LDL levels (Type IIB hyperlipoproteinemia) will also show a significant reduction in LDL-cholesterol (LDL-C) concomitant with a fall in VLDL cholesterol (VLDL-C) and triglycerides.[12]

Often patients with marked hypertriglyceridemia (TG level > 500 mg/dl) have normal or even low plasma concentrations of LDL. In such individuals a rise in LDL may accompany fibrate treatment and increases from 5 percent to 50 percent in LDL-C have been observed.[8,13] However, very large rises in LDL-C are usually observed only in patients with severe hypertriglyceridemia who show marked reductions in the TG level with fibrate therapy. And, an increase in the LDL-C level to above the normal range of 160 mg/dl occurs only rarely with fibrate therapy.

Increases in HDL-C occur with all fibrates,[9] although differences have been described with gemfibrozil being more effective than clofibrate.[14] The magnitude of this change is usually 5 percent to 20 percent with sustained increases of 10 percent to 15 percent in most studies. The large percentage increase in HDL-C is associated with a baseline level below the mean, i.e., level of HDL-C < 45 mg/dl in men[15], < 55 mg/dl in women. On the other hand, some individuals with a very low level of HDL-C, i.e., < 30 mg/dl, may not show a response. This variance in response perhaps reflects the heterogeneous causes of a low HDL-C level.[16]

In a recent review of the literature attempting to compare the efficacy of different fibric acid derivatives, it was suggested that bezafibrate, fenofibrate and ciprofibrate were more effective in lowering LDL-C than clofibrate and gemfibrozil.[9] However, this conclusion was reached after comparing the observed efficacy in separate trials conducted with individual drugs in differing types of patients and in differing settings. Of note, very few direct contemporaneous comparisons of the LDL-C lowering ability of the various fibric acid derivatives are available. Additional randomized objective studies with an adequate number of participants must be done to allow direct comparisons of the individual fibric acid derivatives to determine relative efficacy in TG and LDL reduction as well as HDL elevation. Clofibrate and gemfibrozil have been evaluated in one trial with a double-blind crossover design so that the efficacy could be observed in the same patients.[11] In this study, the TG reduction and HDL elevation were not different. Also, there was no change in mean LDL concentrations in this cohort with either drug.

Apolipoprotein components of lipoproteins are altered by fibrate treatment of hypercholesterolemic individuals. These alterations include reductions in apolipoprotein B, apolipoprotein CIII and apolipoprotein E components of VLDL, IDL and LDL. LDL apolipoprotein B levels may not fall in hypertriglyceridemic patients. Small rises in the apolipoprotein AI, the major apolipoprotein of HDL have been observed in several studies,[17,19] but not all.[18] The second most prevalent HDL apolipoprotein, apolipoprotein AII has usually been found to show the larger and more consistent increases.[18,19]

MECHANISM OF ACTION

The physiologic changes in lipoprotein metabolism following fibrate administration are complex. Hepatic TG synthesis and VLDL transport from the liver are reduced in humans[20,21] and animals.[22,23] This reduction is thought to be secondary to a reduction in the available free fatty acid substrates delivered from adipose tissue[24] and to increased oxidation of fatty acids in the liver.[25] However, radioactive tracer studies in humans suggest that an increased plasma clearance rate for VLDL-TG is the quantitatively more important change explaining the reduced plasma TG level.[26] Also, the activity of lipoprotein lipase, as measured in post-heparin plasma and in muscle tissue, increases after fibrate treatment.[27,28] In addition, there are structural changes in VLDL and chylomicrons with reduced apolipoprotein CIII content.[29] This last mentioned apolipoprotein is a known inhibitor of lipase action[30] and therefore more rapid clearance may be due to the actual change in the nature of the particle. Moreover, there appears to be greater uptake of IDL by the liver,[26] a fraction of which includes partially degraded VLDL.

The elevated LDL level falls, in part because of increased activity of the specific LDL receptor mechanism in the liver and other tissues.[31] LDL receptor activity is known to increase when hepatic cholesterol content falls. Two known effects of fibrates are thought to be responsible for a reduction in the cholesterol level in the hepatocyte: cholesterol excretion into the bile is increased relative to bile acids;[21] and, cholesterol synthesis is reduced, possibly as a result of a fall in HMG CoA reductase activity.[32]

The paradoxical rise in LDL-C seen in persons with hyper-triglyceridemia has at least two contributory mechanisms. First, individuals with low LDL associated with high VLDL and high chylomicron levels have abnormally high LDL clearance.[33] Much of this more rapid clearance is due to pathways other than through the LDL receptor. These so-called nonreceptor-mediated clearance pathways have been found to be reduced by fibrate treatment. Even though LDL receptors may increase in number in the liver of persons with very high TG, the reduced nonreceptor-mediated clearance may predominate and the result is a rise in the apolipoprotein B level and increased LDL particle number. Secondly, the LDL in such patients is usually smaller, more dense and relatively cholesterol poor.[16,18] Fibric acid derivatives cause the LDL composition of hypertriglyceridemic patients to alter, gaining in cholesterol ester content and becoming more similar to that of normal persons. This more cholesterol rich LDL contributes to a rise in the total plasma LDL level. This rise in LDL-cholesterol may occur even if the apolipoprotein B level does not change, indicating a constant number of LDL particles and reflecting a balance in the increasing receptor clearance and decreasing activity of nonreceptor-mediated clearance.[33] Thus, the final LDL level will reflect a balance of these competing physiologic changes.

The HDL in hypertriglyceridemic patients is also TG rich and cholesterol poor.[33] Fibrate treatment reverses this situation, decreasing the relative TG and increasing cholesterol content of HDL particles. There may also be a rise of HDL-C because the number of HDL particles increase as measured by the major protein components, apolipoprotein AI and apolipoprotein AII. In fact, one study has demonstrated increased apolipoprotein AI synthesis with gemfibrozil treatment.[34] However, other studies indicate abnormally high clearance of HDL particles during hypertriglyceridemia that may be corrected with a reduced TG level. In any event, a full explanation of HDL alterations with fibrate treatment has not been adequately developed by physiologic and biochemical studies.

ADVERSE REACTIONS

The adverse event rate with clofibrate has been well described by over 25 years of clinical use but most importantly by careful observation in two large scale, double-blind, randomized, placebo-controlled, clinical trials lasting five years each — the Coronary Drug Project that was conducted in the United States[35] and the World Health Organization (WHO) Study conducted in Europe.[36] In addition, the recently reported Helsinki Heart Study provided five years of observation in a similar controlled trial with gemfibrozil.[37] It should be noted that all of these trials involved exclusively men and therefore possible adverse events in women are less well studied.

TABLE II. Reported adverse drug effects

Gastrointestinal	Nausea eructation, flatulence, diarrhea, abdominal pain
Skin	Rash, urticaria, hair loss, increased sweating
Musculoskeletal	Myalgias, elevated CPK and SGOT
Hepatic	Lithogenic bile, gallstones*, elevated SGPT and SGOT
Psychoneurologic	Dizziness, fatigue, headache, insomnia, impotence
Cardiovascular	Atrial and ventricular arrhythmias*
Hematologic	Leukopenia, anemia
Drug Interactions	Potentiates coumarins. Increases incidence of myositis with reductase inhibitors.

CPK = creatine phosphokinase; SGOT = serum glutamic oxaloacetic transaminase;
  SGPT = serum glutamic pyruvic transaminase
*Documented only for clofibrate in the Coronary Drug Project and the World Health
  Organization Study

Gastrointestinal

Abdominal discomfort, sometimes accompanied by nausea or diarrhea is seen in approximately 10 percent of patients. This finding is probably because of a direct gastric or upper intestinal exposure to the drug, since antacids or food relieve the symptoms in some patients. Increased cholecystitis and cholecystectomy was documented in the Coronary Drug Project and WHO studies with clofibrate. Careful studies of bile composition revealed increased cholesterol content relative to the other solubilizing lipids, i.e., phospholipids and bile acids. Also, with all fibrate derivatives studied[38] the bile is more lithogenic. However, *only* with clofibrate is there documented evidence of increased gallbladder disease.[35,36]

Musculoskeletal

Several cases of muscle tenderness associated with increased creatinine phosphokinase (CPK) have been reported with clofibrate treatment.[39] This CPK increase appears to be much less common with the other fibrates and was not observed with gemfibrozil in the Helsinki Heart Study.

Carcinogenic

In the WHO Study, a trend toward higher cancer rates was noted in clofibrate-treated patients.[36] No single type of cancer stood out in the analysis of the data of the WHO Study. In addition, total mortality from a variety of causes including death from cholecystectomy was higher in the clofibrate-treated patients than in those patients on placebo. These last two findings led to considerable concern about the long-term safety of clofibrate when this study was initially reported. Further follow-up of these patients for a subsequent five-year period failed to show continuation of the increased cancer rates or the increased incidence in total mortality.[41] Therefore, it is quite possible that the observations during the first phase of the trial were spurious. Moreover, no other trials with clofibrate or with other fibric acid derivatives have shown increased cancer incidence or increased incidence in total mortality.

Other Less Common Events

Rarely cardiac arrhythmias have been described with clofibrate and linked to blood level in one study.[40] Less common (1 percent to 2 percent) have been increases in the plasma level of enzymes characteristic of hepatic cellular disease, and skin rash has occurred in an occasional patient. Other reported adverse events are not documented as clearly due to fibrate therapy. These include leukopenia, alopecia, impotence and headaches. Such disorders have usually resolved with discontinuation of treatment.

Drug Interactions

Drug interactions include the well-documented potentiation of the anticoagulative effect of warfarin derivatives. However, it is possible to use warfarin derivatives if the dosage is reduced appropriately. Also, the frequency of myositis appears to increase markedly when lovastatin is combined with fibrate therapy.[42] Of note, a few interesting chemical effects have been noted with fibrate therapy which are usually of little consequence: the uric acid level falls consistently with fenofibrate, which appears rather uniquely uricosuric among the fibrates;[3] blood sugar is reported lower with bezafibrate in nondiabetics; and clofibrate has been reported to reduce the insulin requirements in diabetics.

PREVENTION OF CORONARY HEART DISEASE

The major rationale for lowering blood cholesterol with the fibric acid derivatives has been the potential for preventing coronary heart disease (CHD). The Coronary Drug Project,[35] the WHO Study[36] and the Helsinki Heart Study[37] were designed to test the efficacy of fibrates in this arena. In all three trials, middle-aged men were studied using a design with double-blind, random assignment to active treatment or to placebo control groups. The major endpoints were myocardial infarction (MI) and CHD death.

In the Coronary Drug Project, men aged 30 years to 64 years at entry and having suffered at least one MI were assigned to one of five drug treatment groups or to placebo. There were 1,103 men who received clofibrate and were compared to 2,789 on placebo treatment. All men were monitored for at least five and up to seven years following randomization. Adherence to clofibrate was equivalent to placebo. The mean reduction of total plasma cholesterol was 9 percent and the mean reduction of TG was 22 percent, when compared to the placebo-treated cohort over the period of this study. At five years after initiation of the study there was a 9 percent reduction in CHD death added to nonfatal MI, which had been established as the major endpoint. This reduction was not sufficient to meet the tests of statistical significance. However, when the incidence in new MI was considered alone, there was a 25 percent reduction, which was significant. Of note, a series of other cardiovascular endpoints was measured and in four of these, the group taking clofibrate did significantly worse. These four endpoints included new intermittent claudication, new angina pectoris, pulmonary embolism and cardiac arrhythmias other than atrial fibrillation. Only one class of these clinical events, arrhythmia, has been observed in other studies.[40]

A second trial was sponsored by the WHO and conducted in three centers in Europe: Edinburgh; Budapest; and Prague. In this study, men aged 30 years to 59 years were selected based on their blood cholesterol level. A total of 10,000 men with a cholesterol level in the upper third of the population distribution were randomly assigned to clofibrate 1.6 gm per day, or placebo. In addition, 5,000 men with a cholesterol level in the lower third of the population were placed on placebo as a second control group. A mean reduction of 9 percent in total serum cholesterol was maintained over the 5.3 years of the study. The incidence of coronary heart disease was reduced by 20 percent in the clofibrate treated group (p < 0.05). This difference was due totally to a 25 percent reduction in the incidence of nonfatal MI. Death from CHD was not significantly changed. Men who smoked and who had blood pressure above average for the population appeared to have greater benefit from clofibrate treatment with regard to reduced CHD incidence.[44] Unfortunately, the total mortality in the *high*-cholesterol, clofibrate-treated group was found to be higher than in the *high*-cholesterol, placebo group. Most excess deaths were attributed to conditions in the liver, biliary and intestinal systems. Age adjustment of the patients with fatal events tended to negate the difference between the clofibrate-treated and placebo group. It was also noted that the incidence of such deaths were of comparable incidence in the clofibrate-treated group and in the *low*-cholesterol, placebo control group, raising the question of a spurious low incidence of mortality in the *high*-cholesterol, control group. A subsequent five-year monitoring of this cohort has failed to document continued higher mortality in the clofibrate-treated population[41] and the actual cause of the initial mortality findings have never been answered to full satisfaction. Interestingly, the initial observation of lower mortality in the one control group gained more attention than the observed reduction in nonfatal MI. As a result, the use of clofibrate in the medical therapy of elevated cholesterol began to decline steadily when the outcome of this clinical trial was reported.

The recently completed Helsinki Heart Study was the first fibric acid trial to use lipoprotein measurements to define the study population and to relate therapeutic efficacy of lipoprotein lipid changes to CHD incidence.[37] This study of 4,081 middle-aged, Finnish men, 40 years to 55 years of age, involved the blind random assignment to gemfibrozil 600 mg twice daily or to placebo. In order to enter this study, men were required to have moderate to marked elevations in LDL-C and/or VLDL-C (i.e., total plasma cholesterol minus HDL-C > 200 mg/dl). During five years of observation, mean decreases were 35 percent for total serum triglycerides, 10 percent for total cholesterol and 11 percent for LDL-C. A mean rise of 11 percent above baseline was observed with HDL-C. These lipoprotein changes in the gemfibrozil-treated group were associated with a statistically significant reduction of 34 percent in the summed incidence of MI and CHD death when compared to the placebo group. The reduction in MI and CHD, the major cardiovascular endpoints, were independently associated with the reduction in LDL-C and the rise in HDL-C. Although the TG reduction was the most dramatic of changes in lipid parameters, this reduction was not significantly related to the reduced incidence of cardiovascular disease when the change in lipoprotein cholesterol (LDL and HDL) were taken into consideration. In the subgroup analysis, the greatest reduction in incidence of CHD appeared to occur in those who had lower HDL-C at baseline and in those who had both increased LDL-C and VLDL-C. Gemfibrozil proved to be a very safe drug with only abdominal discomfort and intestinal symptoms occurring with a statistically significant increase in frequency.

COMBINATION THERAPY

Additional lipoprotein reduction can be achieved by using fibrates in combination with other lipid-lowering drugs. The specific use of each combination will be discussed in relation to the clinical presentation of patients.

Elevated VLDL and LDL

Patients who have elevated VLDL triglycerides may also have elevated LDL (Type IIB). Niacin may be the most effective single agent for this disorder but often contraindications such as hyperuricemia or subjective intolerance make this treatment undesirable. Bile acid binding resins will lower LDL-C but the VLDL-C level may rise so significantly that the total plasma cholesterol may show no change or an increase. The use of a fibrate will usually reduce TG by 30 percent to 40 percent. However, LDL may not decline or may even show an increase. After 2 to 3 months of treatment, if the LDL-C persists at a higher than desirable level, addition of cholestyramine (4 mg bid) or colestipol (5 gm bid) will usually lower the LDL-C without raising TG. The resins may then be increased at 4- to 6-week intervals to titrate the LDL to a desirable range.

Elevated LDL-C

Patients with familial hypercholesterolemia may have an LDL-C level well above 200 mg/dl, and single drug therapy even at maximal doses may not produce satisfactory reduction. Jones *et al.*[46] achieved a 44 percent reduction of LDL-C in such patients by combining cholestyramine (12 gm bid) and gemfibrozil (600 mg bid). This reduction compared to only a 33 percent decrease with cholestyramine alone (12 gm bid). Weisweiler and Schwandt found a comparable reduction of LDL-C (41 percent) in a similar patient population using colesipol 5 gm tid and fenofibrate 250 mg daily, similar to the fall in LDL-C with maximal doses of an HMG CoA reductase inhibitor, simvastatin, observed in a randomly assigned parallel group within the same study.[46] Illingworth[41] found only modest additional reduction of LDL-C when gemfibrozil (600 mg bid) was added to maximal doses of lovastatin (40 mg bid) in patients with familial hypercholesterolemia.

The combination of fibrates with nicotinic acid would appear to offer only moderate additional LDL-C and/or TG reduction when compared to either agent alone. However, the recently reported Stockholm Heart Study[47] found a very significant decline in CHD mortality (36 percent) and total mortality (25 percent) in a group of survivors of MI. In the Stockholm Heart Study, 279 patients were treated for five years with both clofibrate (1 gm bid) and a delayed-release form of nicotinic acid (pentaerythrityl-trans-nicotinate) at a dose of 1 gm tid and compared to a parallel, placebo-treated control group of 276 patients. Over the period of the study, the total plasma cholesterol was reduced by 13 percent and the TG by 19 percent when compared to the average values in the control group. Unfortunately, LDL-C and HDL-C measures were not reported. A large rise in HDL-C could have hidden a very profound reduction in LDL-C. Such changes would have been consistent with the known effects of these drugs and with the relationship between lipoprotein alterations and decline in CHD endpoints observed in other studies.

CONCLUSION

The fibric acid derivatives have been documented to be safe and effective agents in the treatment of primary hypertriglyceridemia of several types. Elevated levels of VLDL, IDL and chylomicrons are reduced by these agents. These drugs are particularly effective in patients with dysbetalipoproteinemia (Type III hyperlipoproteinemia) in which both the VLDL and IDL levels are elevated and cholesterol is enriched. These agents are also efficacious in treating patients with elevated LDL-C but normal TG. A reduction in LDL can be achieved by this group of drugs in persons with familial hypercholesterolemia. However, the fibrates are usually less effective in this capacity than are the bile acid sequestrants or HMG CoA reductase inhibitors. In many patients with a low HDL level, the fibric acid derivatives produce a significant rise in the plasma level of HDL-C as well as the apolipoproteins AI and AII. In one study, this last mentioned lipoprotein alteration induced by gemfibrozil was associated with a decline in CHD.[37] Further studies documenting this important relationship are needed.

Adverse events with fibric acid derivatives include the production of lithogenic bile, which appears to be associated with a higher probability of developing cholelithiasis and symptomatic gallbladder disease after many years (particularly with clofibrate). Although uncommon, myositis and hepatocellular dysfunction may occur and these possibilities require the monitoring of appropriate laboratory tests. Drug interactions include the potentiation of the anticoagulant effects of warfarin and more frequently observed episodes of myositis when fibrates were used in conjunction with lovastatin therapy. Patients who have liver and kidney disease should be carefully evaluated before treatment with fibric acid derivatives, since excretion of the metabolites of these agents may be markedly retarded.

REFERENCES

1. Thorp JM, Waring WS. Modification of metabolism and distribution of lipids by ethyl chlorphenoxyisobutyrate. Nature. 1962;194:948-949.
2. Hellman L, Zumoff B, Kessler G, et al. Reduction of cholesterol and lipids in man by Ethyl-p-chlorphenoxyisobutyrate. Ann Intern Med. 1963;59:477-494.
3. Brown WV. Fenofibrate, a third-generation fibric acid derivative. Proceedings of a symposium 1986 Nov 15; Dallas. Am J Med. 1987;83(suppl 5B):1-89.
4. Todd PA, Ward A. Gemfibrozil: a review of its pharmacodynamic and pharmacokinetic properties and therapeutic use in dyslipidaemia. Drugs. 1988;36:314-339.
5. Curtis CG, Danahu TM, Hibbert EA, et al. The fate of gemfibrozil and its metabolites in the rat. Biochem Soc Trans. 1977;13:1190-1191.
6. Desager JD, Costermans J, Verberckmoes R, et al. Effect of hemodialysis on plasma kinetics of fenofibrate in chronic renal failure. Nephron. 1982;31:51-54.
7. Kremer P, Marowski C, Jones C, et al. Therapeutic effects of bezafibrate and gemfibrozil in hyperlipoproteinemia type IIA and IIB. Curr Med Res Opin. 1989;11:293-303.
8. Goldberg AC, Schonfeld G, Feldman EB, et al. Fenofibrate for the treatment of type IV and V hyperlipoproteinemias: a double-blind, placebo-controlled, multicenter U.S. Study. Clin Therapy. 1989;11:69-83.
9. Hunninghake DB, Peters J. Effects of fibric acid derivatives on blood lipid and lipoprotein levels. Am J Med. 1987;83(suppl 5B):44-49.
10. Kuo PT, Wilson AC, Kostis JB, et al. Treatment of type III hyperlipoproteinemia with gemfibrozil to retard the progression of coronary artery disease. Am Heart J. 1988;116:85-90.
11. Rabkin SW, Hayden M, Frohlich J. Comparison of gemfibrozil and clofibrate on serum lipids in familial combined hyperlipidemia: a randomized placebo-controlled, double-blind crossover clinical trial. Atherosclerosis. 1988;73:233-240.

12. Brown WV, Dujovne CA, Farguhar JW, et al. Effects of fenofibrate on plasma lipids: double-blind, hyperlipidemia. Arteriosclerosis. 1986;6:670-678.

13. Wilson DE, Lees RS. Metabolic relationships among the lipoproteins: reciprocal changes in the concentrations of very low- and low-density lipoproteins in man. J Clin Invest. 1972;51:1052-1062.

14. Nye ER, Sutherland WH, Temple WA. The treatment of hyperlipoproteinemia with gemfibrozil compared with placebo and clofibrate. N Zeal Med J. 1980;92:345-349.

15. Manninen V, Huttunen JK, Heinonen OP, et al. Relation between baseline lipid and lipoprotein values and the incidence of coronary heart disease in the Helsinki Heart Study. Am J Cardiol. 1989;63:42H-47H.

16. Eisenberg S, Gavish D, Oschry Y, et al. Abnormalities in very low-, low- and high-density lipoproteins in hypertriglyceridemia: reversal toward normal with bezafibrate treatment. J Clin Invest. 1984;74:470-482.

17. Goldberg AC, Schonfeld G, Anderson C, et al. Fenofibrate affects the composition of lipoproteins. Am J Med. 1987;83(suppl 5B):60-65.

18. Knopp RH, Walden CE, Warnick R, et al. Effect of fenofibrate treatment on plasma lipoprotein lipids, high-density lipoprotein cholesterol subfractions and apolipoproteins B, AI, AII and E. Am J Med. 1987;83(suppl 5B):75-84.

19. Mellies MG, Stein EH, Khoury P, et al. Effects of fenofibrate on lipid, lipoproteins and apolipoproteins in 33 subjects with primary hypercholesterolemia. Atherosclerosis. 1987;63:57-64.

20. Kissebah AH, Alfarsi S, Adams PW, et al. Transport kinetics of plasma free fatty acids, very low-density lipoprotein triglycerides and apoprotein in patients with hypertriglyceridemia. Effects of 2, 2-dimethyl, 5-(2,5 -xyloxy) valeric acid therapy. Diabetologia. 1976;24:199-218.

21. Kesanicmi YA, Grundy SM. Influence of gemfibrozil and clofibrate on metabolism of cholesterol and plasma triglyceride in man. JAMA. 1984;251:2241-2246.

22. Maragandakis ME, Hankin H. On the mode of action of lipid-lowering agents. V. Kinetics of the inhibition *in vitro* of rat acetyl CoA carboxylase. J Biochem. 1971;246:348-354.

23. Rodney O, Uhlendorf D, Maxwell RE. The hypolipidemic effect of gemfibrozil (C1-719) in laboratory animals. Proc R Soc Med. 1976;69:6-9.

24. Rifkind BM. Effect of CPIB ester on plasma free fatty acid levels in man. Metabolism. 1966;15:673-675.

25. Petit D. Effects of ciprofibrate and fenofibrate on liver lipids and lipoproteins synthesis in normo and hyperlipidemic rats. Atherosclerosis. 1988;74:215-225.

26. Grundy SM, Vega GL. Fibric Acids: effects on lipids and lipoprotein metabolism. Am J Med. 1987;83(suppl 5B):9-20.

27. Boberg J, Boberg M, Gross R, et al. The effect of treatment with clofibrate on hepatic triglyceride and lipoprotein lipase activities of post-heparin plasma in male patients with hyperlipoproteinemia. Arteriosclerosis. 1977;267:499-503.

28. Vessby B, Lithel H, Lederman H. Elevated lipoprotein lipase activity in skeletal muscle tissue during treatment of hypertriglyceridemic patients with bezafibrate. Atherosclerosis. 1982;44:113-118.

29. Fruchart JC, Davignon J, Bard JM, et al. Effect of fenofibrate on Type III hyperlipoproteinemia. Am J Med. 1987;83(suppl 5B):71-74.

30. Brown WV, Baginsky ML. Inhibition of lipoprotein lipase by an apoprotein of human very low-density lipoprotein. Biochem Biophys Res Commun. 1972;46:375-382.
31. Stewart JM, Packard CJ, Lovimer AR, et al. Effects of bezafibrate on receptor mediated and receptor independent low-density lipoprotein catabolism in type II hyperlipoproteinemic subjects. Atherosclerosis. 1984;44:355-364.
32. Bernt J, Gaumert R, Still J. Mode of action on the lipid lowering agents clofibrate and BM 15, 075 on cholesterol biosynthesis in rat liver. Atherosclerosis. 1978;30:147-152.
33. Shepherd J, Caslake MJ, Lorimer AR, et al. Fenofibrate reduces low-density catabolism in hypertriglyceridemic subjects. Arterioscleriosis. 1985;5:162-168.
34. Saku K, Gartside DS, Hind BA, Kashyap MK. Mechanism of action of gemfibrozil on lipoprotein metabolism. J Clin Invest. 1985;75:1702-1712.
35. The Coronary Drug Project Research Group. Clofibrate and niacin in coronary heart disease. JAMA. 1975;231:360-381.
36. Committee of Principal Investigators. A cooperative trial in the primary prevention of ischaemic heart disease using clofibrate. Br Heart J. 1978;10:1069-1118.
37. Frick MH, Elo O, Haapa K, et al. Helsinki Heart Study: primary prevention trial with gemfibrozil in middle-aged men with dyslipidemia. N Engl J Med. 1987;317:1237-1245.
38. Palmer RH. Effects of fibric acid derivatives on biliary lipid composition. Am J Med. 1987;83(suppl 5B):37-43.
39. Langer T, Levy RI. Acute muscular syndrome associated with administration of clofibrate. N Engl J Med. 1968;279:856-858.
40. LaRosa JC, Brown WV, Frommer P, et al. Clofibrate-induced ventricular arrhythmia. Am J Cardiol. 1969;23:266-269.
41. WHO Cooperative Trial on primary prevention of ischaemic heart disease with clofibrate to lower serum cholesterol: final mortality follow-up. Lancet. 1984;2:600-604.
42. Illingworth DR, Bacon S. Influence of lovastatin plus gemfibrozil on plasma lipids and lipoproteins in patients with familial hypercholesterolemia. Circulation. 1989;79:590-596.
43. Kremer P, Marowski C, Jones C, et al. Therapeutic effects of bezafibrate on gemfibrozil in hyperlipoproteinemia, types IIA and IIB. Curr Med Res Opin. 1989;11:293-303.
44. Green KG, Heady A, Oliver MF. Blood pressure, cigarette smoking and heart attack in the WHO cooperative trial of clofibrate. Int J Epidemiol. 1989;18:355-360.
45. Jones AF, Hughes EA, Cramb R. Gemfibrozil plus cholestyramine in familial hypercholesterolaemia. Lancet. 1988;1:776.
46. Weisweiler P, Schwandt P. Colestipol plus fenofibrate versus synvinolin in familial hypercholesterolaemia. Lancet. 1986;2:1212-1213.
47. Carlson LA, Rosenhamer G. Reduction of mortality in the Stockholm Ischaemic Heart Disease Secondary Prevention Study by combined treatment with clofibrate and nicotinic acid. Acta Med Scand. 1988;223:405-418.

CHAPTER 6

HMG CoA Reductase Inhibitors

Gustav Schonfeld, M.D.
Saint Louis, Missouri

INTRODUCTION

The therapy of hyperlipoproteinemia has two major aims: (1) the amelioration of symptoms (seen only in the minority of cases) and (2) delaying, halting or reversing rates of atheroma formation and the development of clinically manifest coronary heart disease (CHD).[1-4] In principle, the second aim could be achieved in a number of ways: (a) by altering the functions of the cellular elements of the arterial wall; (b) by inhibiting those chemical transformations of lipoproteins, e.g., oxidation, that render them more atherogenic; and (c) by lowering the plasma concentrations of atherogenic lipoproteins such as low-density lipoprotein (LDL) and intermediate-density lipoprotein. Other approaches may also be possible, such as affecting high-density lipoprotein (HDL) concentrations or platelet functions. At the present time, the most successful and proven approach for the prevention of CHD consists of decreasing the plasma concentrations of atherogenic lipoproteins, and the most potent and widely used drugs for implementing these changes are the β-hydroxymethyl-β-glutaryl Coenzyme A (HMG CoA) reductase inhibitors. However, before any lipid-lowering drugs are used, the correct diagnosis needs to be established and diet therapy attempted.

HMG CoA REDUCTASE ENZYME

The HMG CoA reductase enzyme is a protein consisting of 887 amino acids (Figure 1). About 50 percent of the length of the amino terminal end of protein, containing seven hydrophobic regions, is anchored in the membrane and lumen of the endoplasmic reticulum.[5] The remainder of the molecule protrudes into the cytoplasm. The cytoplasmic domain contains the catalytic site. Enzyme activity is regulated by varying the amounts of enzyme protein present in cells[6] and also by phosphorylation of the protein.[7] The amount of enzyme protein present in cells is the result of several regulated metabolic processes: (1) the rates of transcription of HMG CoA reductase mRNA are determined by interactions of several nuclear transcription factor proteins[8] with each other and with steroid regulatory elements in the 5' non-transcribed promoter regions of the HMG CoA reductase gene;[9] (2) alternate initiation sites and splice sites exist for HMG CoA reductase mRNA, giving rise to mRNAs of different sizes which are probably translated into protein at differing rates. What regulates the use of the various transcription and splice sites and hence the mix of mRNAs present at any given time is unknown, but the rate of

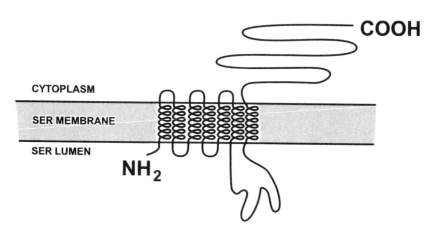

FIGURE 1. Structure of the HMG CoA reductase enzyme (adapted from reference 5)

transcription of the mRNA is known to be regulated by both sterol and non-sterol intermediates; and (3) the intracellular stability of the protein, i.e., its rate of catabolism, is also regulated by sterols.[10] The membrane-spanning portion of the enzyme needs to be present for this intracellular stablity to occur.

The HMG CoA reductase enzyme catalyzes the reduction of HMG CoA to mevalonate (Figure 2). The product of the reaction is the first committed intermediate in the pathways that lead to the synthesis of isopentenyl pyrophosphate, farnesyl pyrophosphate, ubiquinone, dolichol, cholesterol and other molecules.[5] Many of these are important regulatory or structural molecules. For example, farnesyl phosphate serves to anchor several proteins into the cell membrane including the GTP-binding, growth-regulating p21 *ras* protein; thus farnesyl phosphate may be essential for the regulation of cell growth and in oncogenesis. Ubiquinone serves as a component of the mitochondrial electron transport system that generates ATP and metabolic energy. Dolichol functions in the N-glycosylation of proteins. N-glycosylation targets proteins to various intracellular compartments or for secretion. Cholesterol lends rigidity to cell membranes and is a precursor of adrenal and gonadal steroid hormones. Thus complete inhibition of the HMG CoA reductase reaction would adversely affect several important functions of cells.

Fortunately, (1) the HMG CoA reductase inhibiting drugs do not completely inhibit mevalonate production in part because there is a compensatory increase in enzyme synthesis, (2) the reduced amounts of mevalonate available to cells are preferentially shunted into the non-sterol pathways and (3) alternative sources of cholesterol derived from plasma lipoproteins are available to cells. Thus, cells are not deprived of any of these important metabolites. In fact, the situation is quite the opposite, in that mevalonate continues to be synthesized in humans treated with these inhibitors, albeit in reduced amounts.[11-17]

HMG CoA REDUCTASE INHIBITORS

Molecular Structures and Cellular Mechanisms

At the present time, four compounds are either approved for clinical use in the United States or in clinical trials (Figure 3). Three of these originated as fungal extracts or derivatives of fungal extracts (lovastatin, simvastatin and pravastatin) whereas the fourth (fluvastatin) was completely synthesized. The active sites of all the inhibitors resemble HMG CoA, the substrate of the enzyme being inhibited. Three of the compounds are administered as pro-drugs whose active sites are present as closed lactone rings. The fourth, pravastatin, is administered as the active 6-α-hydroxy open acid.[18-23]

There are also differences observed in *in vivo* experiments in animals with respect to the extent to which the liver removes the compounds absorbed from the gut during the first pass of portal blood through the liver ("first pass removal"); hence there are differences in how much of the drugs "escape" the liver to circulate in plasma and remain available for uptake by peripheral tissues. Based on cell culture and *in vivo* animal experiments, it has been proposed that pravastatin, a more hydrophilic compound than the three others, displays tissue selectivity for the liver, a potentially useful trait because this may result in more desirable side effect and toxicity profiles for pravastatin.[23-26] However, this claim has been contested.[27]

The major issue to be settled at this time is whether any significant differences in clinical efficacy and undesirable effects between these compounds are discernable in patients. To date, the three compounds for which clinical information is available, lovastatin, simvastatin and pravastatin, appear quite similar.

Pharmacokinetics and Drug Metabolism

About 30 percent to 80 percent of oral doses of the inhibitors are absorbed from the gut, and 30 percent to 80 percent of absorbed doses are taken up by the liver.[18,19,23,24] The drugs are detectable in plasma in approximately 30 minutes and reach peak concentrations in approximately 1.5 hours. Peak plasma concentrations are dose-dependent, ranging from 10 to 40 ng/ml (for pravastatin, for example) using oral doses ranging from 10 to 40 mg/day. Half-lives of elimination from plasma are approximately 1.5 hours and none of the four drugs is detectable at 18 to 24 hours after a single dose. Within 72 hours following single oral doses of any of the labeled inhibitors, 60 percent to 80 percent are excreted in bile and 10 percent to 50 percent in urine. Following the intake of the

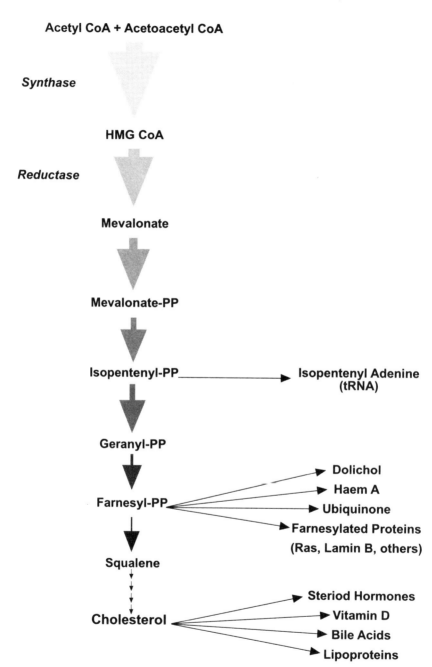

FIGURE 2. The cholesterol synthetic pathway, including the important isoprene compounds (adapted from reference 5)

pro-drug, several hydroxymetabolities, not all of which have been characterized, are found in plasma and urine. Most of these appear to have reduced inhibitory activity. Repeated dosing does not result in increasing peak or nadir concentrations of the drugs in plasma, i.e., at the recommended doses, there is no accumulation.

Mechanisms of Plasma Lipid-Lowering

There are at least two mechanisms by which plasma LDL concentrations are lowered. One of these mechanisms is that reduced rates of cholesterol synthesis result in decreased intracellular levels of cholesterol. This in turn

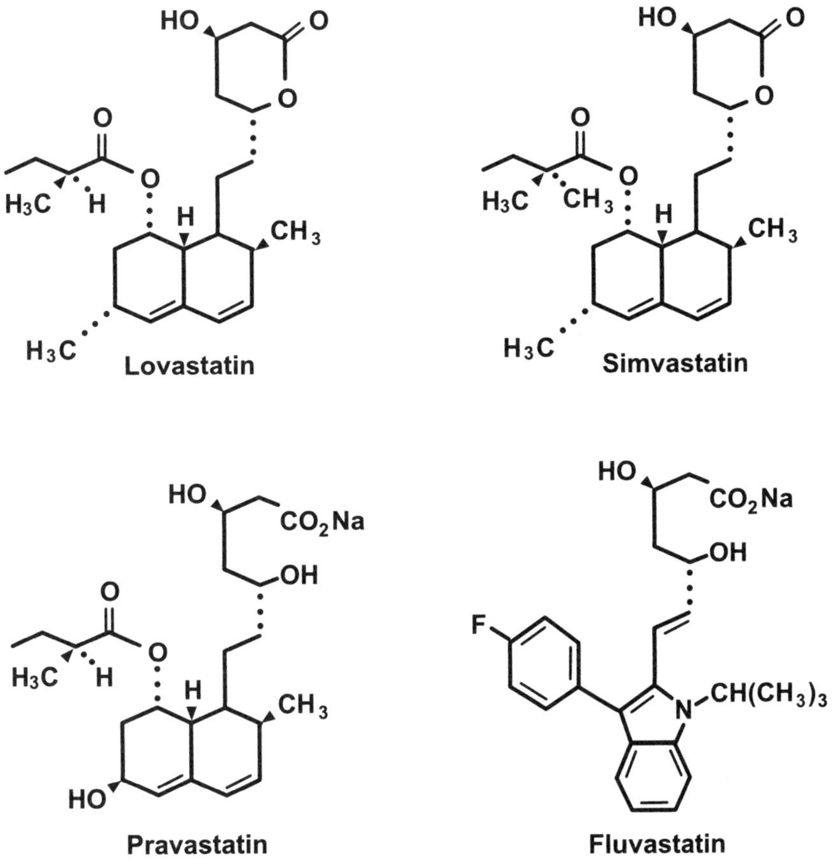

FIGURE 3. The HMG CoA reductase drugs currently on the market in the U.S. or in clinical testing

triggers a compensatory mechanism for replenishing intracellular cholesterol stores, namely increased activity of hepatic LDL-receptors, which in turn results in enhanced rates of clearance of LDL from plasma and reduction in plasma LDL concentrations.[28-37] This mechanism seems important in patients with familial hypercholesterolemia (FH) and normal controls. A second mechanism is that inhibition of cholesterol synthesis in liver reduces the rate of very low-density lipoprotein (VLDL) secretion; since VLDL serve as precursors of LDL, there is also a reduction in LDL concentration. This second mechanism seems more important in patients with familial combined hyperlipidemia.

Clinical Indications

Lovastatin, simvastatin and pravastatin are available in the United States in mid 1992. Fluvastatin is in clinical trials.

Since the inhibitors work in part by up-regulating the expression of LDL-receptors, they are not efficient in lowering LDL-cholesterol (LDL-C) concentrations in patients with the homozygous form of FH,[38] nor would they be expected to be fully effective in patients with homozygous familial defective apoprotein B-100 (apoB-100), because their defective apoB-100 molecules are poorly recognized by LDL-receptors.[39] Lp(a), a lipoprotein, resembles LDL except for the presence of an added apoprotein, apo(a). The apoB in Lp(a) interacts with LDL-receptors, albeit with reduced affinity. Lp(a) concentrations in plasma correlate positively with coronary artery disease risk. Lp(a) levels are not affected by the inhibitors.[40] However, these drugs are highly efficacious in other isolated hypercholesterolemias (hyper-LDL-lipoproteinemia, Type IIa) and in combined hypercholesterolemias and hypertriglyceridemias, i.e., heterozygous FH, polygenic hypercholesterolemia, Type III hyperlipoproteinemia[41-43] and familial combined hyperlipidemia, including those cases that have elevations of both LDL and VLDL, Type IIb. Both fasting and postprandial elevations of lipids are decreased in plasma.[44]

Alternative drugs to be considered for isolated hypercholesterolemia are bile acid binding resins or niacin. Both are effective in lowering LDL concentrations and in decreasing the incidence of cardiovascular endpoints, but both have substantial side effects and niacin can have several toxicities. Niacin and fibric acid derivates are available for Type IIb and IV patients, but while gemfibrozil is effective in reducing cardio-vascular endpoints, it raises LDL levels in many patients.

The HMG CoA reductase inhibitors are also effective in hyperlipo-proteinemia secondary to diabetes mellitus or chronic renal disease. In contrast to other drugs such as nicotinic acid, they do not produce any deterioration in the metabolic control of diabetics[45,46] and, due to their excretion by the liver, they do not accumulate in the plasma of patients with renal disease.[47-49]

Use of the Drugs

After a diagnosis of primary hyperlipidemia has been established and when an adequate trial of diet therapy has been performed with inadequate results, the administration of an HMG CoA reductase inhibitor should be considered. Baseline liver function and creatinine phosphokinase (CPK) activities are tested. Dosing is begun with one 20 mg tablet per day (for lovastatin), taken with the evening meal. Fasting blood samples are drawn every six weeks for determination of plasma triglyceride (TG) and cholesterol concentrations and liver chemistries. Dosages may be adjusted upwards as necessary at three monthly intervals to a maximum dosage of 80 mg/day, which may be taken as 40 mg with breakfast and 40 mg with dinner. The greatest percentage decrease in LDL-C from pre-drug levels occurs with the initial 20 mg/day (approximately 70 percent of the maximum effect); however, there is a clear dose-response relationship and increasing the dose will produce further stepwise decrements in LDL-C concentrations.[50-53] Drops in LDL-C of 20 percent to 45 percent may be expected between dosages of 20 mg/day to 80 mg/day lovastatin. Concomitantly there may be falls of 6 percent to 25 percent in TG and rises of 6 percent to 20 percent in high-density lipoprotein-cholesterol (HDL-C) in patients with Types IIa and IIb hyperlipoproteinemia. Reductions of apolipoprotein B concentration parallel reductions in total cholesterol. Mean apolipoprotein AI concentrations rise by 6 percent to 10 percent, changes that are not statistically significant in many studies. Even greater changes occur in the TG, LDL-C and HDL-C of patients with Type III hyperlipoproteinemia. The efficacies of the three widely tested preparations appear quite comparable (Table I).[50-76] Preliminary data suggest fluvastatin to have similiar efficacy. In many patients with severe FH, monotherapy with inhibitors is insufficient and combination therapy is used. (See Chapter 8 in this volume.)

Side Effects and Toxicities

These drugs are remarkably well tolerated. The incidence of gastro-intestinal side effects such as constipation, diarrhea, dyspepsia, flatus, cramps, heartburn and nausea for lovastatin, simvastatin and pravastatin is similar to that obtained with placebo. However, there is increased incidence of headache and insomnia with lovastatin. These side effects may be related to the ability of the drug to penetrate the blood-brain barrier. Because some experimental animals receiving huge doses of the drug develop ocular cataracts, great care has been taken to monitor this potential side effect in humans. To date, no increased incidence of cataracts has been found,[77] and routine eye examinations are no longer mandated. Fibric acid derivatives increase the lithogenecity of bile but the inhibitors do not.[78,79]

TABLE I. Efficacy of HMG CoA reductase inhibitors in primary hypercholesterolemia. Data represents percentage reductions of triglycerides (TG), total cholesterol (TC) and LDL-C from post-diet baselines, except for HDL-C levels, which are increases. Mean reductions were calculated from the means in the studies reported in references 50 to 76. The values should be taken merely as indications of results expected. Percentage changes were similar for subjects with familial and non-familial hypercholesterolemia.

	TG	TC	LDL-C	HDL-C
Lovastatin* (n=403)	14	27	33	10
Simvastatin** (n=604)	12 (21)	26 (35)	30 (41)	10 (12)
Pravastatin* (n=600)	12	25	32	12

*40 mg/d; **20 mg/d.

Transient mild elevations (< three times normal) of transaminase are found in 5 percent to 10 percent of cases treated with lovastatin, particularly those associated with ethanol consumption. Elevations can begin after a few weeks of therapy or even several months into therapy. Therefore, it is recommended that hepatic enzymes be monitored every six to eight weeks for the first 15 months of therapy and every three months thereafter.[80] Asymptomatic mild elevations of hepatic enzymes need not force cessation of the drug. Liver function tests may be repeated in two to three weeks. Most often the abnormality will have disappeared. If not, the drug should be stopped and liver enzymes checked again in three to four weeks. If the abnormality is gone, patients can be rechallenged with the drug in two to three months. Approximately 1 percent to 3 percent of individuals experience greater than three-fold elevations of hepatic transaminase enzymes on more than one occasion for 72 months. In such patients the drug should be permanently discontinued. The hepatic effects of simvastatin, pravastatin and fluvastatin are similar in nature.

A few percent of patients experience mild elevations (< three times normal) of CPK, which is most often asymptomatic. More dramatic is the myalgia developing in approximately 0.1 percent to 0.2 percent of patients on routine monotherapy with lovastatin.[80] In such patients pain and muscle weakness are associated with 3- to 10-fold elevated CPK levels. Still more dramatic are the rare, severe episodes of myopathy associated with rhabdomyolysis, 10- to 1000-fold rises in CPK and acute renal failure. Many of the myopathic cases have occurred in heart transplant patients with severe hypercholesterolemia taking lovastatin concomitantly with immunosuppressive agents such as cyclosporine and other lipid-lowering drugs, such as gemfibrozil and niacin. Non-transplant hyperlipidemic patients taking gemfibrozil or erythromycin plus lovastatin or lipid-lowering doses of niacin plus lovastatin also have experienced myopathy.[81] In fact, approximately 30 percent of patients taking lovastatin plus immunosuppressive therapy and approximately 5 percent of patients on gemfibrozil and lovastatin and 2 percent of patients on niacin plus lovastatin develop the myopathy of intermediate severity. Less than 0.1 percent develop rhabdomyolysis.[81,82] Approximately 2.3 percent of routine patients taking lovastatin monotherapy stop taking the drug for reasons related to the drug. Of these, 1.3 percent stop because of transaminase elevations and 0.15 percent because of myopathy (Table II).

TABLE II. Lovastatin long-term side effects*

Status	Percent	Side Effect	Percent
Lost to follow-up	8.3	Raised transaminase	1.3
Drug stopped/drug-related	2.3	Rash	0.4
Unrelated event	3.0	GI symptoms	0.3
Poor response	0.1	Myopathy	0.1
		Insomnia	0.1

*Based on 744 patients with hypercholesterolemia followed for approximately three years[81]

Patients taking any statin should be cautioned to report myalgias, and CPK activities should be determined. If greater than three-fold elevations of CPK are noted, the drug should be stopped until levels are normalized. Patients with mild symptoms may be rechallenged after two to three months. Frequently the drug is tolerated upon rechallenge. Patients on lovastatin who experience moderate to severe myopathy with greater than a three-fold rise of CPK levels probably should not take this drug.

The side effect profiles of the available statins appear to be similiar at this time (mid 1992).

Contraindications

Because of their proven proclivity to develop severe coronary heart disease (CHD), heart transplant patients with lipid disorders need to have their lipids controlled. Statins are very effective in such patients,[83] but because of the risks of myopathy, the drugs should be used in minimum effective dosages and with frequent monitoring in these patients, or other patients taking immunosuppressive therapy. Combination lipid-lowering therapies with statins plus gemfibrozil or statins plus niacin should be avoided if possible. On the other hand, combinations of resins and low-dose statins can be highly effective and safe in lowering LDL-cholesterol by 50 percent to 65 percent even in heart transplant patients.[84-86]

The post-marketing experience with lovastatin spans approximately five years and, as noted, the drug appears quite safe. The experience with simvastatin and pravastatin spans shorter periods of time. All of these drugs may be teratogenic in fetuses although this finding has not been demonstrated in animal studies with pravastatin. The long-term carcinogenic potential of these agents is not known in humans. Therefore these agents should not be used in pregnant women and young children. Fertile women need to be warned regarding pregnancy. It also should be pointed out that although all of the inhibitors used in monotherapy do prevent the development of atherosclerosis in experimental animals,[87-89] the clinical end point trials or the vascular end point data available in humans are derived from studies using combinations of statins and resins.

Drug Interactions

Interactions with commonly used drugs such as beta-blockers, digoxin, calcium channel blockers, diuretics and non-steroidal anti-inflammatory drugs appear not to be a problem with statins. In a few patients taking coumarin anti-coagulants in combination with lovastatin, prolonged prothrombin times have been reported. Therefore, if a statin is to be used in a patient taking anti-coagulants, prothrombin times should be measured early in therapy to establish whether any interaction between the drugs does exist. Interaction between anti-coagulants and pravastatin has not been observed, perhaps due to the lower protein binding of pravastatin (approximately 50 percent versus approximately 95 percent for lovastatin and simvastatin).

CONCLUSION

This latest group of cholesterol-lowering drugs work by competitively inhibiting the rate-limiting enzyme of the cholesterol synthetic pathway, HMG CoA reductase. The ring structures of the various inhibitors can vary, but their "active sites" resemble HMG CoA, the substrate of the reaction. Inhibition with the dosages and dose schedules used is incomplete permitting nearly normal rates of synthesis of other important compounds farther down-stream from HMG CoA, e.g., ubiquinone and isoprenyl compounds, such as farnesyl phosphate and also of sex and corticosteroid hormones.

Inhibition of cholesterol synthesis results in increased activity of hepatic LDL-receptors, which enhances the rate of clearance of LDL from plasma as hepatocytes attempt to restore their cholesterol contents by drawing more cholesterol from plasma. The consequence of enhanced LDL clearance is a drop in plasma LDL concentrations by 25 percent to 50 percent depending on the dose of inhibitor used and the susceptibility of the patient.

Agents of this class appear to be well tolerated with hepatic toxicity being responsible for withdrawal of approximately 2 percent of the patients and myopathy for approximately 0.5 percent.

REFERENCES

1. The Lipid Research Clinics Coronary Primary Prevention Trial Results. II. The relationship of reduction in incidence of coronary heart disease to cholesterol lowering. JAMA. 1984;251(3):365-74.

2. The Lipid Research Clinics Coronary Primary Prevention Trial Results. I. Reduction of incidence of coronary heart disease. JAMA. 1984;251(3):351-64.

3. Blankenhorn DH, Nessim SA, Johnson RL, et al. Beneficial effects of combined colestipol-niacin therapy on coronary atherosclerosis and coronary venous bypass grafts. JAMA. 1987;257(23):3233-40.

4. Frick MH, Elo O, Haapa K, et al. The Helsinki heart study: Primary-prevention trial with gemfibrozil in middle-aged men with dyslipidemia. Safety of treatment, changes in risk factors, and incidence of coronary heart disease. N Eng J Med. 1987;317(2):1237-45.

5. Goldstein JL, Brown MS. Regulation of the mevalonate pathway. Nature. 1990;343:425-30.

6. Faust JR, Luskey, KL, Chin, DJ, Goldstein, JL, et al. Regulation of synthesis and degradation of 3-hydroxy-3-methylglutaryl-coenzyme A reductase by low density lipoprotein and 25-hydroxycholesterol in UT-1 cells. Proc Natl Acad Sci USA. 1982;79:5205-9.

7. Beg ZH, Stonik JA, Brewer HB Jr. Phosphorylation of hepatic 3-hydroxy-3-methylglutaryl coenzyme A reductase and modulation of its enzymic activity by calcium-activated and phospholipid-dependent protein kinase. J Biol Chem. 1985;260:1682-7.

8. Levanon D, Hsieh C-L, Francke U. cDNA cloning of human oxysterol-binding protein and localization of the gene to human chromosome 11 and mouse chromosome 19. Genomics. 1990;7:65-74.

9. Metherall JE, Goldstein JL, Luskey KL, et al. Loss of transcriptional repression of three sterol-regulated genes in mutant hamster cells. J Biol Chem. 1989;264:15634-41.

10. Gil G, Faust JR, Chin DJ, Goldstein JL, et al. Membrane-bound domain of HMG CoA reductase is required for sterol-enhanced degradation of the enzyme. Cell. 1985;41:249-58.

11. Hagemenas FC, Pappu AS, Illingworth DR. The effects of simvastatin on plasma lipoproteins and cholesterol homeostasis in patients with heterozygous familial hypercholesterolaemia. Eur J Clin Invest. 1990;20:150-7.

12. Mol MJTM, Stalenhoef AFH, Stuyt PMJ, et al. Effects of inhibition of cholesterol synthesis by simvastatin on the production of adrenocortical steroid hormones and ACTH. Clin Endocrinology. 1989;31:679-89.

13. Fojo SS, Hoegg JM, Lackner KJ, et al. Adrenocortical function in Type II hyperlipoproteinemic patients treated with lovastatin (mevinolin). Hormone Metab Res. 1987;19(12):648-52.

14. Grundy SM, Bilheimer DW. Inhibition of 3-hydroxy-3-methylglutaryl-CoA reductase by mevinolin in familial hypercholesterolemia heterozygotes: Effects on cholesterol balance. Proc Natl Acad Sci USA. 1984;81(8):2538-42.

15. Mastroberardino G, Costa C, Gavelli MS, et al. Plasma cortisol and testosterone in hypercholesterolaemia treated with clofibrate and lovastatin. J Intern Med Res. 1989;17(4):388-94.

16. Mabuchi H, Haba T, Tatami R, et al. Effects of an inhibitor of 3-hydroxy-3-methylglutaryl coenzyme A reductase on serum lipoproteins and ubiquinone-10 levels in patients with familial hypercholesterolemia. N Eng J Med. 1981;305(9):478-82.

17. Laue L, Hoeg JM, Barnes K, Loriaux DL, et al. The effect of mevinolin on steroidogenesis in patients with defects in the low density lipoprotein receptor pathway. J Clin Endocrinol. 1987;64(3):531-5.

18. Henwood JM, Heel RC. Lovastatin-A preliminary review of its pharmacodynamic properties and therapeutic use in hyperlipidemia. Drugs. 1988;36:429-54.

19. Vickers S, Duncan CA, Chen IW, et al. Metabolic disposition studies on simvastatin, a cholesterol-lowering prodrug. Drug Metab Disp. 1990;18(2):138-45.

20. Alberts AW, Chen J, Kuron G, et al. Mevinolin: a highly potent competitive inhibitor of hyproxymethylglutaryl-coenzyme A reductase and a cholesterol-lowering agent. Proc Natl Acad Sci USA. 1980;77(7):3957-61.

21. Moore RN, Bigam G, Chan JK, et al. Biosynthesis of the hypocholesterolemic agent mevinolin by aspergillus terreus. Determination of the origin of carbon, hydrogen and oxygen atoms by 13C-NMR and mass spectrometry. J Am Chem Soc. 1985;107:3694-701.

22. Mantell G. Lipid lowering drugs in atherosclerosis—the HMG CoA reductase inhibitors. Clin and Exper Hyper Theory and Practice. 1989;A-11(5+6):927-41.

23. Pan HY, Funke PT, Willard DA, McKinstry DN. Pharmacokinetics, pharmacodynamics and safety of pravastatin sodium, a potent inhibitor of HMG-CoA reductase, in healthy volunteers. In: LaRosa JC, ed. New advances in the control of lipid metabolism: Focus on pravastatin. London, England: Royal Soc Med Serv Ltd; 1989:9-21.

24. Scott WA, Mahoney EM, Mosley ST. Mechanism of action and differential pharmacology of pravastatin, a hydrophilic and selective HMG CoA reductase inhibitor. In: LaRosa JC, ed. New advances in the control of lipid metabolism: Focus on pravastatin. London, England: Royal Soc of Med Serv Ltd, 1989:1-8.

25. Tsujita Y, Kuroda M, Shimada Y S, et al. SC-514, a competitive inhibitor of 3-hydroxy-3-methylglutaryl coenzyme A reductase: tissue-selective inhibitor of sterol synthesis and hypolipidemic effect on various animal species. Biochem Biophys Acta. 1986;877:50-60.

26. Chen I-W, Vickers S, Duncan CA, et al. Tissue selectivities of three HMG-CoA reductase inhibitors. FASEB J. 1988;2:4445. Abstract.

27. Germershausen JI, Hunt VM, Bostedor RG, et al. Tissue selectivity of the cholesterol lowering agents lovastatin, simvastatin, and pravastatin in rats in vivo. Biochem Biophys Res Comm. 1989;158(3):667-75.

28. Kume N, Kita T, Mikami A, et al. Induction of mRNA for low density lipoprotein receptors in heterozygous Watanabe Heritable hyperlipidemic rabbits treated with CS-514 (pravastatin) and cholestyramine. Circulation. 1989;79:1084-90.

29. Malmendier CL, Lontie JF, Delcroix C, Magot T. Effect of simvastatin on receptor-dependent low density lipoprotein catabolism in normocholesterolemic human volunteers. Atherosclerosis. 1989;80:101-9.

30. Vega GL, Krauss RM, Grundy SM. Pravastatin therapy in primary moderate hypercholesterolemia: Changes in metabolism of apolipoprotein-B-containing lipoproteins. J Intern Med. 1990;227:81-94.

31. Bilheimer DW, Grundy SM, Brown MS, et al. Mevinolin and colestipol stimulate receptor-mediated clearance of low density lipoprotein from plasma in familial hypercholesterolemia heterozygotes. Proc Natl Acad Sci USA. 1983;80(13):4124-8.

32. Reihner E, Rudling M, Stahlberg D, et al. Influence of pravastatin, a specific inhibitor of HMG-CoA reductase, on hepatic metabolism of cholesterol. N Eng J Med. 1990;323(4):224-8.

33. Grundy SM, Vega GL. Influence of mevinolin on metabolism of low density lipoproteins in primary moderate hypercholesterolemia. J Lipid Res. 1985;26(12):1464-75.

34. Hagemenas FC, Illingworth DR. Cholesterol homeostasis in mononuclear leukocytes from patients with familial hypercholesterolemia treated with lovastatin. Arteriosclerosis. 1989;9:355-61.

35. Ma PTS, Gil G, Sudhof TC, Bilheimer DW et al. Mevinolin, an inhibitor of cholesterol synthesis, induces mRNA for low density lipoprotein receptor in livers of hamsters and rabbits. Proc Natl Acad Sci USA. 1986;83(21):8370-4.

36. Traber MG, Kayden HJ. Inhibition of cholesterol synthesis by mevinolin stimulates low density lipoprotein receptor activity in human monocyte-derived macrophages. Atherosclerosis. 1984;52(1):1-11.

37. Vega GL, East C, Grundy SM. Effects of combined therapy with lovastatin and colestipol in heterozygous familial hypercholesterolemia: effects on kinetics of apolipoprotein-B. Arteriosclerosis. 1989;9(1):1136-44.

38. Uauy R, Vega GL, Grundy SM, Bilheimer DM. Lovastatin therapy in receptor-negative homozygous familial hypercholesterolemia: lack of effect on low density lipoprotein concentrations or turnover. J Pediatr. 1988;113(2):387-92.

39. Innerarity TL, Weisgrager KH, Arnold KS, et al. Familial defective apolipoprotein B100: Low density lipoproteins with abnormal receptor binding. Proc Natl Acad Sci USA. 1987;84(19):6919-23.

40. Berg K, Leren TP. Unchanged serum lipoprotein (A) concentrations with lovastatin. Lancet. 1989;2(8666):812.

41. Illingworth DR, O'Malley JP. The hypolipidemic effects of lovastatin and clofibrate alone and in combination in patients with type III hyperlipoproteinemia. Metabolism. 1990;39(4):403-9.

42. Stuyt PMJ, Mol MJTM, Stalenhoef AFH, et al. Simvastatin in the effective reduction of plasma lipoprotein levels in familial dysbetalipoproteinemia (type-III hyperlipo-proteinemia). Am J Med. 1990;88:N42-5.

43. East CA, Grundy SM, Bilheimer DW. Preliminary report: Treatment of type 3 hyperlipoproteinemia with mevinolin. Metabolism. 1986;35(2):97-8.

44. Weintraub MS, Eisenberg S, Breslow JL. Lovastatin reduces postprandial lipoprotein levels in hypercholesterolemic patients with mild hypertriglyceridemia. Eur J Clin Invest. 1989;19(5):480-5.

45. Yoshino G, Kazumi T, Iwai M. Matsushita M, Long-term treatment of hypercholesterolemic non-insulin dependent diabetics (NIDDM) with pravastatin (CS-514). Atherosclerosis. 1989;75(1):67-72.

46. Garg A, Grundy SM. Lovastatin for lowering cholesterol levels in non-insulin-dependent diabetes mellitus. N Eng J Med. 1988;318(2):81-6.

47. Golper TA, Illingworth DR, Bennett WM. Correction of nephrotic hypercholesterolemia with the HMG-CoA reductase inhibitor lovastatin. Kidney Int. 1988;33(1):136.

48. Vega GL, Grundy SM. Lovastatin therapy in nephrotic hyperlipidemia: Effects on lipoprotein metabolism. Kidney Int. 1988;33(6):1160-8.

49. Kasiske BL, Tortorice KL, Heim-Duthoy KL, et al. Lovastatin treatment of hypercholesterolemia in renal transplant recipients. Transplant. 1990;49(1):95-100.

50. Saito Y, Goto Y, Nakaya N, et al. Dose-dependent hypolipidemic effect of an inhibitor of HMG-CoA reductase, pravastatin (CS-514), in hypercholesterolemic subjects. A double blind test. Atherosclerosis. 1988;72(2-3):205-11.

51. Havel RJ, Hunninghake DB, Illingworth DR, et al. Lovastatin (mevinolin) in the treatment of heterozygous familial hypercholesterolemia. A multicenter study. Ann Intern Med. 1987;107(5):609-15.

52. Hunninghake DB, Miller VT, Palmer RH, Schonfeld G, et al. Therapeutic response to lovastatin (mevinolin) in non-familial hypercholesterolemia: a multicenter study. JAMA. 1987;256(2):2829-34.

53. Illingworth DR, Sexton GJ. Hypocholesterolemic effects of mevinolin in patients with heterozygous familial hypercholesterolemia. J Clin Invest. 1984;74(6):1972-8.

54. Tobert JA, Hitzenberger G, Kukovetz WR, et al. Rapid and substantial lowering of human serum cholesterol by mevinolin (MK-803), an inhibitor of hydroxymethyl-glutaryl-coenzyme A reductase. Atherosclerosis. 1981;41:61-5.

55. Illingworth DR. Mevinolin plus colestipol therapy for severe heterozygous familial hypercholesterolemia. Ann Intern Med. 1984;101:598-604.

56. Illingworth DR, Bacon S. Influence of lovastatin plus gemfibrozil on plasma lipids and lipoproteins in patients with heterozygous familial hypercholesterolemia. Circulation. 1989;79:590-6.

57. Itskovitz HD, Flamenbaum W, DeGaetano C, et al. Effect of lovastatin on serum lipids in patients with non-familial primary hypercholesterolemia. Clin Ther. 1989;11(6):862-72.

58. Tikkanen MJ, Helve E, Jaatela A, et al. Finnish Lovastatin Study Group. Comparison between lovastatin and gemfibrozil in the treatment of primary hypercholesterolemia: The Finnish multicenter study. Am J Cardiol. 1988;62:35J-43J.

59. Tobert JA. The Lovastatin Study Group III. A multicenter comparison of lovastatin and cholestryamine therapy for severe primary hypercholesterolemia. JAMA. 1988;260(3):359-66.

60. Vega GL, Grundy SM. Treatment of primary moderate hypercholesterolemia with lovastatin (mevinolin) and colestipol. JAMA. 1987;257(1):33-8.

61. Aubert I, Emmerich J, Charpak Y, Chanu B, et al. The effects of simvastatin on plasma lipids, lipoproteins and apoproteins A-1 and B: 24 cases of major primary hypercholesterolemia. Press Med. 1988;17(18):901-4.

62. Bach LA, Cooper ME, O'Brien RC, et al. The use of simvastatin, an HMG CoA reductase inhibitor, in older patients with hypercholesterolemia and atherosclerosis. J Am Ger Soc. 1990;38:1-14.

63. Bard JM, Luc G, Douste-Blazy P, et al. Effect of simvastatin on plasma lipids, apolipoproteins, and lipoprotein particles in patients with primary hypercholesterolemia. Eur J Clin Pharmacol. 1989;37:545-50.

64. Helve E, Ojala J-P, Tikkanen MJ. Simvastatin and gemfibrozil in the treatment of primary hypercholesterolemia. J Appl Cardiol. 1988;3(6):381-8.

65. Leclercq V, Havengt C. Simvastatin (MK 733) in heterozygous familial hypercholesterolemia: A two-year trial. Int J Clin Pharmacol. 1989;27:76-81.

66. Mol MJTM, Erkelens DW, Gevers Leuven JA, et al. Simvastatin (MK-733): A potent cholesterol synthesis inhibitor in heterozygous familial hypercholesterolemia. Atherosclerosis. 1988;69(2-3):131-7.

67. Molgaard J, von Schenck H, Olsson AG. Effects of simvastatin on plasma lipid lipoprotein and apolipoprotein concentrations in hypercholesterolemia. Eur Heart J. 1988;9(5):541-51.

68. Molgaard J, von Schenck H, Olsson AG. Comparative effects of simvastatin and cholestyramine in treatment of patients with hypercholesterolemia. Eur J Clin Pharmacol. 1989;36:455-60.

69. Morgan T, Anderson A, McDonald P, Hopper J, Macaskill G. Simvastatin in the treatment of hypercholesterolaemia in patients with essential hypertension. J Hypertens. 1990;8:S25-S32.

70. Pietro DA, Alexander S, Mantell G, Staggers JE, et al. Effects of simvastatin and probucol in hypercholesterolemia (Simvastatin Multicenter Study Group II). Am J Cardiol. 1989;63:632-86.

71. Sirtori CR, Arca M, Barone A, Bertolotto A, et al. Clinical evaluation of simvastatin in patients with severe hypercholesterolemia. Curr Ther Res. 1989;46:230-9.

72. Singer II, Scott S, Kazazis DM, et al. Lovastatin, an inhibitor of cholesterol synthesis, induces hydroxymethylglytaryl-coenzyme A reductase directly on membranes of expanded smooth endoplasmic reticulum in rat hepatocytes. Proc Natl Acad Sci USA. 1988;85(14):5264-8.

73. Stein E, Kreisberg R, Miller V, Mantell G, et al. Multicenter Group I. Effects of simvastatin and cholestyramine in familial and non-familial hypercholesterolemia. Arch Intern Med. 1990;150:341-5.

74. Weisweiler P. Simvastatin plus low-dose colestipol in the treatment of severe familial hypercholesterolemia. Curr Ther Res. 1988:44(5);802-6.

75. Betteridge DJ. Clinical efficacy of pravastatin. In: LaRosa JC, ed. New advances in the control of lipid metabolism: Focus on pravastatin. London, England: Royal Soc Med Services Ltd; 1989:23-8.

76. Franceschini G, Sirtori M, Vaccarino V, et al. Plasma lipoprotein changes after treatment with pravastatin and gemfibrozil in patients with familial hypercholesterolemia. J Lab Clin Med. 1989;114:250-9.

77. Hunninghake DB, Miller VT, Goldberg I, Schonfeld G, et al. Lovastatin: Follow-up ophthalmologic data. JAMA. 1988;259(3):354-5.

78. Hoogerbrugge-vd Linden N, de Rooy FWM, Jansen H, et al. Effect of pravastatin on biliary lipid composition and bile acid synthesis in familial hypercholesterolemia. Gut. 1990;31:348-50.

79. Duane WC, Hunninghake DB, Freeman ML, et al. Simvastatin, a competitive inhibitor of HMG CoA reductase, lowers cholesterol saturation index of gallbladder bile. Hepatology. 1988;8(5):1147-50.

80. Merck Sharp & Dohme. Mevacor package insert (lovasatin, MSD). The Hub Newsletter. 1987:83-6.

81. Tobert JA. Efficacy and long-term adverse effect pattern of lovastatin. Am J Cardiol. 1988;62:23J-34J.

82. Catalano PM, Masonson HN, Newman TJ, et al. Clinical safety of pravastatin. In: La Rosa JC, ed. New advances in the control of lipid metabolism: Focus on pravastatin. London, England: Royal Soc of Med Services Ltd; 1989:35-8.

83. Kuo PC, Kirshenbaum JM, Gordon J, et al. Lovastatin therapy for hypercholesterolemia in cardiac transplant recipients. Am J Cardiol. 1989;64(10):631-5.

84. Pan HY, DeVault AR, et al. Pharmacokinetics and pharmacodynamics of pravastatin alone and with cholestyramine in hypercholesterolemia. Clin Pharmacol Ther. 1990;48:201-7.

85. Bard JM, Parra HJ, Douste-Blazy P, et al. Effect of pravastatin, an HMG CoA reductase inhibitor, and cholestyramine, a bile acid sequestrant, on lipoprotein particles defined by their apolipoprotein composition. Metabolism. 1990;39:269-273.
86. DaCol PG, Cattin L, Valenti M, et al. Efficacy of simvastatin plus cholestyramine in the two-year treatment of heterozygous hypercholesterolemia. Curr Ther Res. 1990;48:269-273
87. Kobayashi M, Ishida F, Takahashi T, et al. Preventive effect of MK-733 (simvastatin), an inhibitor of HMG CoA reductase, on hypercholesterolemia and atherosclerosis induced by cholesterol feeding in rabbits. Japan J Pharmacol. 1989;49:133-5.
88. Watanabe Y, Ito T, Shiomi M, et al. Preventive effect of pravastatin sodium, a potent inhibitor of 3-hydroxy-3-methylglutaryl coenzyme A reductase, on coronary atherosclerosis and xanthoma in WHHL rabbits. Biochem Biophys Acta. 1988;960(3):294-302.
89. LaVille ARE, Seddon AM, Shaikh M, et al. Primary prevention of atherosclerosis by lovastatin in a genetically hyperlipidemic rabbit strain. Atherosclerosis. 1989;78(2-3):205-10.

Probucol

John T. Gwynne, M.D.
Chapel Hill, North Carolina

INTRODUCTION AND HISTORICAL DEVELOPMENT

Probucol is an effective and safe hypocholesterolemic drug. Its structure and mechanism of action differ from all other hypolipidemic drugs. Recent investigations suggest that in addition to lowering plasma cholesterol, probucol also has direct anti-atheriogenic actions. Barnhart[1] first noted the hypolipidemic properties of probucol in studies of rats, mice and primates conducted in the late 1960s. The drug gained U.S. Food and Drug Administration approval for treatment of hypercholesterolemia in 1977. Since that time probucol has been widely used both in the United States and other countries for the treatment of hypercholesterolemia (Fredrickson Type IIa and Type IIb). This chapter will concentrate on five aspects of probucol use including: pharmacokinetics; indications and efficacy; mechanisms of action; antioxidant antiatherogenic activity; and side effects.

CHEMISTRY AND PHARMACOKINETICS

Probucol (4,4'-(isopropyleneithio) bis (2,6-dibutylphenol) is a bis-phenol compound (Figure 1) similar in structure to the antioxidant butylated hydroxytoluene.[2] Structurally, it is unlike any other hypolipidemic drug. The two aromatic rings and multiple uncharged organic side chains make probucol much more soluble in lipids than in water. This physical property plays a major role in determining its pharmacokinetics and the time course of the hypocholesterolemic response.

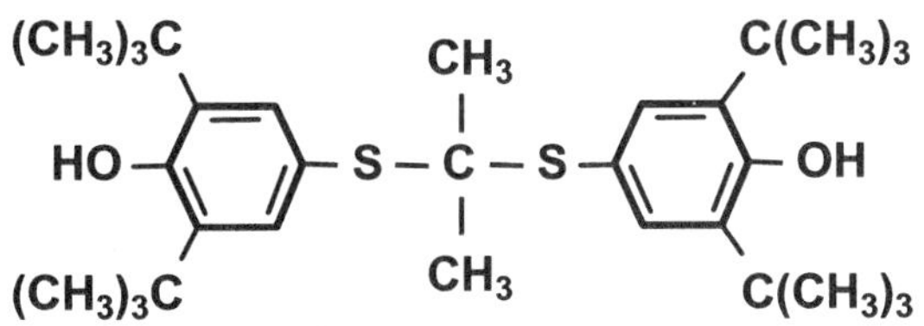

Figure 1.   Structure of probucol

The drug is variably and incompletely absorbed. In animal studies, from 2 percent to 8 percent of the drug is absorbed following a single oral dose when taken without food.[2-4] Arnold *et al.*[2,4] reported that peak plasma levels occurred from 8 to 24 hours after a single radiolabeled dose administered to ten patients treated for 21 days with 500 mg bid. Under these conditions from 0.7 percent to 14 percent of the administered dose was absorbed. The amount absorbed increased when the drug was taken with fatty foods.[3,5] Peak plasma concentrations in normal human volunteers receiving a single 3 gram dose were higher when the drug was taken after a meal than before or fasting.

Circulating steady state probucol levels vary widely among individuals receiving the same oral dose. The magnitude of total cholesterol, low-density lipoprotein-cholesterol (LDL-C) or high-density lipoprotein-cholesterol (HDL-C) lowering is unrelated to circulating steady state levels.[6] In 162 patients reported by Tedeschi et al.[7] there was no relationship between steady state plasma probucol levels and post-treatment cholesterol levels. Because it is hydrophobic, probucol circulates primarily bound to serum lipoproteins. In fasting samples, up to 85 percent is bound to LDL and the remainder to very low-density lipoprotein (VLDL) and HDL.[8-10] The binding of probucol to atherogenic lipoproteins may offer an unexpected advantage. It assures that probucol is present where it can most advantageously exert its antioxidant activity.

Increasingly, attention has been devoted to the possible role of postprandial lipids in atherogenesis. It is therefore of interest to know if probucol is present in postprandial lipoproteins. One study found that probucol redistributes to triglyceride (TG) rich lipoproteins in the postprandial state.[11] Furthermore, in rabbits fed high-cholesterol diets, to induce atherosclerosis, most circulating probucol is found associated with TG-rich lipoproteins, which are believed to be highly atherogenic in this animal model of human atherosclerosis.[12] Although probucol circulates bound to lipoproteins, the steady state concentration is unrelated to total cholesterol, LDL-C or total TG concentration.[7]

The hydrophobic nature of probucol also dictates its tissue distribution. Probucol is stored predominately in fatty tissues. In studies of rhesus monkeys,[13] the tissue concentration of probucol greatly exceeded circulating levels. The highest concentration occurred in adipose tissue and was 100 times greater than in plasma. The concentrations of probucol in adrenal and liver as well as skeletal and cardiac muscle were also greater than in the plasma.

Probucol is removed by hepatic detoxification and biliary excretion.[2-4] Fecal excretion predominates. A small amount (1 percent to 2 percent) is excreted in the urine. At least two inactive metabolites, believed to have no clinical significance, are produced by the liver and may be found in the circulation in small amounts.[3] The incomplete absorption of probucol coupled with the large storage capacity of fatty tissues causes a considerable delay in achieving maximum circulating concentrations. In fact, circulating levels may not reach steady state for up to 4 months.[7-9] Maximum total cholesterol and LDL-C lowering is likewise delayed. Similarly, because of large fatty tissue stores, circulating levels remain elevated for up to 6 to 8 weeks after cessation of treatment. In one study of eight hypercholesterolemic males treated with 500 mg bid, mean probucol levels had declined by 60 percent at 6 weeks and 80 percent at 6 months.[9] However, LDL-C levels generally return to pretreatment levels before tissue stores of probucol are completely depleted. Because of this persistent activity of probucol and its unknown effects on fetal development, probucol treatment should be discontinued well in advance of an anticipated pregnancy. The persistent action of the drug also means that occasionally missing a dose will not significantly diminish efficacy.

INDICATIONS FOR USE AND EFFICACY

Probucol is indicated as an adjunct to diet in the treatment of primary hypercholesterolemia (Fredrickson Type IIA) and combined hyperlipidemia (Fredrickson Type IIB). Since the drug has no effect on TG levels, it is not indicated for treatment of hypertriglyceridemia. Probucol is also effective in management of some types of secondary hypercholesterolemia, particularly those associated with diabetes and nephrotic syndrome. Like other hypolipidemic drugs, probucol has not yet received marketing approval for treatment of hypercholesterolemia in children or adolescents. Attainment of maximum linear growth probably signals the time at which probucol can be confidently used. Like all other hypocholesterolemic drugs, the safety of probucol in pregnancy is unknown and the drug should not be administered during pregnancy.

Total Cholesterol and LDL-C

Probucol lowers total cholesterol, LDL-C and HDL-C levels, but has little effect on fasting levels of TG. More than 40 trials of probucol effects on serum lipid levels have been reported.[3] Clinical trials of probucol efficacy have included a heterogenous group of patients and are summarized in Table I. The mean per person decrease in total cholesterol and LDL-C were 15.2 percent and 14.8 percent, respectively. Response to treatment is variable. The best means of assessing drug response is by long-term randomized placebo-controlled trials. No single such trial with probucol has been reported, and the proven value of hypocholesterolemic therapy precludes future placebo-controlled trials. However, experience in long-term open trials with large numbers of subjects and in short-term randomized placebo-controlled trials of small numbers of subjects are available. When considered together these two complimentary types of trials yield a consistent picture of the response that can be expected when using probucol.

TABLE I. Summary of clinical trials of probucol

No of Pts (M/F)	Rx (Mos)	TC* Pre Rx TC* (mg/dl)	TC* Percent Decrease	LDL-C Pre Rx LDL-C (mg/dl)	LDL-C Percent Decrease	Ref No
778	6	305	13.0			7
766	12		16.0			
414	36		20.0			
(88/0)	6	304	17.2			14
47	84		24.3			
(3/7)	18	812	27.0	735	27	16
6	3	335	9.0	250	(2)>10	17
(15/15)	3	323	13.0	255	18	18
(2/13)	3	400	34.0			19
(8/5)	3	297	16.8			20
(10/9)	2	376	13.0			21
13	4	325	13.0	265	16	22
(13/6)	1	454	9.0			23
(14/6)	6	435	9.9			
7 IIA	2	366	25.0			24
13 IIB	2	384	30.0			24
32	2	295	23.0			25
(11/9)	6-24	339	31.0			27
(18/16)	1-3	396	12.0	294	14	26
12	6	297	12.7	250	11.7	28
34 IIA	3	330	14.6	257	12	29
13 IIB	3	316	17.8	228	18	29
(5/7)	3	377	13.0	300	14	99
(25/12)	4	296	32.0			100
89	4-10	363	13.5			34
10	3	294	14.0	243	11	35

* TC = total cholesterol

Tedeschi et al.[14] have reported long-term experience with probucol treatment in open trials of up to 10 years duration (Figure 2). The average decrease in total cholesterol for this heterogeneous group of 1,133 patients treated with 500 mg bid was approximately 17 percent at six months and 20 percent at three years. In this open trial there was no loss of efficacy with continued treatment in patients who initially responded. About two thirds of patients treated for six months showed greater than a 10 percent decline in total cholesterol while more than 50 percent showed greater than a 15 percent reduction. These observations suggest that there is considerable variability in response to treatment. Some patients exhibit dramatic reduction while others show very little response.

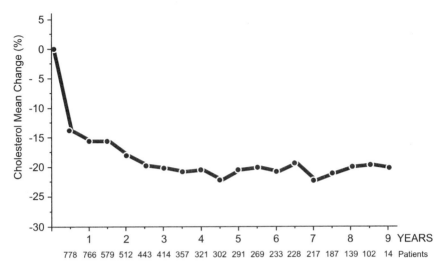

Figure 2. Probucol long-term therapy. All studies combined. (Adapted from reference 45)

Consideration of the individual trials and the types of patients enrolled is informative. The single largest randomized placebo-controlled double-blinded clinical trial of at least one year's duration, reported by McCaughan,[15] enrolled 118 patients (88 treated and 30 placebo controls) with total cholesterol > 250 mg/dl. The mean age and pretreatment total cholesterol for the probucol-treated group (49.6 ± 6.7 years and 304.7 ± 36.4 mg/dl) were the same as the 33 control patients (51.0 ± 5.6 years and 306.6 ± 34.8 mg/dl). Approximately one-third of each group had a history of myocardial infarction. There were no differences between the groups in the prevalence of other cardiovascular disease risk factors. Total cholesterol decreased 17.2 percent at 6 months and 16.2 percent at one year in the probucol-treated group compared to only 5.7 percent and 10.9 percent in the control group. Formal dietary intervention was not provided to either the control or treated group and the substantial lipid lowering exhibited by the control group may have resulted from heightened awareness and self-imposed dietary modifications. At the end of one year, 36 of 77 probucol-treated patients (46.8 percent) had greater than a 20 percent reduction in total cholesterol. In 47 patients subsequently followed for seven years on open protocol, 27 (57.4 percent) showed greater than a 20 percent reduction in total cholesterol. Side effects were minimal. Seventeen (19.3 percent) probucol-treated patients had "diarrhea" in the first year compared to 10 percent of the control group. Significantly, this controlled clinical trial yielded results quantitatively similar to those observed in the open trials summarized by Tedeschi et al.[14]

The response to treatment in groups of patients with a variety of specific lipid disorders has been characterized. A collection of short papers reporting clinical trials in small numbers of patients with various disorders can be found in *Diet and Drugs in Atherosclerosis in 1980.*[16] Probucol lowers total cholesterol and LDL-C not only in polygenic or "common hypercholesterolemia," but also in familial monogenic hypercholesterolemia (FH) and in patients with combined hyperlipidemia. Probucol appears especially effective in FH homozygotes. Baker et al.[17] treated 3 males and 7 females homozygous for FH, ranging in age from 6 years to 46 years, with maximal doses of probucol for an average of 18 months. All patients had previously failed to respond to other available hypocholesterolemic drugs and five patients had undergone portal caval shunt. Total cholesterol and LDL-C were both reduced by approximately 27 percent. At 1 month and 6 months, HDL-C fell by almost 50 percent, but returned to pretreatment levels after 18 months of treatment. There was no relationship between circulating probucol levels and response. Interestingly, cutaneous and tendon xanthoma disappeared in four patients and markedly improved in four others. One patient did not have xanthoma at entry and one showed no change.

However, not all clinical trials in FH patients have been so successful. In a study of six heterozygous patients treated for 12 weeks, Cortese and colleagues[18] reported that only two had a decline in LDL-C which exceeded 10 percent of pretreatment values. LeLorier et al.[19] examined the response to probucol in 30 patients with familial hypercholesterolemia using a cross-over design and formal dietary counseling. Twenty of the 30 patients had tendinous xanthoma, and efforts were made to exclude patients with familial combined hyperlipidemia although 14 patients exhibited a Type IIB phenotype. Sixteen patients had no decrease in total cholesterol on diet while 14 responded to diet alone during a 12-week pretreatment period with a decrease in total cholesterol of at least 8.3 percent. During the subsequent treatment periods, probucol reduced total cholesterol by 13 percent and LDL by 15 percent in diet non-responders. In the diet responders, probucol reduced LDL-C nearly 25 percent. The percent reductions in total cholesterol and LDL-C attributable to probucol were similar in diet responders and non-responders. In the diet responders, the decrease in total cholesterol was approximately the same in patients with Type IIA and Type IIB phenotypes. Males and females exhibited similar reductions. No changes in TG were observed in any group. In another study by Stefanovic et al.[20] of 15 patients with familial hyper-cholesterolemia, serum cholesterol decreased 34 percent from nearly

400 mg/dl to 229 mg/dl. Thus, in patients with familial hyper-cholesterolemia, probucol is effective in both those who do and do not respond to diet. In those who respond to diet the effects of probucol are additive to those of diet.

The efficacy of probucol in "common" or sporadic (non-FH) hypercholesterolemia as well as in FH and non-FH combined hypercholesterolemia has been examined. Probucol in conjunction with diet has been reported to lower total cholesterol 11 percent to 35 percent and to lower LDL-C 9 percent to 33 percent in patients with common non-FH hypercholesterolemia.[3] In a double-blind clinical trial of three months duration, 13 patients studied by Riberio et al.[21] experienced a 13 percent reduction in total plasma cholesterol. Similarly, in a comparison of clofibrate and probucol, De Gennes et al.[22] reported that the 19 patients receiving probucol had a 13 percent decline in total cholesterol from 376 mg/dl to 329 mg/dl. These last investigators commented especially on the variability in response to probucol, noting that one patient showed a 12 percent increase in total cholesterol (which is unusual) while 6 of the 19 patients had greater than a 20 percent reduction in total cholesterol. By comparison, total cholesterol declined only 11 percent in the 19 patients treated with clofibrate.

Mordasini et al.[23] studied 11 females and 16 males (mean age 51 years, range 27 to 71 years) with primary hypercholesterolemia using a double-blind, placebo-controlled protocol with four months of active drug treatment following dietary modification and placebo run-in. In this trial total cholesterol declined 13 percent and LDL-C declined 16 percent. Also, in this study there were no significant changes observed in TG, HDL-C or in apolipoprotein B. There was a decrease in apolipoprotein AI and apolipoprotein AII of 26.9 percent and 54 percent, respectively. A similar decline in apolipoprotein AII was observed in the placebo group suggesting that methodologic problems may render the apolipoprotein AII values meaningless. Beaumont and colleagues[24] reported their experience in 19 patients with severe hypercholesterolemia (mean pretreatment total cholesterol of 454 ± 126 mg/dl), 13 of whom also had tendon xanthoma and presumably had FH. Eight patients had Type IIA and 11 patients had Type IIB phenotypes. Both short-term (1 month) and long-term response in a slightly larger group (n=20) including 17 of the above patients were reported. The mean decline in total cholesterol at 1 month and 6 months were 9 percent and 9.9 percent, respectively.

Carmena and Ascaso[25] compared the response to treatment (500 mg bid, for 2 months) in 7 Type IIA and 13 Type IIB patients treated in a double-blind, placebo-controlled, cross-over design. In the Type IIA patients (baseline cholesterol = 366 mg/dl), total cholesterol fell to 276 mg/dl (-25%) on probucol compared to 345 mg/dl (-5.7%) on placebo. In the Type IIB patients (baseline cholesterol = 384), total cholesterol fell to 270 mg/dl (-30%) in the probucol-treated patients compared to 364 mg/dl (-5.2%) in the placebo group. Thus, probucol proved equally effective for both hypercholesterolemia and combined hyperlipidemia. Gouveia *et al.*[26] reported that probucol decreased total cholesterol 23 percent, from 295 mg/dl to 228 mg/dl, p<0.001), in 32 patients with primary hypercholesterolemia treated for two months with 500 mg bid. Rouffy *et al.*[27] similarly report that probucol produced a 12 percent decline in total cholesterol and 14 percent decline in LDL-C in 34 patients (25 Type IIA and 9 Type IIB) treated for 1 month to 3 months. Rapado and Curiel[28] found that probucol decreased total cholesterol 31 percent in 11 males and 9 females with Type IIA phenotype. Thus, probucol administered at 500 mg bid lowers total cholesterol and LDL-C on the average 11 percent to 14 percent in unspecified or common hypercholesterolemia, phenotype IIA, and combined hyperlipidemia, phenotype IIB, and appears equally effective in both disorders. These studies also demonstrate considerable variation in individual response ranging from no decrease to greater than 30 percent decrease in total cholesterol levels.

The reasons for the variable response have not been clearly identified. Neither age nor gender appear to modify response. Nestruck *et al.*[29] have reported patients with FH and with at least one allele for apolipoprotein E_4 respond better to probucol than those without this allele or those with non-FH. Total cholesterol decreased 18 percent in those with the E_4 compared to only 11 percent in those with $E_{3/3}$ (p<0.03). In one study of 10 patients with heterozygous FH, treated for three months with probucol 500 mg/day, Durrington and Miller[30] found that the magnitude of the decline in LDL was linearly related to pretreatment HDL_2 levels and to the magnitude of the decrease in HDL_2, i.e., the higher the pretreatment HDL_2 level, the greater the decrease of LDL and HDL_2. In this same study, intravenous fat tolerance tests were performed and no differences were found before or after treatment.

Diabetes. Probucol has also been shown to lower total cholesterol and LDL-C in some secondary hypercholesterolemias. Hattori *et al.*[31] examined the effects of probucol treatment (500 mg bid for 16 weeks) on serum lipids, lipoproteins, apolipoproteins and indices of blood glucose control in 50 hypercholesterolemic patients with non-insulin dependent diabetes mellitus (13 men; 37 women). Total serum cholesterol and TG decreased 15.1 percent and 17.3 percent, respectively, while LDL-C and HDL-C decreased 12.5 percent and 17.3 percent, respectively. Both apolipoprotein AI and apolipoprotein CII also decreased significantly but apolipoprotein B did not. Thus, the response to treatment in patients with diabetes is similar to that seen in non-diabetics except that TG levels also declined significantly in the diabetics, an effect not usually observed in non-diabetics. Further study is required to determine if this occurs generally or is peculiar to this single study. There were no consistent changes in hemoglobin AI_C or fasting blood glucose throughout the treatment period. Similarly, blood pressure, liver function tests, serum creatinine and uric acid were likewise unchanged. Thus, probucol possesses the same efficacy in diabetics as in non-diabetics.

Idiopathic nephrotic syndrome. Valeri *et al.*[32] measured serum lipid and lipoprotein changes in five hyperlipidemic adults with idiopathic nephrotic syndrome treated with probucol (500 mg bid) for at least three weeks while on a phase one American Heart Association diet. Total cholesterol, LDL-C and HDL-C decreased 22.6 percent, 23.8 percent and 12.2 percent, respectively, while VLDL-C and TG did not change. The marginal statistical significance in these changes is most likely a result of the small number of subjects examined. Thus, probucol appears to possess the same efficacy in hyperlipidemic patients with diabetes or nephrotic syndrome as it does in hyperlipidemic patients who are otherwise well.

In *summary*, a consistent picture of probucol response emerges from consideration of the various trials noted above. On the average, probucol lowers total cholesterol and LDL-C by approximately 20 percent and 15 percent, respectively.[12] Probucol is effective in all forms of hypercholesterolemia in which it has been examined including primary familial and "common" hypercholesterolemia as well as secondary hypercholesterolemia. However, there is considerable individual variability in response. At either extreme, some patients may show as much as a 30 percent decline in LDL-C while others will show no response at all. Therefore, careful monitoring over a period of at least 3 to 4 months to allow full response is needed to determine the efficacy of this drug in individual patients.

HDL-C

In addition to lowering total cholesterol and LDL-C, probucol lowers HDL-C as well. The degree of HDL-C lowering is greater for higher pretreatment HDL-C than for lower pretreatment HDL-C levels.[33] The decrease in HDL-C produced by probucol averages 20 percent to 30 percent.[34-42] In a double-blind, placebo-controlled, cross-over study of 19 patients with primary FH treated for 24 weeks in each arm of the trial, Mellies *et al.*[34] noted a 10.7 percent decrease in total cholesterol, an 8.4 percent decrease in LDL-C and a 26 percent decrease in HDL-C (Figure 3). The decline in HDL-C was accompanied by a 34 percent decrease in apolipoprotein AI and a 20 percent decrease in apolipoprotein AII. These results are typical of at least five studies of varying designs examining the effects of probucol on HDL-C.[35-39] In general, the decline in HDL-C is accompanied by decreases in both apolipoprotein AI and apolipoprotein AII. However, the decrease in apolipoprotein AII is uniformly less than the decrease in apolipoprotein AI. The study of Mellies et al.[34] differs from other studies in one important way. Most other studies have found that the percent decrease in HDL-C is much greater than the percent decrease in apolipoprotein AI and that the ratio of HDL-C to apolipoprotein AI decreases with treatment.[35-39] In a recent study by Stein et al.,[41] nine patients with primary hypercholesterol were treated for 17 weeks with probucol (500 mg bid) while on a prudent diet. There was a decline in HDL-C of 25.7 percent while apolipoprotein AI declined only 14 percent and apolipoprotein AII declined only 4.2 percent. These observations suggest that probucol treatment not only decreases the number of HDL particles in the circulation, but also changes their physical properties and possibly their function as well. This suggestion has been borne out by direct measurements.

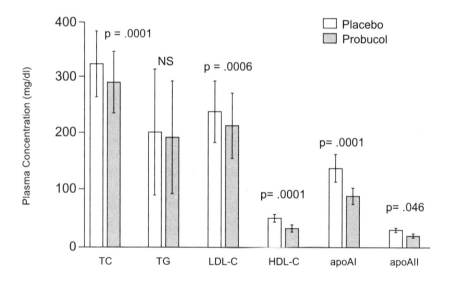

Figure 3. **Changes in plasma lipids, lipoproteins and apolipoproteins resulting from probucol treatment (From reference 34).**

The decline in HDL-C is accompanied by significant changes in HDL compositions and subfraction distribution.[38,42-45] In four representative studies, the average HDL-C to apolipoprotein AI ratio decreased by 18 percent. Berg et al.[35] reported that the greatest decrease in apolipoprotein AI occurred in the HDL_{2b} subfraction. The action of probucol in lowering apolipoprotein AI is selective, since most other apolipoproteins are not decreased. There are also significant changes in the lipid composition of the average HDL particle. The percentage of TG is increased while the percentage of cholesteryl ester is decreased. In one study of nine hypercholesterolemic patients treated for two years, Dachet et al.[8] found that TG increased from 6 percent to 11 percent, and cholesterol decreased from 22 percent to 18 percent of HDL mass. Interestingly, however, the ratio of unesterified cholesterol to cholesteryl ester remained the same.

Probucol also alters the size distribution of HDL particles. Most[35,41-45] but not all[46] investigators have found that HDL_2 decreases much more than HDL_3. Typical of several similar studies, Franceschini et al.[33] found that in 12 hypercholesterolemic subjects treated for eight weeks, HDL_2 decreased 69 percent, but HDL_3 decreased only 21.5 percent.

Gradient gel electrophoresis (GGE) provides a newer, more sensitive way of identifying HDL subfractions than by ultracentrifugation. At least nine subfractions can be identified by GGE as opposed to the traditional two major subfractions by ultracentrifugation. Probucol treatment causes a preponderance of smaller, more dense particles relative to larger, less dense HDL particles. Figure 4 illustrates GGE analysis of HDL subfractions on plasma obtained before and after treatment of a 63-year-old hypercholesterolemic man with probucol 500 mg bid for 6 months.[45]

The changes in HDL produced by probucol treatment result from changes in apolipoprotein synthesis, the level of enzymes which remodel HDL particles within the circulation[47] and the interaction of HDL with cells.[48,49] In general, each HDL particle contains two molecules of apolipoprotein AI. Thus the amount of apolipoprotein AI in the circulation is an estimate of the number of HDL particles. Two groups of investigators, using radiolabeled turnover studies, have measured the synthesis and catabolism of apolipoprotein AI in a total of nine probucol-treated patients with various forms of hyperlipidemia that had proved refractory to other forms of therapy.[37,50-51] Probucol primarily decreased the synthesis of apolipoprotein AI but had no effect on the catabolism of apolipoprotein AI, so that the number of HDL particles in the circulation was decreased. It is of particular interest that the decrease in apolipoprotein AI synthesis is selective. Interestingly, Aburatani et al.[52] have shown that probucol increases apolipoprotein E mRNA in rabbit brain and spleen. McPherson and colleagues[53,54] have reported that apolipoprotein E levels are increased by 67 percent in probucol-treated patients.

Probucol also increases cholesteryl ester transfer protein (CETP) mass[53,54] and cholesteryl ester transfer activity.[38] CETP transfers cholesteryl esters from HDL to other circulating lipoproteins in exchange for TG.[53,55] This action of CETP probably explains, at least in part, the changes in HDL

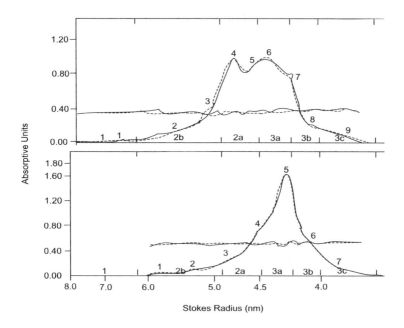

Figure 4. **Size distribution of HDL before (top) and after (bottom) treatment with probucol 500 mg bid for 6 months (From reference 45).** The dotted line indicates the actual spectrographic gel scan. The solid line indicates the model which best describes the actual scan. The center line in each panel indicates the difference between the actual scan and the model. Note the major shift in particle size.

subfraction distribution, lipid composition and the relatively greater decrease in HDL-C than in apolipoprotein AI that results from probucol treatment. In *summary,* probucol treatment decreases HDL-C levels and causes changes in HDL composition and subfraction distribution by decreasing apolipoprotein AI synthesis and increasing CETP.

The clinical consequences of these changes in HDL levels, composition, structure and metabolism are uncertain but may be beneficial in light of current understanding of HDL function and metabolism.[48,50,56] Numerous cross-sectional, prospective population and case-controlled epidemiologic trials[57-61] have, almost without exception, shown that circulating levels of HDL-C are inversely related to the risk of accelerated coronary heart disease. The biologic phenomenon responsible for this epidemiologic relationship are uncertain. The most attractive hypothesis is that HDL promotes "reverse cholesterol transport," the movement of cholesterol out of the arterial wall and back to the liver for excretion.[48,56] This process can be divided conceptually into five steps, which include: (1) loss of cholesterol from cells of the arterial wall to HDL; (2) trapping of cholesterol within HDL particles by esterification; (3) transfer of cholesteryl esters from HDL to apolipoprotein B-containing lipoproteins by cholesteryl ester transfer protein (CETP); (4) delivery to and uptake of cholesteryl esters by the liver; and (5) excretion in the bile as both bile acids and free cholesterol.

Currently, there are no clinical tests to assess the activity of the pathway and the *in vivo* experimental documentation that HDL serves this function is scant. However, HDL has been shown *in vitro* to mediate all the requisite steps in reverse cholesterol transport. Probucol favorably affects many of the *in vitro* steps in reverse cholesterol transport. Goldberg and Mendez[62] have reported that probucol promotes cholesterol efflux from cultured fibroblasts. Both Sirtori *et al.*[42] and McPherson *et al.*[53,54] have shown that probucol increases cholesteryl ester transfer. McPherson *et al.*[53,54] has further shown that the increase in activity is caused by an increase in the amount of CETP. Finally, Barnhart and colleagues[63] and others have presented evidence that probucol promotes hepatic uptake of HDL-C and increases bile acid excretion.

The effects of lowering HDL-C by probucol on atherosclerosis are not known with certainty. However (see *Effects on Atherogenesis* below), probucol treatment retards fatty streak formation, promotes xanthoma regression and as noted in the study by Miettinen and colleagues[64] prevents coronary artery disease events, despite its predictable HDL-lowering effects. Provocatively, when Matsuzawa *et al.*[65] examined the effects of probucol on xanthoma regression in a group of eight heterozygotes with FH, they found that the rate of regression correlated with the decline in HDL-C, but showed no correlation with the change in LDL-C. This latter observation is consistent with the hypothesis that probucol promotes reverse cholesterol transport.

Other Lipoprotein and Apolipoprotein Effects

In a study of 15 hypercholesterolemic patients treated for eight weeks with probucol 500 mg/day, lipoprotein(a) did not change, although the expected decrease in total cholesterol and LDL-C was observed.[66] Thus, like other currently available hypolipidemic drugs, with the possible exception of nicotinic acid and neomycin, probucol does not affect lipoprotein(a) levels.

Several investigators have examined the effects of probucol treatment on apolipoprotein levels. Although without immediate clinical implications these studies are of interest in terms of understanding the mechanism of drug action and will be of value as the role of particular apolipoproteins in atherosclerosis becomes better understood. As noted earlier, probucol decreases apolipoprotein AI but has little effect on apolipoprotein AII.[34,35] The decrease in apolipoprotein AI is less than that seen with HDL-C.[34,35,39,64] Conflicting reports of probucol effects on apolipoprotein E have appeared. In one study, McPherson et al.[54] report that probucol treatment increases apolipoprotein E by 60 percent.

Mechanism of Drug Action

The cholesterol-lowering action of probucol is incompletely understood. No clear single mechanism of cholesterol lowering has been identified and it is possible that the overall effect is attributable to the summation of a variety of activities.

Direct measurements of apolipoprotein B turnover have been conducted by five groups,[37,46,51,64,67] and in the aggregate, suggest that at least a portion of probucol LDL-cholesterol lowering is due to increased apolipoprotein B removal. In the most comprehensive study involving the largest number of patients with a good response to treatment, Kesaniemi and Grundy[67] examined nine hypercholesterolemic patients, one of whom also had hypertriglyceridemia using autologous radiolabeled LDL. Patients were maintained on mixed liquid formula/solid diets for 10-14 days prior to each turnover and treated for two to six months with probucol 500 mg bid. The apolipoprotein B FCR was calculated both from the terminal die away curve and the U/P ratio. Plasma apolipoprotein-LDL decreased by 10.5 percent from 133 ± 8 to 119 ± 7 mg/dl ($p<0.05$) and LDL-C decreased by 14 percent. In this group of patients, treatment produced no change in the mean LDL protein to cholesterol ratio. The FCR increased in 8 of the 9 patients studied. The mean increase was 22.9 percent. There was no change in mean apolipoprotein B synthetic rate. In contrast, Magill et al.[46] reported no change in FCR, but noticed a decrease in apolipoprotein B synthetic rate in two patients.

Several studies suggest that probucol may modestly accelerate apolipoprotein B removal, perhaps by non-receptor mechanisms. In these studies, the decline in LDL-C could not be entirely explained by changes in LDL apolipoprotein B turnover. Interestingly, when LDL obtained from animals treated with probucol is injected into untreated animals, the injected LDL apolipoprotein B is removed more rapidly than the native LDL apolipoprotein B suggesting that probucol accelerates apolipoprotein B removal by an effect on LDL structure rather than on cell receptors.[68-70]

Significantly, probucol lowers total cholesterol and LDL-C in Watanabe hereditable hyperlipidemic rabbits (WHHR), an animal model for FH that lack functional LDL receptors.[71] In addition, the drug is effective in patients with homozygous FH suggesting that it accelerates LDL-C removal by a pathway distinct from the LDL-receptor pathway.[17,72]

At least three observers[51,73-75] have reported that probucol increases bile acid secretion, suggesting that the drug increases hepatic cholesterol excretion. Marecek *et al.*[76] measured bile acid composition in five hypercholesterolemic patients before and after treatment with probucol 500 mg bid for 8 weeks and found no statistically significant change in the lithogenic index. In a group of ten outpatients, this same group of investigators[75] have reported that the lithogenic index decreased markedly, reflecting a statistically significant decline in cholesterol concentration. If not accompanied by compensatory changes, an increase in bile acid secretion would be expected to decrease hepatic cholesterol content and increase LDL-receptor activity and LDL removal.

EFFECTS ON ATHEROGENESIS

Antioxidant Properties and Atherogenesis

There is an increasingly impressive body of evidence that probucol, by virtue of its antioxidant properties, directly inhibits the early steps in formation of atherosclerotic plaques. This is supported by observations *in vitro* and studies of diet-induced atherogenesis in rabbits and primates. Elucidation of these actions have contributed substantially to elucidating the process of atherogenesis and vice versa.

Several lines of evidence, including cross-sectional pathologic observations in man and diet-included atherosclerosis animal models, convincingly demonstrate that fatty streak formation is one of the earliest events in atherogenesis and precedes the formation of more complex lesions.[71,77-79] Structurally, early "fatty streaks" are comprised of subendothelial lipid-laden macrophages derived from both circulating monocytes and medial smooth muscle cells.[78] Lipid and lipoprotein metabolism in isolated macrophage has been extensively characterized. Macrophages derived from human monocyte and mouse peritoneal macrophages bind, internalize and catabolize native LDL poorly, if at all. In contrast, these same cells possess specific membrane receptors, which recognize and metabolize modified forms of LDL.[80] Several modifications, including acetylated, malondialdehyde-modified, glycosylated and oxidized LDL are recognized by these receptors. When present in the extracellular media, these modified forms of LDL cause massive lipid accumulation in cultured macrophages. Such cultured cells resemble, in appearance and in function, the foam cells which characterize fatty streaks in early atherosclerotic lesions.

Oxidized LDL can be produced *in vitro* by incubation with Cu^{++} or with cultured endothelial cells, smooth muscle cells or macrophages. Incubation of LDL under these conditions produces structural changes in both the lipid and protein constituents of the particle. In particular, lysolecithin is generated from lecithin and the apolipoprotein B-100 chain is cleaved. The precise changes which render the molecule recognizable by the "scavenger" receptor are not known. Steinberg *et al.*[81] has elegantly summarized the putative role of oxidatively modified LDL in atherogenesis. It is hypothesized that oxidatively modified LDL plays a pivotal role in early atherogenesis through four mechanisms, which include: (1) attraction of circulating monocytes to the subendothelial space; (2) foam cell formation by interactions with the scavenger receptor; (3) retarding foam cell efflux; and (4) endothelial injury due to cytotoxicity of the oxidatively modified LDL.

Addition of probucol to LDL incubated either with Cu^{++} or cultured cells prevents the oxidative modification otherwise observed in its absence.[82] Considerable evidence indicates that probucol prevents oxidative modification of LDL *in vitro* and *in vivo* and inhibits formation of fatty streaks. Notably, oxidatively modified LDL has been identified in human circulation and moreover is more abundant in patients with clinical manifestations of atherosclerotic disease than in those without.[83,84] Addition of probucol to cultured endothelial cell *in vitro* prevents oxidative modification of added normal human LDL. Similar findings have been reported for cultured human monocyte-derived macrophage and mouse peritoneal macrophage. In addition to preventing oxidative modification, addition of probucol prevents lipid accumulation and foam cell formation by macrophage cultured *in vitro* with modified LDL.[85] The inhibitory effect of probucol resides with the lipoprotein since addition of LDL from probucol-treated patients is much less avidly accumulated and metabolized by cultured macrophage than is LDL from untreated patients. Thus, oxidized LDL exists *in vivo* and its formation can be prevented or retarded by probucol, and inhibiton of oxidative modification prevents foam cell formation *in vitro*. Moreover, the localization of probucol within LDL may impart a considerable advantage over naturally occurring antioxidants such as vitamin E, which is more widely distributed and not targeted to sites of lipoprotein modification.

Prevention of Atherosclerotic Lesions

Several observations suggest that these *in vitro* observations of the antioxidant effects of probucol have relevance to the *in vivo* situation. Using highly specific antibodies, Schwenke *et al.*[86] have shown histocytochemically that oxidized LDL is localized at the sites of fatty streaks, but not in the normal arterial segments of rabbits fed atherogenic diets. Perhaps most persuasive are the findings of Carew *et al.*[87] and of Kita *et al.*[88] that probucol prevents aortic fatty streak formation in WHHR. These animals lack functional LDL receptors and are a good model of human FH. Both groups have reported similar findings. In their studies, Carew and colleagues compared lipid and lipoprotein levels as well as extent of aortic involvement with fatty streaks in probucol-treated and untreated WHHR. A third group of rabbits was treated with lovastatin to achieve as great or greater degree of lipid lowering, allowing the investigators to distinguish the effects of lipid lowering from the antioxidant activity of probucol. The probucol-treated animals had significantly less aortic involvement than either the untreated or lovastatin-treated control rabbits.

Daughtery and Zweifel[89] examined the effects of probucol on fatty streak formation in normal rabbits fed high-fat, high-cholesterol diets to accelerate fatty streak formation. Similar to other investigators, this group found that animals treated with probucol have significantly less fatty streak formation than control animals. Animal studies, conducted prior to the recognition of the antioxidant effects of probucol, also document an antiatherogenic action.[90,91]

EFFECTS ON CLINICAL EVENTS

Xanthoma Regression

Probucol treatment has been associated with regression of cutaneous[17] and tendinous xanthoma[72] in patients with FH. The study of Yamamoto et al.[72] is of particular interest. Achilles tendon thickness in 51 patients with FH was assessed by xeroradiography after two to four years of treatment. In six patients treated with probucol alone, there was an average decrease in total cholesterol and HDL-C of 18.3 percent and 30.2 percent, respectively. All six patients demonstrated a significant decrease in achilles tendon thickness by an average of 2.16 mm. The decrease in achilles tendon thickness correlated well with the decrease in HDL-C and not at all with the change in total cholesterol. These findings suggest that the decrease in HDL-C may play a role in xanthoma regression, perhaps reflecting accelerated reverse cholesterol transport.

Coronary Artery Lesions

Studies in animal models cited previously support the contention that probucol will retard or possibly reverse atherosclerosis. As yet, no well-controlled clinical trials have been conducted in man. However, a large percentage of the 612 high risk males enrolled by Miettinien et al.[92] in a randomized, multifactorial, intervention trial lasting five years were treated with probucol. Overall, the trial failed to demonstrate a reduction in coronary events, although strokes decreased significantly from 1.3 percent in the control population to 0 percent in the treated group. These authors noted that, "In univariate analysis, the coronary events were enriched in subgroups treated with clofibrate and β-blockers, whereas the incidence was low in the subjects using diet only or in those treated with probucol or diuretics."[92]

A unique large-scale trial is currently underway to assess the impact of probucol treatment on peripheral atherosclerosis. The Probucol Quantitative Regression Swedish Trial is a double-blind, randomized, placebo-controlled, three-year intervention trial.[93] The primary endpoint is quantitation of femoral atheroma volume by densitometric assessment of annual femoral angiograms. The trial, which began in 1985, will enroll a total of 240 patients and should be concluded in late 1992. Prior to randomization, an antiatherogenic diet will be initiated; patient response to cholestyramine alone and in combination with probucol will be determined and pre-randomization femoral angiograms will be obtained. Only patients showing greater than an eight percent decline in total cholesterol above that observed with cholestyramine alone and who also have visible femoral atherosclerosis will enter the randomized phase of treatment, which will extend for three years and be accompanied by annual femoral angiograms. For ethical reasons, the control population will receive cholestyramine while the active treatment group will also receive probulcol 500 mg bid. Hypercholesterolemic (total cholesterol > 265, LDL-C > 175 and TG < 350) men and women less than 71 years of age are candidates for participation. Enrollment is now complete and the results are eagerly awaited. In order to reach an alpha level of 0.05 with a two-tailed t-test and have an estimated power of 90 percent to detect a 5 percent greater annual change in atheroma volume in the probucol over the placebo treatment group, 120 patients will be randomized to each group.

SIDE EFFECTS AND TOXICITY

Probucol is virtually free of drug interactions and can be safely taken in combination with a wide variety of cardioactive drugs including β-blockers. Loosening of the stools or diarrhea occurs in 7 percent to 8 percent of treated patients, but resolves in most with continued treatment. Perhaps the side effect of major concern is prolongation of the QT interval. Dujovne et al.[94] examined the consequences of probucol treatment on QT intervals in 40 hypercholesterolemic patients treated for 18 to 24 months in a double-blind clinical trial which includes a combined colestipol group. An increase in corrected QT interval of 10 msec or longer was observed in 48 percent of patients treated with probucol. However, with this number of patients and the large individual variability, the QT interval differences did not reach statistical significance. No patients experienced any adverse clinical events and no significant arrthymias were observed. Nonetheless, a large number of patients can be expected to demonstrate some increase in QT interval when treated with probucol. In one study,[95] 27 percent of patients experienced QT prolongation in excess of 440 msec. There have not been any significant arrhythmias reported in the published series of patients treated with probucol.

Concern regarding the prolonged QT interval seen with probucol and the possibility of arrhythmia arose from studies of primates fed high-fat diets, in whom fatal arryhthmias occurred. In these early studies by

Wissler and Vasselinovitch,[96] ingestion of probucol with high-fat diets lead to cardiac arrhythmias probably because of the unusually high rates of absorption. It is likely that the nature of the diet employed in these animal studies and possibly species susceptibilies lead to unusually high drug concentrations and the associated adverse outcome. However, there was no relationship between arryhthmias and either blood or cardiac tissue levels of probucol.

A number of potential side effects have been examined in clinical trials enrolling only a small number of patients. Such small trials have the power to detect adverse effects of major magnitude only. Rapado and Curiel[28] found no change in [47]Ca absorption in five patients treated for up to six months. These investigators, like others, found no change in prothrombin time for patients taking dicoumarins and treated with probucol.

REFERENCES

1. Barnhart JW, Sefranka JA, McIntosh DD. Hypocholesterolemic effect of 4,4'-(isopropylidenedithio)-bis-(2,6-di-t-butyl-phenol) (probucol). Am J Clin Nutr. 1970;23:1229-1233.

2. Heel RC, Brogden RN, Speight TM, et al. Probucol: a review of its pharmacological properties and therapeutic use in patients with hypercholesterolemia. Drugs. 1978;15:409-428.

3. Buckley MM, Goa KL, Price AH, et al. Probucol: a reappraisal of its pharmacological properties and therapeutic use in hypercholesterolemia. Drugs. 1989;37:761-800.

4. Arnold JA, Martin D, Taylor HL, et al. Absorption and excretion studies of the hypocholesterolemic agent 4,4'-(isopropylidenedithio)bis(2,6-di-t-butyl-phenol) (DH-581). Fed Soc Exp Med Biol. 1970.

5. Heeg JF, Tachigawa H. Taux plasmateques du probucol chez l'homme apres administrtion oral unique ou repetee. Nouvelle Presse Medicale. 1980;9:2990-2994.

6. Riesen WR, Keller M. Mordasinin R. Probucol in hypercholesterolemia. Atherosclerosis. 1980;36:201-207.

7. Tedeschi RE, Martz BL, Taylor HA, et al. Safety and effectivenss of probucol as a cholesterol lowering agent. Artery. 1982;10:22-34.

8. Dachet C, Jacotot B, Buxtorf JC. The hypolipidemic action of probucol: drug transport and lipoprotein composition in Type IIa hyperlipoproteinemia. Atherosclerosis. 1985;58:261-268.

9. Fellin R, Gasparotto A, Valerios G, et al. Effect of probucol treatment of lipoprotein cholesterol and drug levels in blood and lipoproteins in familial hypercholesterolemia. Atherosclerosis. 1986;59:47-56.

10. Uren S, Ruant P, Albengres E, et al. In vitro studies on the distribution of probucol among plasma lipoproteins. Molec Pharmacol. 1984;26322:322-327.

11. Eder HA. The effect of diet of the transport of probucol in monkeys. Artery. 1982;10:105-107.

12. Daugherty A, Lange LG, Sobel BE, et al. Aortic accumulation and plasma clearance of B-VLDL and HDL effects of diet-induced hypercholesterolemia in rabbits. J Lipid Res. 1985;26:955-963.

13. Data on file. Marion Merrell Dow Research Laboratories; Kansas City, Mo.

14. Tedeschi RE, Taylor HL, Martz BL. Clinical experience of the safety and cholesterol lowering action of probucol. In: Noseda G, Lewis B, Paoletti R, eds. Diet and Drugs in Atherosclerosis. New York, NY: Raven Press; 1980:1-259.

15. McCaughan D. The long-term effects of probucol on serum lipid levels. Arch Intern Med. 1981;41:1428-1432.

16. Noseda G, Lewis B. Paoletti R. Diet and Drugs in Atherosclerosis. New York, NY: Raven Press; 1980:1-327.

17. Baker SG, Joffe BI, Mendelsohn D, et al. Treatment of homozygous familial hypercholesterolemia with probucol. S A Med J. 1982;62:7-11.

18. Cortese C, Marenah CB, Miller NE, et al. The effects of probucol on plasma lipoproteins in polygenic and familial hypercholesterolemia. Atherosclerosis. 1982;44:319-325.

19. LeLorier J, BuBreuil-Quidoz S, Lussier-Cacan S, et al. Diet and probucol in lowering cholesterol concentrations. Arch Intern Med. 1977;137:1429-1434.

20. Stefanovic S, Vucic L. Effect of probucol in hypercholesterolemic patients resistant to other hypolipidemic drugs. In: Noseda G, Lewis B, Paoletti R, eds. Diet and Drugs in Atherosclerosis. New York, NY: Raven Press; 1980:257-259.

21. Riberio AC, Viana AP. Clinical trial of a new cholesterol-lowering agent: probucol. In: Noseda G, Lewis B, Paoletti R, eds. Diet and Drugs in Atherosclerosis. New York, NY: Raven Press; 1980:223-226.

22. De Gennes JL, Truffert J. Efficacy and tolerance of probucol and clofibrate. In: Noseda G, Lewis B, Paoletti R, eds. Diet and Drugs in Atherosclerosis. New York, NY: Raven Press; 1980:195-197.

23. Mordasini R, Keller M, Riesen WF. Effect of probucol and diet on serum lipids and lipoprotein fractions in primary hypercholesterolemia. In: Noseda G, Lewis B, Paoletti R, eds. Diet and Drugs in Atherosclerosis. New York, NY: Raven Press; 1980:181-187.

24. Beaumont V, Buxtorf JC, Jacotot B, et al. Short- and long-term trials of probucol in Type II hyperlipoproteinemia. In: Noseda G, Lewis B, Paoletti R, eds. Diet and Drugs in Atherosclerosis. New York, NY: Raven Press; 1980:209-214.

25. Carmena R, Ascaso JF. Treatment of hypercholesterolemia with probucol. In: Noseda G, Lewis B, Paoletti R, eds. Diet and Drugs in Atherosclerosis. New York, NY: Raven Press; 1980:215-218.

26. Gouveia A, Noronha A, Dionisio I, et al. Effect of probucol in primary hypercholesterolemia. In: Noseda G, Lewis B, Paoletti R, eds. Diet and Drugs in Atherosclerosis. New York, NY: Raven Press; 1980:219-222.

27. Rouffy J, Baki R, Chanu B, et al. Probucol: an evaluation of effects on plasma lipids and lipoproteins in 34 cases of primary types IIa and IIb hyperlipoproteinemia. In: Noseda G, Lewis B, Paoletti R, eds. Diet and Drugs in Atherosclerosis. New York, NY: Raven Press; 1980:237-244.

28. Rapado A, Curiel MD. Effect of probucol on intestinal absorption of calcium and on long-term anticoagulant therapy in patients with hypercholesterolemia associated with cardiovascular dieases. In: Noseda G, Lewis B, Paoletti R, eds. Diet and Drugs in Atherosclerosis. New York, NY: Raven Press; 1980:231-236.

29. Nestruck AC, Bouthillier D, Sing CF, et al. Apolipoprotein E polymorphism and plasma cholesterol response to probucol. Metabolism. 1987;36:743-747.

30. Durrington PN, Miller JP. Double-blind, placebo-controlled, cross-over trial of probucol in heterozygous familial hypercholesterolemia. Atherosclerosis. 1985;55:187-194.

31. Hattori M, Tsuda K, Taminato T, et al. Effect of probucol on serum lipids and apoproteins in patients with noninsulin-dependent diabetes mellitus. Curr Ther Res. 1987;42:967-973.

32. Valeri A, Gelfand J, Blum C, et al. Treatment of the hyperlipidemia of the nephrotic syndrome: a controlled trial. Am J Kid Dis. 1966;13:388-396.

33. Franceschini G, Calabresi L, Tosi C, et al. Correlation between high-desity lipoprotein subclass distribution and triglyceridemia. Arteriosclerosis. 1987;7:426-435.

34. Mellies MJ, Gartside PS, Glatfelter L, et al. Effects of probucol on plasma cholesterol, high- and low-density lipoprotein cholesterol, and apolipoproteins A1 and A2 in adults with primary familial hypercholesterolemia. Metabolism. 1980;29:956-964.

35. Berg A, Frey I, Baumstark M, Keul J. Influence of probucol administration on lipoprotein cholesterol and apolipoproteins in normolipemic males. Atherosclerosis. 1988;72:49-54.

36. Miettinen T, Huttunen JK, Kuusi T, et al. Effect of probucol on the activity of postheparin plasma lipoprotein lipase and hepatic lipase. Clin Chem. 1981;113:59-64.

37. Atmeh RF, Stewart JM, Boag DE, et al. The hypolipidemic action of probucol: a study of its effects on high- and low-density lipoproteins. J Lipid Res. 1983;24:588-595.

38. Franceschini G, Sirtori M, Vaccarino V, et al. Mechanisms of HDL reduction after probucol - changes in HDL subfractions and increased reverse cholesteryl ester transfer. Arteriosclerosis. 1989;9:462-469.

39. Atmeh RF, Shepherd J, Packard CJ. Subpopulations of apolipoprotein A-I in human high-density lipoproteins: their metabolic properties and response to durg therapy. Biochem Biophys. 1983;751:175-188.

40. Glueck CJ. Colestipol and probucol: treatment of primary and familial hypercholesterolemia and amelioration of atherosclerosis. Ann Intern Med. 1982;96:475-482.

41. Stein et al. In press.

42. Sirtori CR, Sirtori M, Calabresi L, et al. Changes in high-density lipoprotein subfraction distribution and increased cholesteryl ester transfer after probucol. Am J Cardiol. 1988;62:73B-76B.

43. Johansson J, Carson LA. High-density lipoprotein particle size subclass alterations by treatment with nicotonic acid. In: Carlson LA, ed. Disorders of HDL. London: Smith-Gordon Company Limited; 1990:203-208.

44. Johansson J, Molgaard J, Olsson AG, et al. Effects of probucol treatment on HDL particle size subclass concentrations as assessed by gradient gel electrophoresis. In: Carlson LA, ed. Disorders of HDL. London: Smith-Gordon Company Limited; 1990:209-214.

45. Gwynne JT, Mahaffee DD. Probucol and HDL. In: Carlson LA, ed. Disorders of HDL. London: Smith-Gordon Company Limited; 1990:215-224.

46. Magill P, Whiting C, Hammett F, et al. Probucol: effects on the metabolism of low-density and high-density lipoproteins in moderate hypercholesterolemia. Artery. 1982;10:88-94.

47. Eisenberg S. High-density lipoprotein metabolsm. J Lipid Res. 1984;25:1017-1058.

48. Gwynne JT. HDL and atherosclerosis: an update. Clin Cardiol. 1991;14:I17-I24.

49. Gwynne JT. High-density lipoprotein cholesterol levels as a marker of reverse cholesterol transport. Am J Cardiol. 1989;64:10G-17G.

50. Gwynne JT. Probucol, high-density lipoprotein metabolism, and reverse cholesterol transport. Am J Card. 1988;62:48B-53B.

51. Nestel PJ. Effects of probucol on lipoprotein protein kinetics. Artery. 1982;10:96-98.

52. Aburatani H, Matsumoto A, Kodama T, et al. Increased levels of messenger ribonucleic acid for apolipoprotein E in the spleen of probucol-treated rabbits. Am J Cardiol. 1988;62:60B-65B.

53. McPherson R, Marcel Y. Role of cholesteryl ester transfer protein in reverse cholesterol transport. Clin Cardiol. 1991;14:I-31-I-34.

54. McPherson R, Hogue M, Milne RW, Tall AR, Marcel YL. Increase in plasma cholesterylester transfer protein during probucol treatment: relation to changes in high density lipoprotein composition. Arteriosclerosis and Thrombosis. 1991;11:476-481.

55. Tall AR. Plasma lipid transfer proteins. J Lipid Res 1986;27:361-367.

56. Reichl D, Miller NE. Pathophysiology of reverse cholesterol transport. Arteriosclerosis. 1989;9:785-797.

57. Gordon DJ, Probstfield JL, Garrison RJ, et al. High-density lipoprotein cholesterol and cardiovascular diease. Circulation. 1989;79:8-15.

58. Gordon DJ, Knoke J, Probstfield JL, et al. High-density lipoprotein cholesterol and coronary heart disease in hypercholesterolemic men: the lipid research clinics coronary primary prevention trial. Circulation. 1986;74:1217-1225.

59. Jacobs Dr, Mebane IL, Bangdiwals SI, et al. High density lipoprotein cholesterol as a predictor of cardiovascular disease mortality in men and women: the follow-up study of the lipid research clinics prevalence study. Am J Epidemiol. 1990;131:32-47.

60. Gordon DJ, Rifkind BM. High-density lipoprotein: the clinical implications of recent studies. Curr Concepts. 1989;321:1311-1316.

61. Miller NE. Associated of high-density lipoprotein subclasses and apolipoproteins with ischemic heart disease and coronary atherosclerosis. Am Heart J. 1987;113:589-597.

62. Goldberg RB, Mendez A. Probucol enhances cholesterol efflux from cultured human skin fibroblasts. Am J Cardiol. 1988;62:57B-59B.

63. Barnhart JW, Li DL, Cheng WD. Probucol enhances cholesterol transport in cultured rat hepatocytes. Am J Cardiol. 1988;62:52B-56B.

64. Miettinen TA, Huttunen JK, Ehnholm C, et al. Effect of long-term antihypertensive and hypolipidemic treatment on high-density lipoprotein cholesterol and apolipoproteins A-I and A-II. Atherosclerosis. 1980;36:249-259.

65. Matsuzawa Y, Yamashita S, Funahashi T, Yamamoto A, Tarui S. Selective reduction of cholesterol in HDL2 fraction by probucol in familial hypercholesterolemia and hyper-HDL2 cholesterolemia with abnormal cholesteryl ester transfer. Am J Cardiol. 1988;62:66B-72B.

66. Noma A. Lack of effect on probucol on serum lipoprotein(a) levels. Atherosclerosis. 1989;79:267-269.

67. Kesaniemi YA, Grundy SM. Influence of probucol on cholesterol and lipoprotein metabolism in man. J Lipid Res. 1984;25:780-790.

68. Nestel PJ, Bellington T. Effect of probucol on LDL removal and HDL synthesis. Atherosclerosis. 1981;38:203-209.

69. Naruszewicz M, Carew TE, Pittman RC, Witzum JL, Steinberg D. A novel mechanism by which probucol lowers low-density lipoprotein levels demonstrated in the LDL receptor-deficient rabbit. J Lipid Res. 1984;25:1206-1213.

70. Steinberg D. Studies on the mechanism of action of probucol. Am J Cardiol. 1986;57:16H-21H.

71. Goldstein JL, Toru K, Brown MS. Defective lipoprotein receptors and atherosclerosis. N Engl J Med. 1983;309:288-296.

72. Yamamoto A, Matsuzawa Y, Yokoyama S, et al. Effects of probucol on xanthomata regression in familial hypercholesterolemia. Am J Cardiol. 1986;57:29H-35H.

73. Beynen AC. Mode of hypocholesterolemic action of probucol in animals and man. Artery. 1987;14:113-126.

74. Balasubramaniam S, Beins DM, Simons LA. One the mechanism of plasma cholesterol reduction in the rat given proboucol. Clin Sci. 1981;61:615-619.

75. Jirsa M, Marecek Z, Kerdac V, et al. Effect of probucol on bile composition in man. Artery. 1982;10:44-47.

76. Marecek Z, Jirsa M, Kordac V, et al. Effect of probucol on human bile composition: reliminary observations. In: Noseda G, Lewis B, Paoletti R, eds. Diet and Drugs in Atherosclerosis. New York, NY: Raven Press; 1986;227-236.

77. Small DM. Progression and regression of atherosclerotic lesions. Arteriosclerosis. 1988;8:103-129.

78. Ross R. The Pathogenesis of atherosclerosis - an update. N Engl J Med. 1986;314:488-500.

79. Steinberg D. Lipoproteins and atherosclerosis. Arteriosclerosis. 1983;3:283-301.

80. Kodama T, Freeman M, Rohrer L, Zabrecky J, Matsudaira P, Kreiger M. Type I macrophage scavenger receptor contains helical collagen-like coiled coils. Nature. 1990;343:531-525.

81. Steinberg D, Parthasarathy S, Carew TE, et al. Modifications of low-density lipoprotein that increase its atherogenicity. N Engl J Med. 1989;320:915-924.

82. Parathasarathy S, Young SG, Witztum JL. Probucol inhibits oxidative modification of low-density lipoprotein. J Clin Invest. 1986;77:1-4.

83. Esterbauer H, Striegl G, Puhl H, et al. Continuous monitoring of in vitro oxidation of human low-density lipoproteins. Free Rad Res Comms. 1989;6:67-75.

84. Avogaro P, Bittolo Bon G, Cazzolato G. Presence of a modified low-density lipoprotein in humans. Arteriosclerosis. 1988;8:79-87.

85. Yamamoto A, Hara H, Takaichi S, et al. Effect of probucol on macrophages, leading to regression of xanthomas and atheromatous vascular lesoins. Am J Cardiol. 1988;62:31B-36B.

86. Schwenke DC, Carew TE. Inititiation of atherosclerotic lesions in cholesterol-red rabbits. II: selective retention of LDL vs selective increases in LDL permeability in susceptible sites of arteries. Arteriosclerosis. 1989;9:908-918.

87. Carew TE, Schwenke DC, Steinberg D. Antiatherogenic effects of probucol unrelated to its hypocholesterolemic effect: evidence that antioxidants in vivo can selectively inhibit low-density lipoprotein degradation in macrophage-rich fatty streaks and slow the progression of atherosclerosis in the Watanabe heritable hyperlipidemic rabbit. Proc Natl Acad Sci. 1987;84:7725-7729.

88. Kita T, Nagano Y, Yokode M, et al. Probucol prevents the progression of atherosclerosis in Watanable heritable hyperlipidemic rabbit, an animal model for familial hypercholesterolemia. Proc Natl Acad Sci. 1987;84:5928-5931.

89. Daughtery A, Zweifel BS, Schonfeld G. Probucol attenuates the development of aortic atherosclerosis in cholesterol-fed rabbits. Br J Pharmacol. 1989;98:612-618.
90. Kritchevsky D, Kim HK, Tepper SA. Influence of 4,4'-(Isopropylidenedithio)bis(2,6-dibutylphenol) (DH-581) on experimental atherosclerosis in rabbits (35461). PSEBM. 1971;136:1216-1221.
91. Kritchevsky D. Probucol-lipid pharmacology. Artery. 1982;10:16.
92. Miettinien TA, Huttunen JK, Naukkarinen V, et al. Multifactorial primary prevention of cardiovascular diseases in middle-aged men. JAMA. 1985;254:2097-2102.
93. Walldius G, Carlson LA, Erikson U, et al. Development of femoral atherosclerosis in hypercholesterolemic patients during treatment with cholestyramine and probucol/placebo: probucol quantitative regression Swedish trial (PQRST): a status report. Am J Cardiol. 1988;62:37B-43B.
94. Dujovne CA, Atkins F, Wong B, et al. Electrocardiographic effects of probucol: a controlled prospective clinical trial. Eur J Clin Pharmacol. 1984;26:735-739.
95. Browne KF, Prystowsky EN, Heger JJ, et al. Prolongation of the QT interval induced by probucol: demonstration of a method for determining QT interval change induced by a drug. Am Heart J. 1984;107:680-739.
96. Wissler RW, Vasselinovitch D. Combined effects of cholestyramine and probucol on regression of atherosclerosis in rhesus monkey aortas. Appl Pharmacol. 1983;1:89-96.

CHAPTER 8

Drug Combination Therapy for Lipid Disorders

Conrad B. Blum, M.D.
New York, New York

INTRODUCTION

In most instances, hyperlipoproteinemias can be effectively treated by dietary means. When diet has been insufficient, the use of a single drug generally provides satisfactory control of lipoprotein levels. However, in severe hyperlipoproteinemias, the concurrent use of several agents may be needed. This chapter provides an overview of:

- pharmacological interactions that make certain combinations particularly effective;

- use of combinations of lipid-lowering agents in clinical trials with coronary heart disease (CHD) endpoints; and

- an approach for designing combination therapy in clinical practice.

THE PHARMACOLOGY OF HYPOLIPIDEMIC DRUG COMBINATIONS

Lipid-lowering agents with differing mechanisms of action have been paired in attempts to obtain additive or synergistic effects. Table I summarizes the results of 17 different studies of combination regimens. Most of these studies have involved treatment to lower levels of low-density lipoprotein (LDL) in patients with familial hypercholesterolemia.

The pairing of a *bile acid sequestrant with niacin* (nicotinic acid) was the first combination to receive extensive use. This regimen is attractive because bile acid sequestrants lower LDL levels by enhancing receptor-mediated clearance of LDL from plasma, while niacin limits the production of LDL. Thus, LDL levels are lowered by two distinct mechanisms. With this combination, it has been possible to reduce plasma LDL levels by 31 percent to 55 percent in hypercholesterolemic individuals. Both drugs in this regimen contribute substantially to the reduction in LDL seen with the combination. The combination of niacin with a bile acid sequestrant also causes substantial (approximately 30 percent) increases in high-density lipoprotein cholesterol (HDL-C), an effect primarily due to niacin. Also, as a consequence of niacin, large reductions in plasma triglyceride (TG) levels occur with the use of this combination of medications.

While the bile acid sequestrants are very effective in enhancing the receptor-mediated clearance of LDL, they also enhance hepatic cholesterogenesis. This hepatic response may limit the effectiveness of bile acid

TABLE I. Studies Showing Efficacy of Combination Drug Regimens For Treating Hyperlipoproteinemias

Drugs	Number of subjects	Metabolic disorder	% Change in			% Change on Adding Under-lined Drug [++]	
			LDL	HDL	TG	LDL	HDL
Colestipol + Niacin[1]	22	FH	-55	+17	-27	-31	24
Colestipol + Niacin[2]	13	Type IIa	-31	+23	-35	-31	23
Colestipol + Niacin[3]	80	Cholesterol 185-350 mg/dl; TG < 500 mg/dl	-38	+35	-20	n.a.	n.a.
Colestipol + Probucol[4]	47	LDL > 180	-29	-29	+11	-9	-29
Cholestyramine + Mevastatin[5]	10	FH	-53	+44	-23	-35	6
Colestipol + Lovastatin[6]	8	FH	-52	+8	-2	n.a.	n.a.
Colestipol + Lovastatin[7]	12	FH	-54	-2	+6	-26	-2
Colestipol + Niacin + Lovastatin[8]	21	FH	-66	+32	-42	-46	5
Colestipol + Lovastatin[9]	34	apoB > 125 mg/dl	-48	+14	n.a.	-43	10
Colestipol + Niacin[9]	32	apoB > 125 mg/dl	-34	+41	n.a.	-28	36
Lovastatin + Probucol[10]	17	FH	-37	-21	-25	-1	-27
Lovastatin + Colestipol[10]	16	FH	-52	0	-12	-25	-8
Lovastatin + Colestipol + Probucol[10]	15	FH	-53	-19	-15	-2	-19
Lovastatin + Gemfibrozil[11]	12	FH	-40	+6	-45	-7	4
Bezafibrate + Cholestyramine[12]	21	Type II	-37	+22	-39	-16	0
Colestipol + Fenofibrate[13]	18	FH	-37	+23	-17	-23	13
Gemfibrozil + Colestipol[14]	9	FCH; IIb	-20	+11	-44	-17	-13
	8	FCH; IV	-14	+13	-18	-34	-10
Gemfibrozil + Lovastatin[14]	9	FCH; IIb	-28	+26	-56	-25	0
	8	FCH; IV	-14	+35	-56	-34	7
Gemfibrozil + Lovastatin[**15]	10	NIDDM; TG > 500	-3	+27	-57	-30	1
Gemfibrozil + Lovastatin[+15]	6	NIDDM: TG 250-500	-16	+4	-40	-30	0
Neomycin + Niacin[16]	11	LDL > 200	-39	+16	n.a.	-20	20
Cholestyramine + Neomycin[16]	11	LDL > 200	39	+2	n.a.	-2	-16
Lovastatin + Neomycin[16]	11	LDL > 200	-42	-9	n.a.	-13	-22
Clofibrate + Lovastatin[*17]	6	Type III	-25	+37	-75	-28	6
Lovastatin + Niacin[11]	8	FH	-49	+25	-43	-27	20
Colestipol + Lovastatin + Niacin[11]	3	FH	-62	n.a.	n.a.	-27	n.a.

FH = familial hypercholesterolemia; Type III = Type III hyperlipoproteinemia; IIB = Type IIB hyperlipoproteinemia; NIDDM = non-insulin-dependent diabetes mellitus; TG = triglycerides; FCH = familial combined hyperlipidemia.; IV = Type IV hyperlipoproteinemia; n.a. = not available

[*] 67% reduction in plasma cholesterol with the combination; addition of lovastatin as a second agent gave an additional 31% reduction below the level obtained with gemfibrozil alone

[**] 29% reduction in LDL apolipoprotein B (gemfibrozil plus lovastatin vs. placebo)

[+] 25% reduction in LDL apolipoprotein B (gemfibrozil plus lovastatin vs. placebo)

[++] Percent change in LDL and HDL when the underlined drug is added to treatment with the other drug(s) listed

sequestrants when used alone. However, a β-hydroxy-β-methylglutaryl coenzyme A (HMG CoA) reductase inhibitor may block this enhanced hepatic cholesterogenesis. Thus, a regimen coupling a *bile acid sequestrant with an HMG CoA reductase inhibitor*, that inhibits cholesterol biosynthesis, is an attractive treatment option. There have been at least five published reports on such combination regimens, the results revealing that LDL levels can often be reduced by about 50 percent. The data presented in Table I indicate that with this combination regimen, both agents contribute substantially to the reduction in LDL levels. Increases in HDL-C with a combination of a bile acid sequestrant and an HMG CoA reductase inhibitor have usually been small. Likewise, with this combination of agents, alterations in plasma TG levels have been inconsistent and usually small.

Several investigators have studied the combination of a *fibric acid derivative with a bile acid sequestrant or with an HMG CoA reductase inhibitor*. These combinations have been interesting because the effects of fibric acid derivatives on lipoprotein metabolism differ from those of HMG CoA reductase inhibitors and bile acid sequestrants. While the reductase inhibitors and bile acid sequestrants speed the clearance of LDL from plasma via LDL receptors, fibric acid derivatives enhance lipoprotein lipase activity and increase the clearance of very low-density lipoproteins (VLDL) and chylomicron remnants. Illingworth and Bacon[11] found that the combination of gemfibrozil and lovastatin was barely superior to lovastatin alone in treating patients with heterozygous familial hypercholesterolemia. However, in similar patient populations[12,13] the use of other fibrates (fenofibrate or bezafibrate) with bile acid sequestrants adds substantially to the reduction in LDL; LDL levels fall by nearly 40 percent with the combination. The fibric acid drug in these combinations may reduce LDL concentrations by 7 percent to 30 percent below the level seen with a bile acid sequestrant alone. The fibric acid drug is also responsible for 10 percent to 20 percent increments in HDL levels and 20 percent to 40 percent reductions in fasting TG levels.

In patients with familial combined hyperlipidemia and elevated TG levels, there appears to be less of a reduction of LDL in response to the combination of a bile acid sequestrant or HMG CoA reductase inhibitor with a fibric acid derivative than is the case when such a combination is used in patients with familial hypercholesterolemia.[14] Thus, the combinations of gemfibrozil plus an HMG CoA reductase inhibitor or gemfibrozil plus colestipol may reduce LDL only 15 percent to 30 percent in patients with familial combined hyperlipidemia; for such patients, however, both of these combinations are more effective than monotherapy with gemfibrozil. In patients with familial combined hyperlipidemia, the combination of gemfibrozil plus lovastatin appears to have a more beneficial effect on plasma lipoproteins than does the combination of gemfibrozil plus colestipol: (1) a greater increment in HDL was seen with the lovastatin regimen; (2) patients with a type IIB lipoprotein pattern (elevated LDL and elevated TG) also had a greater reduction in LDL with the lovastatin regimen; and (3) for patients with a type IV lipoprotein pattern, the colestipol-gemfibrozil combination reduced LDL as well as the lovastatin-gemfibrozil combination.

However, the somewhat better lipoprotein results found with a gemfibrozil and lovastatin combination must be balanced against risks of myositis seen when these drugs are used together.[20-22] Therefore, in most cases, the combination of gemfibrozil and lovastatin should be avoided.

Probucol has been studied less extensively in combinations with other agents. This drug enhances the clearance of LDL from plasma by non-receptor mechanisms. Thus, probucol might be expected to provide additive results when paired with colestipol or HMG CoA reductase inhibitor which speed receptor-mediated clearance of LDL. However, this is not the case. When probucol is combined with colestipol[4] or lovastatin[10], it adds only modestly (1 percent to 10 percent) to the reduction of LDL cholesterol (LDL-C). A potential disadvantage to the combination of probucol with colestipol or lovastatin is the substantial (20 percent to 30 percent) fall in HDL, attendant to the use of probucol. Witztum *et al.*[10] reported that probucol added nothing to the reduction in LDL when it was used in combination with colestipol and lovastatin; however, probucol did cause a 19 percent reduction in HDL.

The most dramatic changes in lipoprotein levels have occurred with the three-drug regimen including *lovastatin, colestipol and niacin*.[8,11] With this three-drug regimen, a 66 percent reduction in LDL, 32 percent increase in HDL and 42 percent reduction in TG have been reported.

While neomycin[16] alone has been reported to reduce LDL-C levels by as much as 25 percent, adding it to cholestyramine does not at all enhance the reduction of LDL-C. Adding neomycin to lovastatin, however, yields a 13 percent additional reduction in LDL-C. With both of these last two mentioned combinations, the use of neomycin resulted in a substantial 16 percent to 22 percent reduction in HDL levels. Thus, combination drug therapy with neomycin appears to offer little.

USE OF COMBINATION REGIMENS IN CLINICAL TRIALS TO PREVENT CORONARY HEART DISEASE AND ATHEROSCLEROSIS

Three clinical trials involving combinations of hypolipidemic drugs have been reported: the Stockholm Ischaemic Heart Disease Secondary Prevention Study;[18] the Cholesterol Lowering Arteriosclerosis Study (CLAS);[3] and the Familial Arteriosclerosis Treatment Study (FATS).[9] These three studies have demonstrated that combined drug regimens for treating hyperlipidemia can reduce coronary heart disease (CHD) risk and can limit coronary atherosclerosis.

In the Stockholm Ischaemic Heart Disease Secondary Prevention Study, 555 survivors of myocardial infarction were randomly assigned in unblinded fashion to treatment with clofibrate plus niacin or to no lipid-altering therapy. The participants were then followed for five years for the occurrence of the primary endpoints of total mortality, CHD mortality and non-fatal myocardial infarction (MI). There were no lipid criteria for entry into the Stockholm Study. In the course of the trial, total serum cholesterol was lowered by 13 percent in the treated group; TG was reduced by 19 percent. The response of LDL and HDL levels to the treatment was not reported. The relatively small degree of cholesterol lowering, less than is usually seen in monotherapy with niacin, raises questions about the degree of adherence to the study regimen. Nonetheless, the combined drug regimen of clofibrate plus niacin led to a statistically significant 26 percent reduction in all-cause mortality (p < 0.05), and a 36 percent reduction in CHD mortality (p < 0.01). The incidence of non-fatal MI was reduced by 30 percent.[18]

The CLAS investigated the effects of the combined drug regimen of colestipol plus niacin on coronary atherosclerosis. In this randomized, double-blind trial, 162 men with a history of coronary artery bypass surgery and baseline serum cholesterol levels 185 mg/dl to 350 mg/dl were treated either with colestipol plus niacin and an intensive cholesterol-lowering diet or with placebos for these two agents and a less intensive cholesterol-lowering diet. Coronary angiograms were performed at baseline and after two years of treatment. In response to the treatment, LDL-C fell by 38 percent and HDL-C rose by 35 percent (both as compared to placebo). The treatment with colestipol plus niacin significantly reduced the progression of atherosclerotic lesions (p < 0.01), and regression of lesions was seen more frequently in the treated group (16 percent) than in the control group (2 percent).[3]

The FATS enrolled 103 individuals with elevated plasma levels of apolipoprotein B and a family history of premature CHD. The participants were randomly assigned to treatment with colestipol, or lovastatin plus colestipol, or niacin plus colestipol. They underwent coronary angiograms at baseline and after 2.5 years. Plasma LDL levels fell by 9 percent in the colestipol monotherapy group, 48 percent in the lovastatin plus colestipol group, and 34 percent in the niacin plus colestipol group. HDL levels rose by 3 percent, 14 percent and 41 percent, respectively, in the three groups. In the colestipol monotherapy group, atherosclerotic lesions progressed at an average rate of 1.7 percent per 2.5 years (change in percent stenosis). The combination drug regimens led to regression at rates of 0.3 percent per 2.5 years for lovastatin plus colestipol and 0.9 percent per 2.5 years for niacin plus colestipol. It is of note that although niacin plus colestipol did not yield the greatest reduction in LDL-C, it did yield the greatest regression of lesions. Perhaps this finding is due to the larger effect of the regimen of niacin plus colestipol on HDL levels. The incidence of cardiovascular events (death, proven MI, or newly refractory ischemia requiring bypass surgery or angioplasty) was noted. Both of the combined drug regimens resulted in a reduction in cardiovascular events compared to the colestipol control.

PRACTICAL ISSUES IN PLANNING AND IMPLEMENTING COMBINATION DRUG THERAPY FOR HYPERLIPIDEMIA

Combination drug regimens may be used for many reasons (Table II): (1) in order to attain greater lowering of LDL than is possible with a single agent; (2) in order to optimize lipoproteins while using low doses of lipid-lowering drugs and, thus, limit side effects; (3) in order to allow the use of a bile acid sequestrant to lower LDL in hypertriglyceridemic patients; and (4) in order to treat the increased LDL level that is often found when hypertriglyceridemia is treated with a fibric acid derivative.

Therapy with a combined drug regimen should be considered only after treatment with diet and with a single-drug regimen have been found to be insufficient. The National Cholesterol Education Program (NCEP) guidelines[19] call for a trial of dietary therapy, in most cases for at least six months, before beginning any lipid-lowering medication. When therapy with a single agent is initiated for elevated LDL levels, plasma lipoproteins should be assessed at four- to six-week intervals on at least two occasions. If the target LDL level has not been achieved (130 mg/dl for persons with CHD or with at least two other risk factors, 160 mg/dl for persons without CHD and with fewer than two other risk factors), the addition of other agent(s) should be considered. Combination therapy should be approached in a stepwise fashion, adding one drug at a time. Plasma lipoproteins and potential drug side effects should be assessed four to six weeks after a new drug has been added. The addition of a third drug should be considered only after the effects of a two-drug regimen have been determined at least twice at intervals of no less than four to six weeks. If a patient is found not to respond beneficially to a newly added drug, that drug should be discontinued.

Selection of a Combination Regimen in Order to Maximize Reduction of LDL

Since a bile acid sequestrant will usually be the drug of first choice for lowering LDL-C, a combination regimen will usually include a bile acid sequestrant. The most effective two-drug regimens for lowering LDL are: (1) bile acid sequestrant plus niacin; (2) a bile acid sequestrant plus lovastatin; and (3) an HMG CoA reductase inhibitor plus niacin.

The FATS[9] suggests that a bile acid sequestrant plus niacin may be more effective in limiting coronary artery disease than a bile acid sequestrant with lovastatin. There may be an increased risk of myositis when lovastatin is paired with niacin. Thus, in the absence of a contraindication to either a bile acid sequestrant or niacin, the combination of these two agents may be the first choice. However, when the use of niacin is precluded (e.g., by gastrointestinal intolerance, hepatitis, diabetes, etc.), a bile acid sequestrant plus lovastatin should be considered. When a bile acid sequestrant cannot be prescribed (e.g., because of gastrointestinal side effects or concerns about adsorption of other drugs in patients with complicated medical regimens), the combination of an HMG CoA reductase inhibitor and niacin may be used with careful attention to the status of liver function tests. While combinations involving fibric acid drugs are less effective in lowering LDL-C, a fibrate plus niacin may warrant consideration because this combination reduced all-cause mortality in the Stockholm Study.[8] Regimens involving neomycin will usually offer little advantage. Those combinations containing probucol are generally to be avoided because this drug contributes only modestly to reduction of LDL, and it substantially reduces HDL levels.

Use of a Combination Regimen to Optimize Lipoprotein Levels While Using Low Dosages of Drugs to Limit Side Effects

Occasionally a patient experiencing intolerable side effects to high dosages of a drug will have no difficulty with small dosages. For example, cholestyramine 4 to 12 g/d is generally very well tolerated, while gastrointestinal side effects become more common at higher doses. Similarly, administration of niacin in low doses (e.g., 500 mg t.i.d.) or lovastatin in doses as low as 10 mg/day may be permissible in persons who cannot tolerate larger quantities of these drugs. Such dosages may be insufficiently effective in monotherapy. However, these small dosages of lipid-lowering medications may be quite adequate as components of a combination regimen.

Combination Regimens to Allow the Use of a Bile Acid Sequestrant in Hypertriglyceridemic Persons With Elevated LDL

Bile acid sequestrants increase plasma TG levels by stimulating the hepatic secretion of VLDL. When used in patients with baseline hypertriglyceridemia, these agents may cause marked elevation of TG and precipitate pancreatitis. For this reason, bile acid sequestrants should not be used as monotherapy in patients with baseline TG levels over 250 mg/dl. However, these drugs may be considered for hypertriglyceridemic persons with elevated LDL if their TG levels are first brought under control. The preferred means for controlling hypertriglyceridemia are eliminating obesity, increasing exercise, restricting alcohol and stopping TG-elevating drugs. When these measures are unsuccessful, niacin, a fibric acid drug or somatic fish oils may be used to lower TG levels. It should be noted that in the setting of hypertriglyceridemia, the fibric acid drugs and fish oils often **elevate** LDL. When TG levels have been brought below 250 mg/dl, a bile acid sequestrant may be added to control the LDL concentration.

Combination Regimens When Elevated LDL Occurs in Response to the Use of a Fibric Acid Derivative

The use of fibric acid derivatives or somatic fish oils to treat hypertriglyceridemic individuals will often elevate plasma LDL levels. Thus, treatment of hypertriglyceridemia may create a new problem which itself requires treatment. LDL levels may then be reduced by adding a bile acid sequestrant (if TG levels have been brought below 250 mg/dl), niacin or an HMG CoA reductase inhibitor. However, the increased risk of myositis requires special caution when lovastatin is combined with a fibric acid derivative.[20-22] Since niacin does not tend to elevate LDL levels, treatment of hypertriglyceridemic patients with niacin may obviate the use of a second drug.

Table II. Rationale for combination drug therapy

1. To maximize reduction of LDL
2. To limit doses of individual drugs, thus limiting side effects
3. To allow the use of a bile acid sequestrant to treat high LDL levels in hypertriglyceridemic patients
4. To treat elevated LDL levels occurring as a result of using a fibric acid derivative

INFLUENCE OF COMBINATION REGIMENS ON HDL LEVELS

Combination drug regimens alter HDL levels as the sum of their component drugs. Thus, when niacin is added to a regimen, it will increase HDL by 20 percent to 40 percent. The addition of a fibric acid derivative increases HDL levels by 10 percent to 20 percent. The addition of lovastatin generally increases HDL levels by 5 percent to 10 percent. Bile acid sequestrants usually increase HDL levels slightly (2 percent to 5 percent), but they may cause substantial reduction of HDL levels in persons with baseline hypertriglyceridemia and in those who develop hypertriglyceridemia with these drugs. On the other hand, probucol causes HDL levels to fall.

Of the combination regimens the greatest increases in HDL-C levels (40 percent to 50 percent) have been reported with colestipol plus niacin. In the FATS,[9] much of the reduction of atherosclerosis in the colestipol plus niacin group appears to have been due to increased HDL levels.

COMBINATION REGIMENS FOR TREATMENT OF HYPERTRIGLYCERIDEMIA

While the literature is replete with studies on combination drug regimens for lowering LDL, there is a dearth of material on treatment of hypertriglyceridemia with combination drug regimens. In theory, the possibilities are limited to combinations of the various agents known to be effective as monotherapy for hypertriglyceridemia. These include: niacin (limits secretion of VLDL); fibric acid derivatives (stimulate non-splanchnic clearance of VLDL); and somatic fish oils with omega-3 fatty acids (limit secretion of VLDL). Of note, the use of bile acid sequestrants in combination regimens raises plasma TG levels just as in monotherapy (Table I).

SIDE EFFECTS OF COMBINATION DRUG REGIMENS FOR HYPERLIPOPROTEINEMIAS

Special considerations apply to the combination of lovastatin with gemfibrozil (and probably other fibric acid derivatives as well). With this combination the risk of myositis is increased, occurring in approximately five percent of patients.[20] Also, rhabdomyolysis with acute renal failure may occur.[21,22] Thus, special caution should attend the use of this combination, and it should probably be reserved for unusual cases.

When probucol is added to a bile acid sequestrant, the frequency of constipation is less than with a bile acid sequestrant alone.[4] However, as noted above, the effects of this regimen on lipoprotein levels mitigate against its widespread use.

Combination drug regimens may also be associated with any of the side effects of their component drugs. Thus, regimens with a bile acid sequestrant may lead to constipation, abdominal bloating or pain and adsorption of other drugs impairing their bioavailability; those combinations with niacin may lead to flushing, ichthyosis, gastritis, hepatitis, hyperuricemia or hyperglycemia; those combinations with lovastatin may lead to hepatitis or myositis; and those combinations with a fibric acid derivative may lead to cholelithiasis, nausea, abdominal pain, weight gain, decreased libido and drowsiness.

CONCLUSIONS

Combinations of lipid-lowering agents can be powerful tools in the management of severely hyperlipidemic patients. Most hyperlipidemic patients, however, are best treated with diet alone or with diet plus a single lipid-lowering drug. The drugs found to be most effective as monotherapy are the ones most useful in combination regimens. In designing a regimen for a patient, it is important to proceed stepwise, adding one drug at a time and carefully assessing the effect of each addition before considering another. Combination regimens have been capable of reducing LDL-C by more than 60 percent and of raising HDL-C by 35 percent to 40 percent. More importantly, these combination regimens have been shown to reduce CHD events, all-cause mortality and coronary atherosclerosis.

REFERENCES

1. Kane JP, Malloy MJ, Tun P, et al. Normalization of low-density lipoprotein levels in heterozygous familial hypercholesterolemia with a combined drug regimen. N Engl J Med. 1981;2304:251-258.

2. Illingworth DR, Phillipson BE, Rapp JH, et al. Colestipol plus nicotinic acid in treatment of heterozygous familial hypercholesterolemia. Lancet. 1981;1:296-298.

3. Blankenhorn DH, Nessim SA, Johnson RL, et al. Beneficial effects of combined colestipol-niacin therapy on coronary atherosclerosis and coronary venous bypass grafts. JAMA. 1987;3233-3240.

4. Dujovne CA, Krehbiel P, Cecoursey S, et al. Probucol with colestipol in the treatment of hypercholesterolemia. Ann Intern Med. 1984;100:477-482.

5. Mabuchi H, Sakai T, Sakai Y, et al. Reduction of serum cholesterol in heterozygous patients with familial hypercholesterolemia: additive effects of compactin and cholestyramine. N Engl J Med. 1983;308:609-613.

6. Grundy SM, Vega GL, Bilheimer DW. Influence of combined therapy with mevinolin and interruption of bile-acid reabsorption on low-density lipoproteins in heterozygous familial hypercholesterolemia. Ann Intern Med. 1985;103:339-343.

7. Illingworth DR. Mevinolin plus colestipol in therapy for severe heterozygous familial hypercholesterolemia. Ann Intern Med. 1984;101:598-604.

8. Malloy MJ, Kane JP, Kunitake ST, et al. Complementarity of colestipol, niacin, and lovastatin in treatment of severe familial hypercholesterolemia. Ann Intern Med. 1987;107:616-623.

9. Brown BG, Lin JT, Schaefer SM, et al. Niacin or lovastatin, combined with colestipol, regress coronary atherosclerosis and prevent clinical events in men with elevated apolipoprotein B. Circulation. 1989;80(suppl 2):II-266.

10. Witztum JL, Simmons D, Steinberg D, et al. Intensive combination drug therapy of familial hypercholesterolemia with lovastatin, probucol, and colestipol hydrochloride. Circulation. 1989;79:16-28.

11. Illingworth DR, Bacon S. Influence of lovastatin plus gemfibrozil on plasma lipids and lipoproteins in patients with heterozygous familial hypercholesterolemia. Circulation. 1989;79:590-596.

12. Series JJ, Caslake MJ, Kilday C, et al. Effect of combined therapy with bezafibrate and cholestyramine on low-density lipoprotein metabolism in type IIa hypercholesterolemia. Metabolism. 1989;38:153-158.

13. Weisweiler P. Low-dose colestipol plus fenofibrate: effects on plasma lipoproteins, lecithin: cholesterol acyltransferase and postheparin lipases in familial hypercholesterolemia. Metabolism. 1989;38:271-275.

14. East C, Bilheimer DW, Grundy SM. Combination drug therapy for familial combined hyperlipidemia. Ann Intern Med. 1988;109:25-32.

15. Garg A, Grundy SM. Gemfibrozil alone and in combination with lovastatin for treatment of hypertriglyceridemia in NIDDM. Diabetes. 1989;38:364-372.

16. Hoeg JM, Maher MB, Bailey KR, et al. Comparison of six pharmacologic regimens for hypercholesterolemia. Am J Cardiol. 1987;59:812-815.

17. Illingworth DR, O'Malley JP. The hypolipidemic effect of lovastatin and clofibrate alone and in combination in patients with type III hyperlipoproteinemia. Metabolism. 1990;39:403-409.

18. Carlson LA, Rosenhamer G. Reduction of mortality in the Stockholm Ischaemic Heart Disease Secondary Prevention Study by combined treatment with clofibrate and nicotinic acid. Acta Med Scand. 1988;223:405-418.

19. Expert Panel on Detection, Evaluation, and Treatment of High Blood Cholesterol in Adults. Report of the National Cholesterol Education Program Expert Panel on Detection, Evaluation, and Treatment of High Blood Cholesterol in Adults. Arch Intern Med. 1988;148:36-69.

20. Tobert JA. Letter. N Engl J Med. 1988;318:48.

21. Norman DJ, Illingworth DR, Munson J, Hosenpud J. Myolysis and acute renal failure in a heart-transplant recipient receiving lovastatin. N Engl J Med. 1988;318:46-47.

22. East C, Alivizatos PA, Grundy SM, Jones PH, Farmer JA. Rhabdomyolysis in patients receiving lovastatin after cardiac transplantation. N Engl J Med. 1988;318:47-48.

CHAPTER 9

Effect of Antihypertensive Agents and Other Cardioactive Drugs on Lipid and Lipoprotein Levels

Donald B. Hunninghake, M.D.
Minneapolis, Minnesota

INTRODUCTION

While not used specifically to lower lipid or lipoprotein levels, a number of therapeutic agents have an effect on these levels. The effect of these changes in lipid and lipoprotein levels on coronary heart disease (CHD) risk or cardiovascular disease (CVD) is not available. However, there is increasing evidence that changes in lipid and lipoprotein levels, irrespective of the method of producing the change, are associated with an altered risk for CHD.

CLINICAL SIGNIFICANCE OF DRUG-INDUCED CHANGES IN LIPIDS AND LIPOPROTEINS

Total Cholesterol and Low-Density Lipoproteins

Epidemiological studies indicate that total cholesterol and low-density lipoprotein cholesterol (LDL-C) levels are positively associated with increased risk for CHD.[1,2] Published reports have documented that lowering of total cholesterol and LDL reduces the risk of CHD in both primary and secondary intervention trials (as well as more recently in regression analysis studies).[3-8] These results have been obtained for interventions with dietary therapy and with treatment by several different classes of pharmacologic agents.[3-8] Thus, it appears that any prolonged increase in total and LDL levels will be associated with an increased risk for CHD.

HDL-Cholesterol

Epidemiological studies clearly demonstrate that high-density lipoprotein (HDL) levels are inversely associated with risk of CHD.[9] However, controversy remains about the benefits of pharmacologic intervention to increase HDL levels.[10] Studies such as the Helsinki Heart Study and other studies suggest that CHD risk is decreased when HDL levels are increased.[4,11] A major problem in assessing the importance of changes in HDL levels relates to the fact that in the major studies conducted to date circulating levels of total HDL, HDL_2 or apolipoprotein AI were measured, but in individual patients these levels may not always correlate with the proposed function of HDL in reverse cholesterol transport. On the other hand, it is likely that decreases in HDL levels will be associated with increased CHD risk.

Triglycerides

Triglyceride (TG) levels are correlated with risk of CHD if there is no adjustment for other factors, i.e., obesity, diabetes mellitus, low HDL levels.[12] Even when corrected for confounding variables in certain populations, including postmenopausal women in the United States and patients in Sweden, TG levels have been predictive of CHD risk.[13,14,15] Elevated TG levels are also associated with abnormal lipoproteins, such as small dense LDL, which are considered to be atherogenic. Severe hypertriglyceridemia can also precipitate pancreatitis.

Clinical Trial Results

There are many potential sources of error and variability in clinical trials, especially those designed to detect modest drug-induced changes in lipids and lipoproteins. Conclusions should always be based upon the results of all available data rather than a single clinical trial. Studies with a limited number of participants and those that do not have a control group and are conducted in an unblinded fashion must be interpreted with extreme caution. Life style changes, including diet, must be kept constant. Both the number and accuracy of the lipid and lipoprotein determinations are important considerations. The potential effects of age, gender, hormonal status, presence or absence of hyperlipidemia and drug dosage are rarely considered, but they can be important variables.

Selection of Drug

Although one would generally prefer to select a drug which does not adversely affect lipid and lipoprotein levels, other factors must be considered. These factors include cost of the drug, clinical condition being treated, adherence and side effects. Occasionally, the life expectancy of the patient without treatment would be so short that a potential increased risk for CHD during the course of the remaining lifespan of the patient would be a needless worry.

MAJOR AREAS OF CONCERN

The greatest area of concern regarding drug-induced changes in lipids and lipoproteins has been in the treatment of hypertension. Initially the thiazide diuretics were used primarily for treatment of hypertension followed by popularity of the beta-adrenergic blocking agents. Thiazide diuretics increase blood levels of total cholesterol, LDL and TG.[16-18] Both the nonselective and selective beta-blockers lower HDL and increase TG levels.[16,18-20]

Intervention trials with antihypertensive agents have shown protection against stroke, congestive heart failure, progression to more severe forms of hypertension and complications such as renal failure.[21-23] Protection against the complications of CHD has been minimal. A meta-analysis of nine clinical trials showed a trend toward reduced CHD mortality, but the difference was not statistically significant.[24] However, additional post-trial follow-up has indicated a reduction in mortality from CHD.[25,26] Of note, the thiazide diuretics were the primary class of drugs used in these trials and were the drugs of first choice in the treatment of hypertension for many years. Because of the concerns mentioned and other metabolic abnormalities produced by the thiazides, there has been a decreased emphasis on thiazides as drugs of first choice for the treatment of hypertension. However, thiazides continue to be used, albeit less frequently and in lower doses, either because of cost considerations or the inability to control hypertension with other antihypertensive agents alone.

The beta-blockers are also used extensively in the treatment of hypertension. Both the selective and nonselective agents lower HDL and increase TG levels. However, there is little evidence for an adverse effect of these lipid changes on CHD in the reported intervention trials on hypertension, and a recent report suggests that six months post-myocardial infarction (MI) the lipid effects of the beta-blockers were not predictive of subsequent CHD mortality.[27] Actually, the estimated increase in mortality due to the propranolol-induced changes in HDL was two percent. In addition, both selective and nonselective beta-blockers have been shown to reduce CHD morbidity and mortality when administered to patients post-MI.[28-30] Therefore, beta-blockers should not be withheld from patients who have had a MI because of the lipid-altering effects of these agents.

Recently, there has been concern of the effect of drugs on lipid and lipoprotein levels in patients undergoing organ transplantation, especially kidney and heart transplantation.[31-32] Accelerated coronary atherosclerosis is a major cause of long-term heart graft failure after heart transplantation.[33,34] Although the etiology of this accelerated atherosclerosis has not been conclusively established, there is concern that the immunosuppressant-induced changes in lipid and lipoprotein levels could be a contributory factor. In addition, both prednisone and cyclosporine have been shown to cause significant abnormalities in lipid and lipoprotein levels.[31,32]

DRUGS USED FOR THE TREATMENT OF HYPERTENSION AND/OR OTHER CARDIOVASCULAR ABNORMALITIES

Diuretics

Thiazide diuretics The thiazide diuretics increase total cholesterol, LDL-C and TG levels.[16-18] Generally, either no change or a slight decrease in HDL-C levels has been noted with these agents. A summary of a previous meta-analysis of these studies is indicated in Table I. Although the majority of studies have been conducted with hydrochlorothiazide, similar findings have been reported with most of the other available thiazides, including polythiazide, cyclopenthiazide, clopamide, bendroflumethiazide, mefruside and chlorothiazide.

TABLE I. Effect of thiazide diuretics on serum lipid and lipoprotein levels (adapted from reference 44)

	Change as Percent of Baseline	
	Mean	Range
Total cholesterol	+ 6	+ 4 to + 13
LDL	+ 8	- 20 to + 29
VLDL	+ 22	- 10 to + 70
HDL	- 2	- 30 to + 12
Triglycerides	+ 15	- 22 to + 38

Most of the reported studies used hydrochlorothiazide in total daily doses of 50 mg/day to 100 mg/day. Such doses are higher than those commonly used to treat hypertension today. While there is considerable variability in the results of the different studies (Table I), the increase in total cholesterol and LDL-C has generally been in the range of 5 percent to 10 percent. In these studies TG have usually shown an increase of 10 percent to 20 percent with the majority of studies showing no change in HDL-C levels.

Most studies have been short term, i.e., months, with only a few studies evaluating the effect of diuretics after years of therapy. There is general agreement that diuretics adversely affect lipid and lipoprotein levels in short-term studies, but there is more disagreement about whether the adverse effect on lipids persists for many years.

In evaluating the long-term effects of therapies on lipid and lipoprotein levels, it is very important to determine whether or not changes occurred in the control group or whether or not there were associated therapies (usually diet) to control the adverse lipid effects. Many of the long-term studies do not include a control group. Several studies suggest that the effects of therapies on lipid and lipoprotein levels persist for many years.[16-18] In the six-year observation period of the Multiple Risk Factor Intervention Trial (MRFIT), there was less reduction in total cholesterol following dietary intervention in the diuretic-treated group.[23] Also, in the Lipid Research Clinics' Coronary Primary Prevention Trial, the reduction in total cholesterol and LDL-C following cholestyramine administration was less in the group receiving diuretics.[35] Although other factors could explain the observed results, the lack of significant reduction in CHD risk in the early intervention trials which used diuretics could be related to the adverse lipid and lipoprotein effects of the diuretics.

While not carefully verified in clinical trials, anecdotal clinical experience suggests that patients with hyperlipidemia may experience greater adverse effects on lipids and lipoproteins after administration of thiazides and beta-blockers than patients with relatively normal levels. For example, a patient with hypertriglyceridemia is likely to experience both a greater percentage and absolute increase in TG following administration of a thiazide diuretic or beta-blocker than one with normal TG levels.

Extensive prospective clinical trials with doses of hydrochlorothiazide equivalent to 12.5 mg/day and 25 mg/day are not available. Such doses are now used in the treatment of hypertension, and it would be helpful to know if there are significant adverse effects. Many clinicians feel that if diuretic therapy with thiazides is necessary for the treatment of hypertension, total daily doses of thiazides equivalent to 12.5 mg or 25 mg of hydrochlorothiazide should be used.

In addition to their adverse effect on lipids, there is also concern about other metabolic effects of diuretics. These effects include the hypokalemia, increased glucose and insulin levels, and hyperuricemia. Because there is increasing evidence that insulin resistance may be an important contributor to hyperlipidemia and hypertension, these metabolic effects seen with diuretic administration could contribute to increased CHD risk.[36]

Chlorthalidone. The observed lipid and lipoprotein effects seen following chlorthalidone administration appear to be similar to those observed with hydrochlorothiazide.[37] Also, while there has not been further confirmation, there was a suggestion of a greater adverse effect on CHD mortality with hydrochlorothiazide than with chlorthalidone in the MRFIT Study.[38]

Loop diuretics. Studies have been conducted with the more commonly administered loop diuretics, i.e., furosemide, ethycrynic acid, bumetanide and metolazone. However, the number of studies which have been reported are few in number and primarily involve furosemide.[18,39,40] It appears that the loop diuretics also increase total cholesterol, LDL-C and TG, but the magnitude of change may be less than reported with chlorthalidone and hydrochlorothiazide. The studies are inconclusive, but suggest that the decrease in HDL-C may be greater than seen with chlorthalidone and hydrochlorothiazide.[18]

Potassium-sparing diuretics. Spironolactone, triamterene and amiloride are used frequently in combination with other antihypertensive agents. Several studies suggest only minimal lipid changes in lipids and lipoproteins following spironolactone administration.[18,41] Indapamide has been studied more extensively, and the results suggest no significant effect of this agent on lipid and lipoprotein levels.[42,43] It should be emphasized that these studies have been conducted with an indapamide dose of 2.5 mg/day. It is possible that this low dose of indapamide does not adversely affect lipids and lipoproteins, but that higher doses could do so.

In summary, the currently available evidence suggests that all patients receiving diuretics for the treatment of hypertension should be on a diet for lowering blood cholesterol. Although dietary therapy will not completely negate the adverse lipid and lipoprotein effects of the diuretics,[18] such therapy will tend to minimize these effects.[37]

Beta-Blockers

The beta-blockers have generally been characterized as follows:

1. *Non-selective:* Drugs in this category would include propranolol, nadolol and timolol.
2. *Beta₁-selective:* Prototype drugs would include metoprolol and atenolol.
3. *Beta-blockers with intrinsic sympathomimetic activity (ISA):* Drugs in this class would include pindolol, oxprenolol and acebutolol.
4. *Beta-blockers with alpha blocking properties:* Labetalol has been used primarily in the United States.
5. *Beta-blockers with beta-agonist or vasodilator properties:* For the most part this category reflects a new nomenclature replacing ISA in group 3 above. Drugs will be categorized as to whether the beta-blockade is selective or non-selective, and their type of agonist properties. Beta₂-agonists appear to have a beneficial effect on lipid and lipoprotein levels. Although drugs using this nomenclature have not yet been marketed in the United States, celiprolol is an example of a drug under current investigation. It is a selective beta₁-antagonist and appears to be a beta₂-agonist.

Of the beta-blockers, propranolol, a nonselective beta-blocker, has been studied most extensively for its effect on lipids.[19,20] Both the selective and nonselective beta-blockers decrease HDL-C and increase TG lipoprotein levels.[16,18-20] Agents in the other three categories do not produce significant lipid abnormalities and are considered lipid neutral, although there is evidence in some studies for moderately beneficial effects on lipids with these compounds.

TABLE II. Meta-analysis of the effects of beta-adrenergic blockers on lipoprotein levels (adapted from reference 44)

| | Mean Percent Change From Baseline | | |
	Nonselective	Selective	With ISA
Cholesterol	n.s.	n.s.	n.s.
HDL-C	-16	- 7	- 1
Triglycerides	+32	+20	+18

n.s. = not significant (1 to 4 percent increase)

A meta-analysis of the earlier studies with the beta-blockers is summarized in Table II.[44] Subsequent studies have confirmed these earlier observations.[18] Studies of propranolol or sotalol show a mean increase of 36 percent in TG and a reduction of 16 percent in HDL-C.[18,19,44] Most studies with selective and nonselective beta-blockers have demonstrated an increase in TG of 25 percent to 45 percent and reductions in HDL-C of 5 percent to 25 percent.

Atenolol and metoprolol have been the selective beta-blockers that have been studied most frequently. The effects of these agents on TG and HDL-C may be somewhat less than the nonselective compounds, but this point has not been established.[44] Beta-blockers with ISA, such as oxprenolol and pindolol, show even less effect on TG and HDL-C.[44] Oxprenolol, which has very weak ISA, accounts for most of the increase in TG noted in the data presented in Table II.[44] Pindolol and acebutolol appear to be lipid neutral and some studies even demonstrate that administration of these agents is associated with a slight increase in HDL.[17,44] In addition to the observed effects on HDL and TG levels, there is some evidence that nonselective and selective agents without ISA may also cause compositional changes in LDL-C; smaller, more dense LDL particles, which are considered more atherogenic, have been noted with such agents.[45]

Labetalol blocks both beta$_1$- and beta$_2$-adrenergic receptors and also has peripheral alpha$_1$-blocking properties. Studies have shown that this compound has no appreciable effect on lipid and lipoprotein levels.[46,47] Also, celiprolol, a beta$_1$-antagonist with beta$_2$-agonist properties, has not been shown to adversely effect lipid and lipoprotein levels. In addition, there is some evidence that celiprolol can modestly lower total cholesterol and LDL levels and increase HDL levels.[48]

Alpha-Blockers

There are a number of drugs that possess alpha$_1$-blocking properties. Prazosin, which has been available for use in the United States for a number of years, has been evaluated most extensively for its effect on lipid and lipoprotein levels.[18,49-51] The overall results indicate a 5 percent to 10 percent decrease in total cholesterol and LDL-C and no significant effect on TG levels. Although there is greater variability in the HDL-C levels and the evidence is less conclusive, studies indicate a 5 percent to 10 percent increase in HDL-cholesterol levels. Similar results appear to occur with all other alpha$_1$-blockers, including doxazosin, trimazosin, terazosin and indormin. Therefore, the alpha$_1$-blockers appear to have beneficial effects on lipids and lipoproteins that may offer some advantages for the treatment of hypertension. However, other factors such as cost and incidence of side effects must be considered when using these agents.

Angiotensin Converting Enzyme (ACE) Inhibitors

Captopril, enalapril and lisinopril are the agents that are currently most widely used in the United States. Captopril and enalapril have been studied extensively, and the effects of lisinopril would be expected to be similar.[52-55] The overall results of all these studies show that the ACE inhibitors do not produce any significant adverse effect on lipid and lipoprotein levels.

Recently there has been a great amount of interest in the effects of ACE inhibitors on glucose and insulin levels and insulin resistance. This interest stems from the fact that hypertension is more prevalent in hyperlipidemic patients and less prevalent in patients with normal lipid levels, as well as increasing evidence that insulin resistance may be an important etiologic factor in patients presenting with the combination of hyperlipidemia, hypertension, hyperglycemia or Type II diabetes mellitus.[56] Therefore, it is believed that insulin resistance can contribute both to the development of hypertension and hyperlipidemia. Of note, a preliminary study comparing hydrochlorothiazide and captopril indicates that captopril increased insulin sensitivity, while hydrochlorothiazide decreased insulin sensitivity.[57] This study also indicated that hydrochlorothiazide significantly increased total cholesterol, LDL-C and TG, while captopril showed no significant effect on these lipid levels. Captopril has also been shown to decrease the severity of atherosclerosis in the aorta of Watanabe rabbits, an animal model for hypertensive familial hypercholesterolemics.[58]

A point to be made is that because of the significant increased risk of CHD in patients with diabetes mellitus, the effects of an antihypertensive agent on the entire metabolic profile should be considered — not just the effect on lipids and lipoproteins.

Calcium Channel Blockers

There are a wide variety of calcium channel blockers either available for clinical use or under investigation. Verapamil, diltiazem and nifedipine have been used extensively in the United States. for a variety of cardiovascular conditions. More recently, nicardipine has become available for use in the United States. The available studies suggest that agents in this class are basically lipid neutral, although there are some studies which do suggest some modest lowering of the total cholesterol and LDL-C.[59-61]

There is also interest in the potential effect of these compounds on the atherogenic process. There is preliminary evidence in animals that indicates that the severity of atherosclerosis is reduced by calcium channel blockers and various clinical trials are currently underway. Preliminary evidence from the International Nifedipine Trial on Antiatherosclerotic Therapy (INTACT) Study shows that long-term treatment with nifedipine may have a beneficial effect in preventing the development of coronary artery disease.[62] In this placebo-controlled study, there were 28 percent fewer new lesions in the nifedipine-treated group and the number of patients with new lesions was reduced by 18 percent in the nifedipine-treated group. However, there was no apparent effect on lesions which were detectable at the time of initial angiography.

Centrally-Acting Drugs

Clonidine therapy has generally been associated with decreases in total cholesterol, LDL-C and TG and increases in HDL-C.[51,63] The effects are usually modest and generally not exceeding a five percent change. Guanabenz, which has similar pharmacologic effects to clonidine, also has been reported to produce a similar favorable lipid profile.[51,63]

The reported effects of methyldopa have been less consistent. Many studies show no significant effect, while others have shown a tendency toward a decrease in HDL-C levels.[64] Another study reported an increase in TG levels in patients with normal cholesterol levels, while LDL-C levels decreased in hypercholesterolemia patients.[65] Overall, the effects of methyldopa on serum lipid and lipoprotein levels appears to be negligible.

Vasodilators

Drugs in this class include hydralazine, minoxidil, nitrates and carprazidil. Available data is quite limited. Hydralazine has been reported to lower blood cholesterol levels,[66] while carprazidil has been reported to increase HDL levels.[67]

Postganglionic Neuronal Inhibitors

In many areas, guanethidine, guanadrel and reserpine are rarely used as antihypertensive agents. These agents were used primarily prior to the current interest in lipid and lipoprotein levels and hence there is essentially no information available as to the effect of these compounds on such levels. Of note, reserpine has been reported to have no adverse effect on either lipid or lipoprotein levels.[68]

Combination Antihypertensive Drug Therapy

The effect of a variety of combinations of antihypertensive agents on serum lipids and lipoproteins has been recently reviewed.[18] It was found that many of these studies involved small numbers of patients and were not carefully controlled. Generally, two drugs given in combination tend to have an additive effect on lipid and lipoprotein levels. If both classes of drugs produce similar effects, i.e., increase in LDL-C or TG or a decrease in HDL-C, a greater effect will be seen with combination therapy than with either drug alone. If the two drugs have opposing effects, e.g., one increases and the other decreases LDL-C levels, combination therapy will generally be associated with no significant change in LDL-C levels.

Do the Lipid and Lipoprotein Effects of Antihypertensive Agents Result in Altered Risk for Coronary Heart Disease?

To answer this question, a double-blind, randomized trial utilizing various classes of antihypertensive agents to evaluate the effect on cardiac endpoints is needed. Such a study has not been completed. A preliminary report on the Treatment of Mild Hypertension Study (TOMHS) has been reported.[69] TOMHS is a double-blind, randomized, placebo-controlled study which compares placebo and five active treatments: beta-blocker (acebutolol); calcium channel blocker (amlodipine); diuretic (chlorthalidone); alpha$_1$-blocker (doxazosin); and ACE inhibitor (enalapril). The lipid effects, changes in blood pressure and quality of life are being assessed. The lipid effects after 18 months of therapy are similar to those previously described for each class of drug. Hopefully, a larger study can be completed to ascertain whether or not there is a difference in CHD clinical events between the various treatments. A summary of the qualitative changes in lipid and lipoproteins for drugs frequently used as antihypertensive agents is shown in Table III.

TABLE III. Lipid and lipoprotein effects of drugs frequently used for the treatment of hypertension

Drug Classes	TC	LDL	HDL	TG
Thiazide, cholorthalidone and loop diuretics	+	+	+/−	+
Beta-adrenergic antagonists selective/nonselective	nc	nc	−	+
Beta-adrenergic antagonists with ISA	nc	nc	nc	nc
Combined alpha/beta	nc	nc	nc	nc
Alpha$_1$-antagonists	−	−	nc	nc
ACE inhibitors	nc	nc	nc	nc
Calcium channel blockers	nc/−	nc/−	nc	nc

TC = total cholesterol; LDL = low-density lipoprotein; HDL = high-density lipoprotein; TG = triglycerides; ACE = angiotensin converting enzyme; − = decrease; + = increase; nc = no change; nc/− = no change or decrease.

DRUGS USED IN ORGAN TRANSPLANTATION

Severe forms of hyperlipidemia are noted frequently in patients who have received kidney or heart transplants and other transplant procedures requiring intense immunosuppressive therapy.[31,32,70] The incidence of stroke and CHD is increased in corticosteroid-treated patients.[68,69] Notably, CHD is the leading cause of death in heart transplant patients one or more years post-transplant and CHD also appears to be a significant long-term problem for kidney transplant patients. Although cholesterol lowering has not been proven to reduce CHD risk in transplant patients, it does appear prudent to correct the lipid abnormalities with dietary therapy, exercise and drug therapy, if necessary. Post-transplant patients can have a variety of lipid disorders, but combined hyperlipidemia with elevated cholesterol, LDL and TG levels is very common. Factors contributing to hyperlipidemia in these patients include a genetic predisposition to hyperlipidemia, weight gain, which is common, and the fact that they are taking many medications including corticosteroids and cyclosporine.

Corticosteroids

It is generally accepted that corticosteroids increase levels of total cholesterol, LDL-C, HDL-C and TG. There is very little data from controlled, prospective studies, but the effects appear to be dose-related, probably more severe in women and less severe when administered on an alternate-day dosage schedule (not feasible in most transplant patients).[31,32,73,74] Steroids can also increase glucose levels and increase appetite, with associated weight gain, which can further accentuate the lipid abnormalities.

Cyclosporine

Cyclosporine A is an immunosuppressant agent which is used in transplant procedures and for treating many other conditions. Double-blind, placebo-controlled studies have been conducted in patients with psoriasis and amyotrophic lateral sclerosis.[75,76] These studies suggest that cyclosporine increases total cholesterol and LDL-C and apolipoprotein B levels by approximately 20 percent. Triglyceride levels are increased, while the effects of this agent on HDL-C appear to be minimal. Thus, it would appear that cyclosporine is a major contributor to the observed hyperlipidemias in transplant patients.

OTHER DRUGS

The following drugs have also been reported to have effect on lipid and lipoprotein levels. In many instances, the results are derived from limited studies, but the observations appear to be valid. Many of these drugs will be administered to patients who have cardiovascular disease.

Amiodarone

The studies are limited with this antiarrhythmic agent, but its use appears to be associated with modest increases in cholesterol and TG levels. These lipid changes occur irrespective of any changes in thyroid function.[77]

Anticonvulsants

There have been a number of studies which indicated that anticonvulsant drugs increase HDL levels by at least 10 percent to 15 percent and that the effect appears to be dose-dependent. Although there is also an increase in total cholesterol, the ratio of total cholesterol to HDL-C is decreased. Phenobarbital, primidone, phenytoin and carbamazepine definitely increase HDL-C levels.[78] There is less evidence that other anticonvulsants, i.e., valproic acid, produce similar effects. There are anecdotal suggestions that there is less CHD in patients who receive any of these anticonvulsant drugs chronically.[79]

Para-Aminosalicylic Acid (PAS)

This drug, which was commonly used in the past for the treatment of tuberculosis, decreases total cholesterol, LDL-C and TG levels.[80]

Phenothiazine and Haloperidol

While studies are not conclusive, these agents appear to increase total cholesterol levels.[81] The effects of these agents on other lipid and lipoprotein levels have not been carefully evaluated.

Retinoids

The retinoids are analogs of Vitamin A and are used in the treatment of various skin disorders, including psoriasis and acne. Drugs in this class include isotretinoin, etretinate and acitretin. All of these drugs increase TG levels, primarily very low-density lipoprotein-TG. Additionally, isotretinoin significantly increases total cholesterol and LDL-C and decreases HDL-C levels.[82,83] These drugs are frequently used for months rather than years and thus the effect on atherosclerosis may be limited. However, these agents can significantly increase TG levels in a patient with preexisting hypertriglyceridemia, which may increase the risk of pancreatitis.

Terbutaline

This beta$_2$-agonist is primarily used as a bronchodilator. It increases HDL-C levels by approximately 10 percent.[84]

Ticlopidine

This drug has been used in clinical trials because of its ability to inhibit platelet aggregation. It increases total cholesterol and LDL in the range of 10 percent to 15 percent.[85,86]

Miscellaneous Agents

There are a number of other drugs which have been reported to alter lipid and lipoprotein levels, but the evidence is less convincing, either because the data is derived from cross-sectional studies, uncontrolled studies or variable effects that have been observed in different clinical trials.

The following are primarily observations and have not been demonstrated conclusively: both allopurinol and benzodiazapines have been reported to increase TG levels; certain antacids decrease total cholesterol and LDL-C levels; cimetidine has occasionally been reported to increase HDL-C levels; the antifungal agent, ketoconazole, has been reported to lower total cholesterol and LDL-C levels at higher doses; and nicotine chewing gum can increase total cholesterol levels.

CONCLUSION

There are a number of drugs used for the treatment of clinical conditions that alter lipid and lipoprotein levels, either adversely or positively. Although the effects of these lipid and lipoprotein changes in clinical CHD events have not been defined in controlled clinical trials, these changes should be considered clinically significant.

If a drug increases total cholesterol by 5 percent, the current evidence suggests that chronic administration of this drug should increase the risk of CHD by 10 percent and some evidence would suggest a 15 percent increase.[5] While the absolute increase in CHD risk for an individual patient may not be dramatic, a significant increase in risk of CHD for the entire population would occur if the drug were used extensively.

The evidence is not conclusive, but it appears that patients with preexisting hyperlipidemia are likely to have greater changes in lipids and lipoprotein levels if they receive a drug that adversely effects the specific abnormality for which the patient is being treated. For example, a drug causing hypertriglyceridemia is likely to produce a greater effect in a patient who has hypertriglyceridemia. Patients may be taking several drugs which adversely effect lipid and lipoprotein levels, and the combined effect of these drugs on lipid and lipoprotein levels could be significant. The use of alternative drugs that do not adversely effect lipid and lipoprotein levels could either reduce the required dose of a particular lipid-lowering agent or reduce the need for additional lipid-lowering drugs.

Specific quantitative change in lipids and lipoproteins for many of the classes of drugs discussed in the earlier portions of this chapter has not been provided. The reason is that there is considerable variation in the quantitative response of individual patients to a particular agent. Thus, it is probably important simply to suspect that a drug may have an adverse effect in a particular patient based on the pharmacologic and/or clinical profile of the drug. Using such information, a clinical decision can be made about the selection of an alternative drug.

The specific mechanisms producing the lipid and lipoprotein changes for the various classes of drugs was also not provided in the preceding portion of this chapter. In some cases, the mechanisms are poorly understood or multiple mechanisms have been proposed. It is also difficult to envision a single mechanism as being responsible for the effects of many different classes of drugs. However, it is possible that vasodilation associated with antihypertensive therapy may increase lipoprotein lipase activity and the associated beneficial lipid effects.[48] Conversely, vasoconstriction would decrease lipoprotein lipase activity and adversely effect lipids. Drugs which stimulate the hepatic cytochrome P-450 system (anticonvulsants, cimetidine) increase HDL-C levels. Much more work remains to be done in this area.

In summary, consideration of the potential effect of various drugs on lipid and lipoprotein levels is required for the appropriate management of hyperlipidemia. The adverse effects of certain agents on lipids and lipoproteins could theoretically increase the risk in particular patients for CHD and pancreatitis. Therefore, if alternative drugs are available that do not adversely affect lipid and lipoprotein levels, such agents should be used.

REFERENCES

1. The Pooling Project Research Group. Relationship of blood pressure, serum cholesterol, smoking habit, relative weight, and ECG abnormalities to incidence of major coronary events: final report of the Pooling project. J Chronic Dis. 1978;31:201-236.
2. Stamler J, Wentworth D, Neaton J. Is the relationship between serum cholesterol and risk of death from CHD continuous and graded? JAMA. 1978;256:2823-2828.
3. The Lipid Research Clinics. Coronary Primary Prevention Trial results. I. Reduction in incidence of coronary heart disease. JAMA. 1984;251:351-364.
4. Frick MH, Elo O, Haapa K, et al. Helsinki Heart Study: Primary-prevention trial with gemfibrozil in middle-aged men with dyslipidemia. N Engl J Med. 1987;317:1237-1245.
5. Yusuf S, Wittes J, Friedman L. Overview of results of randomized clinical trials in heart disease. II. Unstable angina, heart failure, primary prevention with aspirin, and risk factor modification. JAMA. 1989;260:2259-2263.
6. Buchwald H, Varco RL, Matts SP, et al. Effect of partial ileal bypass surgery on mortality and morbidity from coronary heart disease in patients with hyper-cholesterolemia. N Engl J Med. 1990;323:946-955.
7. Blankenhorn DH, Nessim SA, Johnson RL, et al. Beneficial effects of combined colestipol-niacin therapy on coronary atherosclerosis and coronary bypass grafts. JAMA. 1987;257:3233-3240.
8. Brown G, Albers JJ, Fisher LD, et al. Regression of coronary artery disease as a result of intensive lipid-lowering therapy in men with high levels of apolipoprotein B. N Engl J Med. 1990;323:1289-1298.
9. Gordon T, Castelli WP, Hjortland MC, et al. High-density lipoprotein as a protective factor against coronary heart disease: the Framingham Study. Am J Med. 1977;62:707-714.
10. Grundy SM, Goodman DS, Rifkind BM, Cleeman JI. The place of HDL in cholesterol management. Arch Intern Med. 1989;149:505-510.
11. Gordon DJ, Probstfield JL, Garrison RJ, et al. High-density lipoprotein cholesterol and cardiovascular disease. Circulation. 1989;79:8-15.

12. Austin MA. Plasma triglyceride as a risk factor for coronary heart disease: the epidemiologic evidence and beyond. Am J Epidemiol. 1989;129:249-259.

13. Castelli WP. The triglyceride issue: a view from Framingham. Am Heart J. 1986;112:432-437.

14. Aberg H, Lithell H, Selinas I, et al. Serum triglycerides are a risk factor for myocardial infarction but not for angina pectories: results from a 10-year follow-up of Uppsala Primary Preventive Study. Atherosclerosis. 1985;54:89-97.

15. Austin MA. Plasma triglyceride and coronary heart disease. Arterioscler Thromb. 1991;11:2-14.

16. Weidmann P, Ferrier C, Saxenhofer H, Uehlinger DE, Trost BN. Serum lipoproteins during treatment with antihypertensive drugs. Drugs. 1988;35(suppl 6):118-134.

17. Ames RP. The effects of antihypertensive drugs on serum lipids and lipoproteins. I. Diuretics. Drugs. 1986;32:250-278.

18. Lardinois CK, Neuman SL. The effects of antihypertensive agents on serum lipids and lipoproteins. Arch Intern Med. 1988;148:1280-1288.

19. Johnson BF. The everyday problem of plasma lipid changes during antihypertensive therapy. J Cardiovasc Pharmacol. 1982;4(suppl 2):213-221.

20. Ames RP. The effects of antihypertensive drugs on serum lipids and lipoproteins. II. Non-diuretic drugs. Drugs. 1986;32:335-337.

21. Grimm RH, Neaton JD, Prineas RJ. Primary prevention trials and the rationale for treating mild hypertension. Clin Ther. 1987;9(suppl D):20-30.

22. Hypertension Detection and Follow-up Program Cooperative Group. Five-year findings of the Hypertension Detection and Follow-up Program. JAMA. 1979;242:2562-2571.

23. Multiple Risk Factor Intervention Trial. Risk factor changes and mortality results. JAMA. 1982;248:1465-1477.

24. McMahon SW, Cutler JA, Fuberg CD, Payne GH. The effects of drug treatment for hypertension on morbidity and mortality from cardiovascular disease: a review of randomized controlled trials. Prog Cardiovasc Dis. 1986;29(suppl 1):99-118.

25. Hypertension Detection and Follow-up Program Cooperative Group. Persistence of reduction in blood pressure and mortality of participants in the Hypertension Detection and Follow-up Program. JAMA. 1988;259:2113-2122.

26. Multiple Risk Factor Intervention Trial Research Group. Mortality after 10-1/2 years for hypertensive participants in the Multiple Risk Factor Intervention Trial. Circulation. 1990;82:1616-1628.

27. Byington RP, Worthy J, Craven T, Furberg CD. Propranolol-induced lipid changes and their prognostic significance after a myocardial infarction: the beta-blocker heart attack trial experience. Am J Cardiol. 1990;65:1287-1291.

28. β-Blocker Heart Attack Trial Research Group. A randomized trial of propranolol in patients with actue myocardial infarction. I. Mortality results. JAMA. 1982;247:1707-1714.

29. β-Blocker Heart Attack Trial Research Group. A randomized trial of propranolol in patients with actue myocardial infarction. II. Morbidity results. JAMA. 1983;250:2814-2819.

30. Yusuf S, Peto R, Lewis J, Collins R, Sleight P. Beta-blockade during and after myocardial infarction: an overview of the randomized trials. Prog Cardiovasc Dis. 1985;27:335-371.

31. Becker DM, Chamberlain B, Swank R, et al. Relationship between corticosteroid exposure and plasma lipid levels in heart transplant recipients. Am J Med. 1988;85:632-638.

32. Vathsala A, Weinberg RB, Schoenberg L, et al. Lipid abnormalities in cyclosporine-prednisone-treated renal transplant recipients. Transplant. 1989;48:37-43.

33. Bilodeau M, Fitchett DH, Guerraty A, Sniderman AD. Dyslipoproteinemias after heart and heart-lung transplantation: potential relation to accelerated graft arteriosclerosis. J Heart Transplant. 1989;8:454-459.

34. Eich DM, Johnson DE, Hastillo A, et al. Accelerated coronary atherosclerosis in cardiac transplantation. Cardiac Transplant. 1990;20:199-211.

35. Glueck CJ. Increased total and low-density lipoprotein cholesterol levels associated with diuretic use in the lipid research clinic's coronary primary prevention trial. Clin Res. 1986;34:365A. Abstract.

36. Weinberger MH. Optimizing cardiovascular risk reduction during antihypertensive therapy. Hypertens. 1990;16:201-211.

37. Grimm RH, Leon AS, Hunninghake DB, et al. Effects of thiazide diuretics on plasma lipids and lipoproteins in mildly hypertensive men. Ann Intern Med. 1981;94:7-11.

38. Multiple Risk Factor Intervention Trial Research Group. Baseline rest electrocardiographic abnormalities, antihypertensive treatment, and mortality in the Multiple Risk Factor Intervetnion Trial. Am J Cardiol. 1985;55:1-15.

39. Bloomgarden ZT, Ginsberg-Fellner F, Rayfield EJ. Elevated hemoglobin A and low-density lipoprotein cholesterol levels in thiazide-treated diabetic patients. Am J Med. 1984;77:823-827.

40. Gluck Z, Baumgartner G, Wiedmann P. Increased ration between serum β- and α- lipoproteins during diuretic therapy: an adverse effect? Clin Sci. 1978;55:325-328.

41. Grimm RH Jr, Leon AS, Hunninghake DB, et al. Diuretics and plasma lipids effects of thiazides and spironolactone. In: Noseda G, Fagiacomo C, Fumagalli R, eds. Lipoproteins and Coronary Atherosclerosis. Amsterdam, Holland: Elsevier Science Publishers; 1982:371-376.

42. Gerber A, Weidmann P, Bianchetti MG. Serum lipoproteins during treatment with the antihypertensive agent indapamide. Hypertens. 1985;7(suppl 2)164-169.

43. Perry HM. Some wrong-way chemical changes during antihypertensive treatment: comparison of indapamide and related agents. Am Heart J. 1983;106:251-257.

44. Weidmann P, Uehlinger DE, Gerber A. Antihypertensive treatment and serum lipoproteins. J Hypertens. 1985;3:297-306.

45. Superko HR, Wood PD, Krauss RM. Effect of alpha- and selective beta-blockade for hypertension control on plasma lipoproteins, apoproteins, lipoprotein subclasses, and postprandial lipemia. Am J Med. 1989;86(suppl 1B):26-31.

46. Ponti GB, Carnovali M, Banderali G. Effects of labetalol on the lipid metabolism in hypertensive patients. Curr Ther Res. 1983;33:466-471.

47. Thulin T, Henningsen NC, Karlberg BE. Clinical and metabolic effects of labetalol compared with atenolol in primary hypertension. Curr Ther Res. 1981;30:194-204.

48. Hunninghake DB. Effects of celiprolol and other antihypertesive agents on serum lipids and lipoproteins. Am Heart J. 1991;121:696-701.

49. Goto Y. Effects of α- and β-blocker antihypertensive therapy on blood lipids: a multicenter trial. Am J Med. 1984;76:72-8.

50. Torvik D, Madshu HP. Multicentre 12-week double-blind comparison of doxazosin, prazosin and placebo in patients with mild to moderate essential hypertension. Br J Clin Pharmacol. 1986;21:69S-75S.

51. Kirkendall WM, Hammond JJ, Thomas JC. Prazosin and clonidine for moderately severe hypertension. JAMA. 1978;240:2553-2556.

52. Weinberger MH. Influence of an angiotensin converting-enzyme inhibitor on diuretic-induced metabolic effects in hypertension. Hypertens. 1983;5(suppl 3):132-138.

53. Kochar MS, Kaur M, Zeller JR, et al. Treatment of essential hypertension with a twice-daily dose of captopril. Curr Ther Res. 1984;35:905-912.

54. Gomez HJ, Cirillo VJ, Irvin JD. Enalapril: a review of human pharmacology. Drugs. 1985;30(suppl 1):35-46.

55. Herra-Acosta J, Perez-Grovas H, Fernandez M, et al. Enalapril: A review of human pharmacology. Drugs. 1985;30(suppl 1):35-46.

56. Reaven GM. Non-insulin dependent diabetes mellitus, abnormal lipoprotein metabolism and atherosclerosis. Metabolism. 1987;36:2(suppl 1):1-8.

57. Pollare T, Lithell H, Berne C. A comparison of the effects of hydrochlorothiazide and captopril on glucose and lipid metabolism in patients with hypertension. N Eng J Med. 1989;321:868-873.

58. Chobanian AV, Haudenschild CC, Nickerson C, Drago R. Antiatherogenic effect of captopril in the Watanabe heritable hyperlipidemic rabbit. Hypertens. 1990;15:327-331.

59. Wallidus G. Effect of verapamil on serum lipoproteins in patients with angina pectoris. Acta Med Scand. 1984;215:43-48.

60. Klein WW. Treatment of hypertension with calcium channel blockers: European data. Am J Med. 1984;77(suppl 4A):143-146.

61. Massie BM, Hirsch AT, Inouye IK, et al. Calcium-channel blockers as antihypertensive agents. Am J Med. 1984;77(suppl 4A)135-142.

62. Lichtlen PR, Hugenholtz PG, Rafflenbeul W, et al. Retardation of coronary artery disease in humans by the calcium-channel blocker Nifedipine: Results of the INTACT Study (International Nifedipine Trial on Antiatherosclerotic Therapy). Circulation. 1989;80(suppl II):II-382.

63. Walker BR, Hare LE, Ditch MW. Comparative antihypertensive effects of guanabenz and clonidine. J Int Med Res. 1982;10:6-14.

64. Leon AS, Agre J, McNally C. Blood lipid effects of antihypertensive therapy: a double-blind comparison of the effects of methyldopa and propranolol. J Clin Pharmacol. 1984;24:209-217.

65. Dujovne CA, DeCoursey S, Krehbiel P. Serum lipids in normo- and hyperlipidemics and after methyldopa and propranolol. Clin Pharmacol Ther. 1984;36:157-162.

66. Perry HM Jr, Mills EJ. The effect of oral hydralazine on circulating human cholesterol. Am J Med Sci. 1962;243:564-572.

67. Weidmann P, Gerber A, Mordasini R. Effects of antihypertensive therapy on serum lipoproteins. Hypertens. 1983;5(suppl 3):120-131.

68. Deming JB, Hodes ME, Baltazar A, et al. The changes in concentration of cholesterol in the serum of hypertensive patients during antihypertensive therapy. Am J Med. 1958;24:882-892.

69. Grimm R, Neaton J, Elmer P, et al. The Treatment of "Mild" Hypertension Study (TOMHS): blood pressure results 18 months. Circulation. 1989;80(suppl II):II-301. Abstract.

70. Stamler JS, Vaughn DE, Rudd MA, et al. Frequency of hypercholesterolemia after cardiac transplants. Am J Cardiol. 1988;62:1268-1272.

71. Ibels LS, Stewart JH, Mahony JF, Sheil LG. Deaths from occlusive renal disease in renal transplant recipients. Br Med J. 1974;3:552-554.

72. Stern MP, Orville G, Kolterman OG, Fries JF, et al. Adrenocortical steroid treatment of rheumatic diseases: effects on lipid metabolism. Arch Intern Med. 1973:132:97-101.

73. Curtis JJ, Galla JH, Woodford SY, Lucas BA, et al. Effect of alternate-day prednisone on plasma lipids in renal transplant recipients. Kidney Intl. 1989;22:42-47.

74. Jeffreys DB, Lessof MH, Mattock MB. Corticosteroid treatment, serum lipids and coronary artery disease. JAMA. 1986;256:3110-3116.

75. Ellis CN, Gorsulowski DC, Hamilton TA, et al. Cyclosporine improves psoriasis in a double-blind study. JAMA. 1989;265:53-56.

76. Ballantyne CM, Podet EJ, Patsch WP, et al. Effects of cyclosporine therapy on plasma lipoprotein levels. JAMA. 1989:265:53-56.

77. Albert SG, Alves LE, Rose EP. Thyroid dysfunction during chronic amiodarone therapy. J Am Coll Cardiol. 1987;9:175-181.

78. Reddy MN. Effect of anticonvulsant drugs on plasma total cholesterol, high-density lipoprotein cholesterol, and apolipoproteins A and B in children with epilepsy. Proc Soc Exp Biol Med. 1985:180:359-363.

79. Muuronen A, Kaste M, Nikkila EA, et al. Mortality from ischemic heart disease among patients using anticonvulsive drugs: a case control study. Br Med J. 1985;291:1481-1483.

80. Barter PJ, Connor WE, Spector AA, et al. Lowering of serum cholesterol and triglyceride by aminosalicylic acid in hyperlipoproteinemia: studies in patients with type II-A and II-B. Ann Intern Med. 1974;83:619-624.

81. Clark ML, Ray TS, Paredes A, et al. Chlorpromazine in women with chronic schizophrenia: the effect on cholesterol levels and cholesterol behavior relationships. Psychosom Med. 1967;29:634-642.

82. Jones DH, King K, Miller AJ, Cunliffe WJ. A dose-response study of 13-cis-retinoics acid in acne vulgaris. Br J Dermatol. 1983;108:333-343.

83. Vahlquist C, Michaelsson G, Vahlquist A, et al. A sequential comparison of etretinate (Tigason®) and isotretinoin (Roaccutane®) with special regard to their effects on serum lipoproteins. Br J Dermatol. 1985;112:69-76.

84. Hooper PL, Woo W, Visconti L, et al. Terbutaline raises high-density lipoprotein cholesterol levels. N Eng J Med. 1981;305:145-107.

85. Berglund U, Wallentin, L. Influence on lipoprotein metabolism of the platelet inhibitory drug ticlopidine. Atherosclerosis. 1986;59(3):241-246.

86. Hass WK, Easton JD, Adams HP Jr, et al. A randomized trial comparing ticlopidine hydrochloride with aspirin for the prevention of stroke in high-risk patients. N Engl J Med. 1989;321(8):501-507.

CHAPTER 10

Exogenous Hormones and Their Effects on Circulating Lipids

Valery T. Miller, M.D.
Washington, D.C.

INTRODUCTION

The same lipid risk factors causing heart disease in men may also cause heart disease in women.[1] These risk factors include high total cholesterol, its surrogate low-density lipoprotein cholesterol (LDL-C) and low levels of high-density lipoprotein cholesterol (HDL-C), the latter conveying a greater risk in men than in women.[2,3] Hypertriglyceridemia is also a risk factor for women.[4] Another dissimilarity in lipid risk factors between men and women is the fact that clinical expression of coronary heart disease (CHD) occurs 10 to 15 years later in women than in men.[5] Some researchers have suggested that among the reasons for women to have some protection from CHD are their higher HDL-C levels (about 10 mg/dl higher for women as a group than observed in men) and a direct benefical effect of endogenous estrogen on the endothelial wall.[5,6]

Nevertheless, of the 500,000 people who die of CHD each year in the United States, fully half are women. Thus, while there are differences in the atherosclerotic process between the sexes, the similarities and the extent of mortality in women make it imperative that CHD prevention applies to women as well as men. One way of doing this besides the usual hygienic recommendations of better diet, more exercise, and weight loss, is the appropriate use of exogenous hormones in women. This chapter will review the cholesterol/lipoprotein changes, both beneficial and non-beneficial, that are produced by contraceptive hormone use and postmenopausal hormone replacement.

LIPID EFFECTS OF ESTROGENS AND PROGESTOGENS

Commonly used estrogens are presented in Table I. All oral estrogens, whether natural or synthetic, affect cholesterol and lipoprotein levels in a dose-dependent fashion. Also, with the exception that triglyceride (TG) levels are increased, the changes are generally beneficial in that reduction in LDL-C and an increase in HDL-C levels are antiatherogenic (Table II). While all the metabolic pathways for these changes have not been clarified, estrogen's main effects occur in the liver, and a high concentration of estrogen via the portal vein is necessary to obtain consistent and significant lipoprotein changes. Only orally administered estrogen appears to meet this condition. In fact, results of published studies reveal that transdermal estrogens do not compare favorably in this regard.[7,8]

Progestogens also act in the liver to produce lipid changes and, in general, these changes can be said to be atherogenic except for the decrease in TG levels (Table II). Newer progestogens that are not yet available in the United States are reported to demonstrate little or no adverse change in lipids.[9] These and other progestogens are presented in Table III.

Both estrogens and progestogens have an individual dose effect on lipids and a specific potency that is characteristic of each; synthetic hormones are more potent than the natural hormones. Progestogens are further characterized by their androgenicity, a property that, in most cases, translates into increased potency and an adverse effect on lipids.

TABLE I. Synthetic and natural estrogens

Natural Estrogens	Synthetic Estrogens
• 17-beta-estradiol	• Ethinyl estradiol
• Conjugated equine estrogen	• Mestranol
• Estropipate	• Diethylstilbestrol
• Estradiol cypiopate*	
• Estradiol valerate*	

* Not widely used in this country

TABLE II. Comparison of effects on lipids of estrogens and progestogens

Lipid	Estrogen Effect	Progestogen Effect
Total cholesterol	Variable	Variable
Total triglycerides	Increased	Decreased
LDL-cholesterol	Decreased	Increased
Apolipoprotein B	Decreased	Increased
HDL-cholesterol	Increased	Decreased
HDL_2	Increased	Decreased
Apolipoprotein AI	Increased	Decreased

TABLE III. Progestogens

Synthetic	Natural	New Synthetics*
Levonorgestrel	Progesterone	Desogestrel
Norethindrone acetate	Micronized progesterone	Norgestimate
Norethindrone		Gestodene
Ethynodiol diacetate		
Medroxyprogesterone acetate		

* Not yet approved for use in the United States

LIPID EFFECTS OF CONTRACEPTIVE HORMONES

The lipid effects of oral contraceptives (OCs) have been well studied. Changes are the result of the sum of the opposing effects of the estrogen and of the progestogen.

In general, norgestrel-containing preparations decrease HDL-C and HDL$_2$ significantly more than do the less androgenic progestogens, norethindrone and ethynodiol diacetate.[10,11] Even in the low-dose preparations, so called because they contain 30 to 35 mg of ethinyl estradiol and in the triphasic preparations, which have varying doses of estrogen and/or progestogen during the month, cholesterol and lipoprotein levels are changed adversely by norgestrel-containing perparations. In fact, LDL levels increase 10 percent to 18 percent with these preparations.[11-13] While HDL-C level change is variable among these formulations (-9 percent to +2 percent change), triphasic oral contraceptives have been shown to decrease HDL$_2$ 40 percent to 47 percent (p < 0.001).

Furthermore, apolipoprotein B levels increase with these low-dose preparations, which may be an additional adverse effect. Also, apolipoprotein A levels increase in the presence of decreasing HDL-C and HDL$_2$ levels, which suggests qualitative changes, the consequence of which is currently unknown.[12,13]

Thus, the potential for some increased risk for atherosclerosis exists for all current preparations with the least androgenic preparations offering the least adverse lipid changes, even among the new low-dose formulations.

Recently a contraceptive subdermal implant, which lasts five years and contains only levonorgestrel, has been approved for use in the United States. Initial studies of cholesterol level effects over the first three years of use are encouraging.[14,15] By the end of the first and second years, the LDL-C/HDL-C ratio had declined 20 percent, p < 0.001 and 10 percent, p < 0.05, respectively, a beneficial effect over that time period. However, by three years, mainly because of a decline in HDL-C below baseline levels and a return to baseline levels of LDL-C, that ratio had risen 13 percent above baseline, p < 0.05.[15] While the LDL-C/HDL-C ratio always remained within the normal range during the first three years, there appears to be a trend upwards. More studies are needed to clarify the sum of effects on lipids of this long-term contraceptive.

RISK OF HEART DISEASE AND ORAL CONTRACEPTIVES

Newer low-dose OCs described previously in this chapter were developed to reduce the risk of venous thrombosis and heart attacks with which high-dose pills (> 50 µg ethinyl estradiol) had been associated.[16] Evaluation of the morbidity and mortality reflecting OC use up to the early 1980s is encouraging, with less CHD being reported.[17]

A more difficult question and one more germane to this discussion, however, remains largely unanswered. *Does past use of OCs convey increased risk of heart disease? More precisely, will the newer pill increase the amount of atherosclerosis in arteries of some women and will they as a result have early clinical disease?*

Several studies evaluating this question are in disagreement.[18-20] In addition, the published studies reflect results from higher dose formulations no longer commonly in use. Some interesting data from Clarkson *et al.* suggest that cynomolgus monkeys receiving hormones in doses similar to current OC formulations did not develop atherosclerosis even in the presence of reduced HDL-C and HDL_2 levels.[6] Whether the findings from this study have any bearing on the atherosclerotic process in humans is unclear.

Several large studies have concluded that lipid changes from OCs in the average woman with normal or modest cholesterol levels and no other significant risks will not lead to premature heart disease later in life.[18,20] It is not at all clear that long-term use of a formulation that alters lipids atherogenically in a woman who has modestly high cholesterol and possibly other risk factors, would not ultimately contribute enough atherosclerotic plaque to lead to early heart disease. Thus, until there is further information about estrogen's protective effect on the endothelial wall in humans, OC preparations that are prescribed should be those that change cholesterol and lipoprotein levels the least.

RISK OF PANCREATITIS WITH ORAL CONTRACEPTIVES

Oral contraceptives and non-contraceptive estrogen administration has been reported to cause hypertriglyceridemia and chylomicronemia, which resulted in pancreatitis.[21,22] It is not uncommon for affected patients to undergo laparoscopy for abdominal pain before the correct diagnosis is recognized. After recovery these women demonstrate Type IV or Type V hypertriglyceridemia. A lipid profile prior to prescribing OCs or non-contraceptive hormones and the avoidance of OCs in those with TG > 250 mg/dl is the best way to identify the woman who may develop pancreatitis. Obtaining a follow-up profile a month or two after the woman has been taking the pill is of little use because the pancreatitis develops usually within two to three weeks of initiation of therapy.

RECOMMENDATIONS FOR ORAL CONTRACEPTIVE USE

Oral contraceptives are for some women the only acceptable birth control at certain times in their lives. In some clinical situations the immediate risk of pregnancy outweighs the possible future risk of coronary disease. Thus, physicians find themselves prescribing OCs in other than ideal situations. Only in women over 35 years of age who smoke are there such strong indications of CHD risk that OC administration is flatly to be condemned. All else appears relative. Short-term therapy (two to three years) with formulations that alter the lipid profiles the least most likely do not contribute measurably to the atherosclerotic process, even in the presence of other risk factors. Long-term use, however, which today can mean 10 to 15 years of OC use, may have later as yet undefined consequences of cardiovascular disease, especially in the presence of other risk factors.

Thus, a baseline measurement of a total cholesterol and TG level is recommended before the initiation of contraceptive hormones. Further, an assessment of other cardiovascular risks is necessary before advising about continued use. Smoking should be discontinued, whatever the age of the woman, if possible. Reexamination of the continued need for an OC in the presence of CHD risk factors is probably as important as reassessment of the lipid profile at some future date. Women who have familial hypercholesterolemia should be treated with the appropriate drug therapy, even when they are taking OCs.

POSTMENOPAUSAL HORMONE REPLACEMENT

Estrogen has been used since the 1960s for the treatment of menopausal symptoms - mainly hot flashes and night sweats. It is now approved for use in the prevention of osteoporosis, and the Food and Drug Administration (FDA) is currently considering approving the use of estrogen for the prevention of heart disease in women who have no uterus. The rationale for approval of this indication is that epidemiological studies show that cardiovascular risk is reduced 40 percent to 50 percent in women who take estrogen.[23,24] The supporting information is that postmenopausal women who use estrogen replacement have LDL-C levels that are 11 percent to 19 percent lower and HDL-C levels that are 13 percent higher than those of non-users.[25] Prospective studies indicate similar beneficial changes in these lipids[26] as well as in HDL_2 and apolipoprotein AI and apolipoprotein B levels.[27-29] Table IV reflects these changes secondary to 0.625 mg of unopposed conjugated equine estrogen.

TABLE IV. Percent change in lipids from 0.625 mg/day unopposed conjugated equine estrogen

	Ref.	(n)	LDL-C	Apo-B	HDL-C	HDL_2	Apo-AI
Miller et al.	27	(11)	-11.8	—	10.9	27.3	11.4
Sonnendecker et al.	28	(10)	-19.7	-17.8	13.8	56	7.1
Sherwin et al.	29	(27)	- 0.3	—	13.7	—	—
Sherwin et al.	29	(23)	-17.6	—	19.0	—	—

Lipid changes due to estrogen are dose-related.[26-29] Furthermore, the degree of LDL-C lowering appears to be correlated with the baseline level of LDL-C.[30] Thus, the higher the baseline LDL-C, the greater the lowering of that lipoprotein level; this finding has led to the use of estrogen postmenopausally to treat hypercholesterolemia.[30,31]

ESTROGEN TREATMENT OF HYPERCHOLESTEROLEMIA

Tikkanen et al.[30] treated 29 Type II postmenopausal women who had a mean total cholesterol of 325 mg/dl and LDL-C of 241 mg/dl for 12 months with 2 mg of estradiol valerate. The mean LDL-C level was reduced by 22 percent, but one woman's LDL-C level declined by 128 mg/dl. The LDL-C levels dropped within three months and there was a significant correlation between the pretreatment levels of LDL-C and the decrease in LDL-C, in that those individuals with the highest levels responded best. High-density lipoprotein cholesterol levels rose 21 percent after six months; interestingly, those women who had the lowest pretreatment levels responded best to treatment. Conversely, all but one of the non-responders initially had higher than average HDL-C levels (greater than 62 mg/dl).

Estrogen has also been reported to correct the lipid levels in patients, men and women, who have Type III hypercholesterolemia;[31] this is a familial disorder, also known as *broad beta disease*, characterized by the accumulation of intermediate-density lipoproteins and by both high cholesterol and high TG. Classically, patients with this condition have levels of cholesterol and TG that are both in the range of 300-500 mg/dl. In these patients, whose very low-density lipoprotein remnant removal capacity is impaired, estrogen appears to promote remnant removal. While lipid profiles of some patients showed only an improvement in cholesterol and TG levels, others were completely corrected. Further, estrogen appeared to work synergistically with clofibrate, a drug used to treat the disorder.

Despite these benefits, estrogen has a limited role in the treatment of Type III hyperlipidemia. Given the usual positive effects of diet and gemfibrozil, estrogen is rarely needed. The doses of estrogen used in the study described were 1 µg/kg body weight per day of ethinyl estradiol, which approximates the estrogen content in higher dose OCs (50 µg to 100 µg). Nevertheless, in the occasional female patient, the therapeutic benefits of estrogen may outweigh the associated risks of hyperlysoproteinemia.

LIPID RESPONSES TO ESTROGEN/PROGESTOGEN REGIMENS

Notably, the data presented in the previous section of this chapter refer to the lipid changes and to their cardiovascular risk reduction due to estrogen administered alone, i.e., unopposed by a progestogen. However, the standard of practice today is to oppose estrogen with a progestogen to prevent endometrial cancer[32] in those women who have a uterus. (Women who do not have a uterus should be prescribed unopposed estrogen.) As with OCs, the resulting lipid profiles from combined regimens reflects the contribution of both hormones.[27-29,33]

In general, all regimens, whether involving cyclic or continuous administration of progestogen, allow an 11 percent to 21 percent reduction in LDL-C levels. Reported levels of HDL-C, however, have been quite variable and the reason for this discrepancy between studies is unclear.[33] There is now a report of the first cross-sectional study comparing the lipids of women using unopposed estrogen to those of women using the combined hormone regimen. Women who reported using estrogen plus progestogen replacement therapy for more than three years, had HDL-C levels that were equal to those levels of women using unopposed estrogen and 11 percent above the levels of women not using estrogen.[34] The reduction in LDL-C levels below levels of non-users was also similar between the two groups (10 percent to 14 percent).

RECOMMENDATIONS FOR POSTMENOPAUSAL HORMONE USE

While estrogen replacement therapy has not yet been approved by the FDA for preventing cardiovascular disease, it is clear that replacement affords significant beneficial changes in cholesterol levels, subfractions and apolipoproteins. Commonly with any regimen currently prescribed, LDL-C levels can be reduced 10 percent to 20 percent, which has been shown at least in men to translate into a 20 percent to 40 percent reduction in risk of cardiovascular disease.[35] More importantly for women, HDL-C and its subfraction HDL_2 are increased. HDL levels may be more significant in women than in men and a 10 mg change in HDL-C correlates with a 30 percent to 47 percent reduction in risk of cardiovascular disease according to the Framingham and Lipid Research Clinic data.[3] Further, there are angiographic data that support the concept that women who take estrogen are less likely to have significant atherosclerosis, defined as greater than 70 percent stenosis.[36] Thus, it does not seem premature to prescribe postmenopausal estrogen replacement for women who have hypercholesterolemia and, considering the substantial epidemiological data in support of cardiovascular risk reduction from hormone replacement, it would appear that, unless there is a contraindication to hormonal replacement, most postmenopausal women will benefit from estrogen replacement therapy.

REFERENCES

1. Lerner DJ, Kannel WB. Patterns of coronary heart disease morbidity and mortality in the sexes: a 26-year follow-up of the Framingham population. Am Heart J. 1986;111:383-390.

2. Castelli WP, Garrison RJ, Wilson PWF, et al. Incidence of coronary heart disease and lipoprotein cholesterol levels. JAMA. 1986;256:2835-2838.

3. Gordon DJ, Probstfield JL, Garrison RJ, et al. High-density lipoprotein cholesterol and cardiovascular disease. Circulation. 1989;79:8-15.

4. Castelli WP. The triglyceride issue: a view from Framingham. Am Heart J. 1986;112:432-437.

5. Kannel WB. Metabolic risk factors for coronary heart disease in women: perspective from the Framingham Study. Am Heart J. 1987;114:413-419.

6. Clarkson TB, Adams MR, Kaplan JR, et al. From menarche to menopause: coronary artery atherosclerosis and protection in cynomolgus monkey. Am J Obstet Gynecol. 1989;160:1280-1285.

7. Chetkowski RJ, Meldrum DR, Steingold KA, et al. Biologic effects of transdermal estradiol. N Engl J Med. 1986;314:1615-1620.

8. Stanczyk FZ, Shoupe D, Nunez V, et al. A randomized comparison of non-oral estradiol delivery in postmenopausal women. Am J Obstet Gynecol. 1988;159:1540-1546.

9. Runnebaum B, Rabe T. New progestogens in oral contraceptives. Am J Obstet Gynecol. 1987;157:1059-1063.

10. Lipson A, Stoy DB, LaRosa JC, et al. Progestins and oral contraceptive-induced lipoprotein changes: a prospective study. Contraception. 1986;34:121-134.

11. Burkman RT, Robinson JC, Druszon-Moran D, et al. Lipid and lipoprotein changes associated with oral contraceptive use: a randomized clinical trial. Obstet Gynecol. 1988;71:33-38.

12. Notelovitz M, Feldman EB, Gillespy M, et al. Lipid and lipoprotein changes in women taking low-dose, triphasic oral contraceptives: a controlled, comparative, 12 months clinical trial. Am J Obstet Gynecol. 1989;160:1269-1280.

13. Lussier-Cacan S, Nestruck AC, Arslanian H, et al. Influence of a triphasic oral contraceptive preparation on plasma lipids and lipoproteins. Fertil Steril. 1990;53:28-34.

14. Dash DC, Das S, Nanda U, et al. Serum lipid profile in women using levonorgestrel contraceptive implant, Norplant®. Contraception. 1988;37:371-382.

15. Singh K, Viegas OAC, Ratnam SS. A three-year evaluation of metabolic changes in Singaporean Norplant acceptors. Advances in Contraception. 1990;6:11-21.

16. Further analysis of mortality in oral contraceptive users. Royal College of General Practitioners' Oral Contraception Study. Lancet. 1981;1:541-546.

17. Porter JB, Hunter JR, Jick H, et al. Oral Contraceptives and non-fatal vascular disease. Obstet Gynecol. 1985;66:1-4.

18. Stampfer MF, Willett WC, Colditz GA, et al. A prospective study of past use of oral contraceptive agents and risk of cardiovascular diseases. N Engl J Med. 1988;319:1313-1317.

19. Slone D, Shapiro S, Kaufman DW, et al. Risk of myocardial infarction in relation to current and discontinued use of oral contraceptives. N Engl J Med. 1981;305:420-424.

20. Croft P, Hannaford PC. Risk factors for acute myocardial infarction in women: evidence from the Royal College of General Practitioners' Oral Contraception Study. Br Med J. 1989;298:165-169.

21. Glueck CJ, Scheel D, Fishback J, et al. Estrogen-induced pancreatitis in patients with previously covert familial Type V hyperlipoproteinemia. Metabolism. 1972;21:657-666.

22. Davidoff F, Tishler S, Rosoff C. Marked hyperlipidemia and pancreatitis associated with oral contraceptive therapy. N Engl J Med. 1973;289:552-555.

23. Bush TL, Barrett-Connor E, Cowan LD, et al. Cardiovascular mortality and non-contraceptive use of estrogen in women: results from the Lipid Research Clinic Program Followup Study. Circulation. 1987;75:1102-1109.

24. Knopp RH. Cardiovascular effects of endogenous and exogenous sex hormones over a women's lifetime. Am J Obstet Gynecol. 1988;158:1630-1643.

25. Wahl P, Walden C, Knopp R, et al. Effect of estrogen/progestogen potency on lipid/lipoprotein cholesterol. N Eng J Med. 1983;308:862-867.

26. Bush TL, Miller VT. Effects of pharmacologic agents used during the menopause. In: Mishell DR, Jr., ed. Menopause: Physiology and Pharmacology. New York, NY: Year Book Medical Publishers, Inc; 1987;197-208.

27. Miller VT, Muesing RA, LaRosa JC, et al. Effects of conjugated estrogen with and without three different progestogens on lipoproteins, high-density lipoprotein subfractions and apoprotein-AI. Obstet Gynecol. 1991;77:235-240.

28. Sonnendecker EWW, Polakow ES, Spinnler Benade AG, et al. Serum lipoprotein effects of conjugated estrogen and sequential conjugated estrogen-medrogestrone regimen in hysterectomized postmenopausal women. Obstet Gynecol. 1989;160:1128-1134.

29. Sherwin BB, Gelfand MM. A prospective one-year study of estrogen and progestin in postmenopausal women: effects on clinical symptoms and lipoprotein lipids. Am J Obstet Gynecol. 1989;73:159-166.

30. Tikkanen MJ, Kuusi T, Vartianinen E, et al. Treatment of postmenopausal hypercholesterolemia with estradiol. Acta Obstet Gynecol Scand Suppl. 1979;88:83-88.

31. Kushwaha RS, Hazzard WR, Gagne C, et al. Type III hyperlipoproteinemia: paradoxical hypolipidemic response to estrogen. Ann Intern Med. 1977;87:517-525.

32. Estrogen Replacement Therapy. ACOG Technical Bulletin; 1986:93.

33. Miller VT. Dyslipoproteinemia in women: special considerations. In: LaRosa JC, ed. Lipid Disorders. Philadelphia, Pa: WB Saunders Co; 1990;19:381-395.

34. Barrett-Connor E, Wingard DL, Crigui MH. Postmenopausal estrogen use and heart disease risk factors in the 1990's. JAMA. 1989;261:2095-2100.

35. The Lipid Research Clinics Coronary Primary Prevention Trial Results II. The relationship of reduction in incidence of coronary heart disease to cholesterol lowering. Lipid Research Clinics Program. JAMA. 1984;251:265-374.

36. Sullivan JM, Zwaag RV, Lemp GF, et al. Postmenopausal estrogen use and coronary atherosclerosis. Ann Intern Med. 1988;108:358-363.

CHAPTER 11

Ensuring Compliance to Dietary and Drug Regimens

Diane B. Stoy, R.N., M.A.
Washington, D.C.

INTRODUCTION

The development and publication of the National Cholesterol Education Program (NCEP) guidelines for cholesterol treatment brings an enormous challenge for physicians. In the years ahead, millions of patients will begin the first step of cholesterol treatment with a low-fat, low-cholesterol diet. And, while the dietary treatment will be sufficient for the majority of patients, there will be millions who will need cholesterol-lowering drugs to lower their blood cholesterol level and their risk of heart disease. The long-term success of diet and drug therapy depends, of course, on how well patients comply with their treatment regimens - not just for a week or two - but for a lifetime. Given the very realistic limitations on time and resources, physicians often wonder how to best help patients "stick with it."

The challenge of ensuring compliance is really a *bad news/good news story.* The *bad news* is that ensuring compliance is difficult and time-consuming work because changing behavior is a complex process. Also, maintaining those new behaviors for prolonged periods of time requires some strategic planning, lots of effort, motivation and plenty of cheerleading.

The *good news* is that practitioners can draw upon the rich body of research and clinical experience in the compliance area. This chapter reviews this research and clinical experience and translates it into a compendium of practical guidelines that can guide physicians to be more effective when counseling patients about complying with a heart-healthy diet and cholesterol-lowering medication.

GENERAL FACTORS THAT INFLUENCE COMPLIANCE

In 1690, John Locke, in his *Essay Concerning Human Understanding,* said that "good and evil, reward and punishment, are the only motives to a rational creature: these are the spur and reins whereby all mankind are set on work and guided."[1] Locke's theory is relevant to compliance because we know that a patient's decision to make a change in any health habit such as eating or taking medication will be guided by perceptions of this good vs. evil, or reward vs. punishment, concept as it relates to disease.

There are, of course, many factors which can influence a patient's compliance to a medical regimen. Key factors among these include the perspectives of the patient, patient characteristics, the patient-physician relationship, and the characteristics of the medical regimen itself.

PATIENT PERSPECTIVES

The Health Belief Model

The association between what the patient believes and willingness to follow treatment plans is well documented in the literature.[2] Although there are many models for identifying the beliefs that are involved in health-related decisions,[3] most models have incorporated the basic tenets of the "health belief model."

Initially developed for an evaluation of compliance with preventive health recommendations such as immunizations,[4-7] the *health belief model* suggests that a patient's compliance to a treatment regimen is influenced by their belief about their personal susceptibility to a particular disease, the severity of their disease, and their perception of the benefits and barriers that result from the recommended action, such as changing their diet or taking a medication.[2]

Compliance experts have long debated the strengths and weaknesses of the *health belief model*. Some critics charge that the model fails to include factors such as failure to behave consistently with one's beliefs or the role of fear arousal on health behavior.[8] Others point out that there have been studies which have not supported the model's hypothesis.[9] Nevertheless, the *health belief model*, which has been revised to include drug compliance,[10-12] is a standard of reference in any discussion of compliance.

In cholesterol counseling, the *health belief model* is addressed by presenting the objective data about the cholesterol-heart disease connection, and then relating it to the individual patient's risk of heart disease, as well as the proven benefits of lowering elevated blood cholesterol with diet and drug therapy, and the fact that such therapy has proven successful with large numbers of patients.

Other Models

Another perspective involves the concept of *self-efficacy*.[13] This view suggests that the ability of a patient to comply has a more practical base. In order to make a successful change in behavior, patients need to believe that they are capable of making the change, i.e., switching to a healthier diet, and that the change can be accomplished with a reasonable amount of effort. Another model of patient behavior, *decision analysis*, suggests that patients consider not only the critical trade-offs between benefit and risk, but that they also consider issues related to the quantity and quality of life.[14,15] Both of these perspectives suggest that, when confronted with directives to change eating patterns and take medication, the patient wonders, *"Can I do this? What kind of effort will it require? How will I feel? What will this do to my everyday life?"*

To answer such questions through counseling requires teaching the patient that a heart-healthy diet is *not* synonymous with deprivation and that cholesterol-lowering medications are generally well-tolerated and successfully integrated into the lives of busy individuals. Counseling must include, of course, giving patients the information that will empower them to select and prepare heart-healthy foods or to successfully build medication-taking into their daily routine. Setting realistic goals, as practitioners well know, is critical to patient success.

Social influence is another variable that affects patient compliance. Numerous reports in the literature have lead to the general hypothesis that the *significant others in a patient's life influence the patient's willingness and success in behavior change.*[16-20] In the real life setting this means that the compliance of a patient can be either positively or negatively influenced by family, co-workers, media spokespersons or, in fact, any individual considered a "significant other" by the patient. In particular, there is general agreement among clinicians and researchers that successful, long-term behavioral change is dependent upon an environment that supports the change,[16,21] and that significant others are an influential part of that environment. The obvious corollary in counseling, of course, is that the support of family members and significant others should be enlisted and that these individuals should be, whenever possible, involved in educational sessions such as meal planning, food preparation or medication instructions.

PATIENT CHARACTERISTICS

There is continuing controversy about the relationship of individual patient characteristics and the patient's ability to comply with a medical regimen. A review of the compliance literature conducted in 1970 found that when examined separately, demographic variables such as age, sex, socioeconomic status, education, religion, marital status and race were not predictive of compliance with medical recommendations.[22] A subsequent review article, which analyzed over 185 original research reports, as well as reports by other reviewers, have also found no consistent relationship between compliance and demographic variables.[11,23,24]

While a recent study of compliance found that compliance problems occurred in all study populations,[25] there have been other reports that noncompliance increases with extremes of age, lower socioeconomic status, less education and language barriers between the physician and the patient.[26]

These types of conflicting findings suggest that, although there may not be a proven association, any individual patient characteristic may have potential impact on the patient's ability and willingness to comply with a long-term regimen such as dietary and drug treatment of hypercholesterolemia. Every individual patient and his/her ability to comply must be assessed from this pragmatic point of view. As one family physician who studied compliance so aptly said, "Every patient is a potential defaulter; compliance can never be assumed."[27]

PATIENT-PHYSICIAN RELATIONSHIP

While there are conflicting data on the association between demographic variables and compliance, there seems to be little doubt in the literature about the strong influence of the doctor-patient relationship on compliance. Compliance has been reported to be greater when patients feel that their expectations of response to therapy prescribed by the physician have been fulfilled;[11] the physician elicits and respects the patient's concerns;[28] the physician provides responsive information about the patient's condition and progress;[29] and the physician also offers sincere concern and sympathy for the patient.[30]

TABLE I. Factors related to patient diet and/or drug therapy compliance success

- Realistic goals
- Perceived versus fulfilled expectations[11]
- Physician sympathy, respect and concern[28,30]
- Physician feedback[29]

Conversely, patients have been found to be less likely to comply if they feel they are not held in adequate esteem by their physician,[31] if their physician seeks information from them without feedback about the rationale of the inquiry,[32] if tension emerges during the interaction between the patient and physician and is not resolved,[32] and if the physician was not behaving in a "friendly" manner.[33]

Beyond these obvious essentials the patient-physician relationship lies a more subtle and critical variable relevant to long-term preventive health care — the spirit of partnership between the physician and patient. Historically, as one reviewer reminds us, physicians were active and the patients were passive, i.e., the physicians prescribed a treatment and the patient followed.[34]

However, the more contemporary view is that preventive health measures are encouraged and supported through mutual participation between patients and their physicians. In a study of the treatment of hypertensive patients, those who were treated as "active" participants in the treatment showed higher compliance with medical advice.[35] Results of another study suggest that physicians could increase compliance to antihypertensive therapy by not only being compassionate and communicative, but also by sharing the responsibility for treatment with the patient in a spirit of mutual participation.[36] The corollary of these perspectives in cholesterol counseling is similar to that in counseling hypertensive patients. To reduce the risk of disease, the physician and patient must work together as partners. Each plays a distinct role, although the success of treatment depends on both.

TABLE II. **Factors implicated in patient noncompliance with diet and/or drug therapy**

- Perception of inadequate esteem by physician
- Inadequate support system by "significant others"
- Lack of physician feedback regarding effects of therapy
- Unresolved patient-physician tension

CHARACTERISTICS OF THE MEDICAL REGIMEN

In addition to psychosocial factors, compliance is also influenced by specific features of the medical regimen itself. Reviews in the literature[22,26,37-39] have shown that there are five major considerations for physicians:

- *Complexity of the regimen.* Poor compliance appears to increase with the complexity of the regimen. More difficulty with compliance is seen in patients who receive prescriptions for multiple medications or who are given more than one medical recommendation to follow.

- *Frequency of dosing.* Frequent dose regimens have also been associated with lower levels of compliance. Three- and four-times-a-day dosing patterns have been associated with lower compliance because patients omit one or more doses. This association was confirmed in a recent study which found that compliance rates fell from 87 percent on a once-a-day regimen to 81 percent with twice daily, 77 percent with three-times-a-day, and 39 percent with four-times-a-day.[38]

- *Alteration of the patient's life style.* Compliance is more difficult with regimens that require major changes in the patient's life style. Conversely, compliance can be enhanced by incorporating new regimens into the patient's existing routine.

- *Presence of side effects.* Compliance is likely to be poor with medical regimens that produce adverse effects. This point is particularly relevant to the care of asymptomatic patients with hypercholesterolemia.

- *Length of treatment.* Not surprisingly, compliance generally tends to decrease over the length of treatment. This factor may well be the single and most difficult compliance challenge facing patients and physicians.

In any event, the fact that there are so many different perspectives on compliance reaffirms the concept that the process of simply changing behavior and then "sticking with it" is not simple at all. Indeed, compliance is influenced by a mosaic of psychosocial, cultural and situational factors – which are complicated, which change over the course of time, and which present physicians and patients with continuing challenges as they work together to reduce the patient's risk of heart disease.

HELPING PATIENTS EAT HEALTHIER

Changing any behavior is a process that involves a series of actions such as learning new skills, deciding about whether to use the new skills, and then figuring out how to incorporate the new skills into the routine of daily life.[40,41] These changes, as previously discussed, are influenced by a variety of factors ranging from the degree of family support for an individual to the work schedule and cultural background of the individual.

The factors that influence how successful individuals are at making dietary changes were the focus of a recent study. Researchers found that individuals were more likely to make dietary changes if they believed that diet-related diseases were severe, that they were personally vulnerable to disease, that changing eating habits would reduce that vulnerability, and that they were confident in their ability to make the dietary changes. Social influence factors were also important in distinguishing dietary "changers" from "non-changers."[42]

Therefore, the practitioner should take into consideration that just one directive for dietary change, i.e., reducing the consumption of saturated fat, involves a constellation of skills and activities. These include learning about the sources of saturated fat in the diet, developing the assertiveness skills needed to "say no" to fatty foods offered by friends who expect continued preferences for foods, time management and decision-making skills needed for finding and selecting healthier foods, and experimenting with and adjusting to "new" foods.[43]

The following are some suggestions physicians can use in helping patients succeed at switching to and then sticking with a healthier diet:

- *Begin with a discussion of the patient's risk.* Since there is evidence that an increased personal conviction of risk is related to good compliance, be sure to begin the counseling session with a review of the patient's cholesterol level and what that level means in terms of the patient's *personal* risk of cardiovascular disease.

- *Emphasize the beneficial outcomes of the heart-healthy diet.* Since many patients who begin the diet worry about "giving up" favorite foods, being hungry on the healthier diet, or finding healthy food to be bland or unsatisfying, it's important to emphasize that a healthy diet is tasty and appealing, that the diet is good for the whole family, and that many people lose weight when they decrease the total fat content in their diet. The good news is that most patients with high blood cholesterol will be able to control their cholesterol with diet alone. And, those who will eventually need drug therapy may require less medication if they strictly adhere to their diet.

- *Involve family/significant others whenever possible.* Since food selection and preparation is often shared by family members, it is prudent, whenever possible, to include the family/significant others in counseling sessions involving the diet.

- *Teach patients the basics about food selection and preparation.* Since there are not enough registered dieticians to meet the increased demands for nutrition counseling, physicians and members of the office staff need to be able to teach the basics about selecting and preparing health foods. Excellent teaching materials are now available from both the American Heart Association and the NCEP. Key issues covered in these teaching materials include identification of the difference between saturated fat and dietary cholesterol as well as the types of fat found in foods, interpretation of food labels, preparation of food in a "healthy" manner and control of portion sizes.

- *Assess the patient's current diet.* Asking the patient to keep a three-day record of food intake is a helpful way to increase the patient's awareness of eating habits and to provide information on those eating patterns which will need to be changed.

- *Set specific and realistic goals with the patient.* After reviewing the patient's food record, it's helpful to suggest small increments of change rather than major changes. Be careful to avoid directions that are too general, such as "cutting down on meat and dairy products." Instead, suggest small, more specific changes. Limited changes are easier to adjust to, and can be achieved more successfully than changes of greater magnitude. For example, it is better to suggest an initial change in milk from whole milk (which is about four percent fat) to milk with two percent fat rather than to suggest a radical change from whole milk to skim milk. First, suggest the change to milk with two percent fat and then gradually work downward to milk with one percent fat content and then to skim milk. Or, with a patient who eats in fast food restaurants frequently, you might suggest a healthier selection from the fast food menu along with a decrease in the number of, times the patient eats in fast food restaurants each week, rather than flatly suggesting that the patient "stop eating fast food."

- *Provide feedback and plenty of positive reinforcement for dietary changes.* The use of a chart showing the sequential results of cholesterol testing can be an effective method for providing feedback to the patient and that important "pat-on-the back" for effort. Be careful to avoid well-meaning but authoritative, non-reinforcing messages. Remember that making dietary changes is difficult and takes time, and that many small changes add up over a period of time.

- *Be realistic.* With most patients, dietary changes and weight loss are best accomplished in small increments over long periods of time. Don't expect speedy changes or perfection.

- *Prepare patients for the "what-ifs."* Most motivated patients do well with a new diet while at home, but have difficulty sticking with the diet during special circumstances, i.e., eating out, celebrating, traveling, etc. It's important to remind patients that their overall eating pattern is what matters — not the occasional indiscretion at a birthday party or business meeting. Again, there are many helpful educational materials available that can assist patients in making healthy eating choices when not at home. These educational materials provide helpful suggestions about making the best food selection when the available menu offers limited heart-healthy choices.

- *During long-term follow-up, don't forget to review the patient's diet compliance.* As the "new" diet becomes routine, the patient's compliance to the diet should be reviewed by the physician on a regular basis. The physician should continue to reinforce the benefits of eating healthier food, in conjunction with a review of the patient's cholesterol level, weight and overall risk status.

MEDICATION COMPLIANCE

Although dietary intervention will be sufficient for most patients with elevated blood cholesterol levels, there will still be millions of patients who require drug therapy to reduce blood cholesterol levels. Cholesterol intervention for such patients means not only changing their eating habits, but also building medication-taking into their daily schedule for a lifetime. Physicians in all areas of practice are, of course, well acquainted with the fact that writing a prescription in no way ensures that a patient will take the medication as prescribed, and that compliance to medication is often far less than ideal.

Reviews in the literature support longstanding clinical impressions that compliance to medications has a high rate of patient default. Although these data are drawn from many types of settings, with a variety of medications and operational definitions of compliance, they nevertheless present a discouraging picture about the scope of the compliance problem.

Results of reviews published in the early 1970s estimated that the percentage of noncompliance to drug regimens ranged from 4 percent to 92 percent.[38] Another reviewer estimated that complete failure to take medication often occurred in one fourth to one half of all outpatients.[26]

The most recent experience with the treatment of hypertension confirms the rather bleak findings of the 1970s. In a review published in 1984 by Eraker and colleagues,[39] it was estimated that there was an average of 50 percent patient compliance with medication regimens used to treat chronic diseases, while the specific experience with hypertension has shown that "only two thirds of those who remain in care consume enough medication to adequately control their hypertension."[39] And, when the results of the experience by Eraker are compared with similar results of Sackett published in 1966,[44] it is clear that there has been little improvement in medication compliance rates over the last 20 years.

The implications of these data are significant. To succeed with cholesterol intervention, physicians and other health care professionals must develop more successful strategies for helping patients take their medication. In reality, compliance must be given equal time and resources, along with the screening, diagnosis, and prescription of dietary and drug treatment of hypercholesterolemia.

HELPING PATIENTS TAKE CHOLESTEROL-LOWERING MEDICATION AS PRESCRIBED

The following are some practical suggestions that physicians can use to increase patient compliance to cholesterol-lowering medication.

- *Begin with a clear description of the cholesterol-heart disease connection and relate it to your patient's personal risk.* Just as with dietary intervention, patients need to have a clear view of their personal vulnerability to cardiovascular disease before they begin a long-term treatment with medication. This understanding of the increased risk of heart disease caused by lipid abnormalities is particularly important for hypercholesterolemic patients, the majority of whom are asymptomatic, healthy individuals who may not understand the basis for treatment. Without a clear description of risk, healthy patients who feel well have every reason to wonder why they should take a medication that may cause side effects and possibly affect the quality of their life.

- *Be sure to review the sources of cholesterol.* Many patients who become candidates for drug therapy have a natural sense of failure. "I tried so hard on the diet," they say, "Why do I now have to take medication?" A simple explanation of the role of the liver in producing cholesterol can be very beneficial in reinforcing the patient's effort on the diet and to explain that the diet alone will be insufficient for some patients who have an internal production of cholesterol which is genetically too high.

- *Discuss the patient's options for drug therapy.* The NCEP's guidelines for the drug treatment of hypercholesterolemia provide a variety of medication selections based on safety, efficacy and proven ability to reduce cardiovascular risk. Since these guidelines allow for individual physician and patient preferences, it is best to take the time to review all the possible options with the patient. Participative decision-making should be encouraged since the literature suggests that goals originating from the "shoulds" of others are weakened by insufficient personal commitment.[43] That is, a patient will be more motivated if he has been involved in making the decision about the "right" medication(s) for him. Factors which should be included in such a discussion include the physician's clinical experience, clinical trial data, costs, convenience factors and the patient's medical history.

- *After deciding on the drug of choice for the patient, describe the drug's mechanism of action.* Since knowledge of drug function has been shown to be correlated with higher medication compliance,[45] it is important to describe to the patient how the drug works and why certain follow-up procedures are required. For example, patients on lovastatin or any HMG CoA reductive inhibitor will understand the importance of follow-up testing for liver enzymes if they understand that the drug is processed through the liver. And, whenever possible, it is helpful to provide patients with written materials which can be read at a later time.

- *Assess the patient's daily routine.* Since success in taking medication is directly related to building it into the daily routine, physicians need to know some of the basics of the patient's daily routine. A simple form, completed by the patient, can provide the physician with important information about meal and work schedules, exercise routine, leisure time, etc. — all of which are important variables that can influence medication compliance.

- *Tailor the drug regimen to the patient's schedule.* The general rule-of-thumb with medication compliance is that medication-taking should be incorporated into a patient's normal schedule rather than changing the patient's schedule to accommodate the medication. For example, a patient who normally leaves home immediately upon arising in the morning will be most successful with a morning dose taken upon arrival at work, rather than one prescribed upon arising. A patient who eats out frequently after work may be most successful with cholestyramine by taking the dose before leaving the office, rather than waiting until later in the evening. A patient who eats lunch in a restaurant every day may not feel comfortable taking a pill or mixing cholestyramine in a public place. Or, a patient who spends many evenings at meetings or social activities may be more successful taking medication in the morning when a schedule is more predictable. The important thing for practitioners to remember is that what appear to be small details regarding medication scheduling can have a considerable impact on patient compliance.

- *Involve the family/significant others whenever possible.* As previously discussed, the significant others in a patient's life can have positive or negative influences on patient compliance. Involving significant others in counseling sessions can help to assure their understanding of the basis for drug treatment, as well as the expected procedures for follow-up and possible side effects. And, although medication-taking is the patient's responsibility, a supportive significant other can help as a back-up reminder, should the patient forget to take a dose or pack medication for a vacation.

- *Explain what to expect.* In their attempt to gain control and understanding, patients need answers to a variety of practical questions. Generally, these questions involve: (1) the required type and extent of follow-up, such as liver function tests, other blood tests, office visits, etc; (2) the probability and type of anticipated side effects, such as constipation with cholestyramine or flushing with nicotinic acid; and (3) realistic expectations for cholesterol lowering, such as average decrease in LDL-cholesterol after four- to six-weeks of therapy, etc.

- *Graduate the dose of the medication whenever possible.* The 10-year clinical experience in the Coronary Primary Prevention Trial (CPPT) with cholestyramine has shown that a gradual increase in dosage allows patients to successfully adjust to small dosage increases before reaching the maximum dosage.[46] In clinical practice many patients have been declared "treatment failures" on cholestyramine because they were initially prescribed the full dosage, rather than a small dosage that was slowly increased over a period of weeks. The same recommendations apply to nicotinic acid which can cause extreme flushing and headache even at the lower initial doses.[47]

- *Provide written instructions with "what-if's."* Beginning a medication for the remainder of one's life can be an overwhelming experience for some patients who may, in many instances, hear only part of the instructions. Be sure to always send the patient home with a clear set of instructions which review the basics of scheduling and the answer to a series of "what if" questions. These questions, which patients often forget to ask, and which are important for coordinating medication scheduling with daily life, include: What do I do if I miss a dose of medication? Can I make up a missed dose? What is the maximum dose of medication I can take in one day? Can I drink alcohol while I'm taking the medication? Must I take the medication with meals or can I take the medication on an empty stomach? How should I take the medication on the weekends when my sleeping and eating patterns change? Can I take my cholesterol-lowering medication at the same time as other medications?

- *Teach patients about cues or reminders.* It is helpful to teach patients about cues or reminders which can help medication taking become a habit. Keeping the medication visible is one helpful reminder. Keeping it near the alarm clock, coffee pot, bathroom sink or any regular spot at home can be another way to "trigger" memory. Some patients find that a colorful heart-shaped magnet on the refrigerator is a good reminder of both diet and medication. Other individuals prefer to keep a small calendar that can be checked off after taking the medication. And many patients find pill boxes helpful, particularly those that hold a week's supply of pills.

- *Pay attention to side effects when they first occur.* Patients and their physicians should maintain close communication with one another during the early weeks of treatment. In fact, the experience with cholestyramine in the CPPT showed that most side effects *and* dropouts from therapy occurred in the first month of treatment.[46] Patients should be encouraged to report side effects because, as we learned in the CPPT, small changes in scheduling or mixing vehicle can make a significant difference in the symptoms. And, in reality, many patients need an extra dose of reassurance that they will be able to adjust to the medication and that they will be able to take the medication successfully over a long period of time.

- *During follow-up visits, be sure to include a discussion of adherence.* Since the patient's compliance to the medication is directly related to the amount of cholesterol lowering achieved, it is important to discuss compliance at all follow-up visits. It is often helpful to use open-ended inquiries such as "describe your medication routine for me" or "how would you describe those occasions when you miss your medication." If the patient regularly misses medication on the weekends, one might suggest a different medication schedule for Saturday and Sunday. Remember that special times of the year, such as holidays or vacations, as well as times of family crisis, can play havoc with patient's schedules and medication compliance. Such times may require changing the amount or scheduling of daily medication doses.

- *Provide the patient with regular, specific feedback.* Since most patients with hypercholesterolemia are asymptomatic, the only reward that patients receive for strict adherence to diet and medication is the knowledge that their cholesterol level has decreased. Therefore, an excellent form of feedback is a graph that shows both the patient's baseline cholesterol levels and response to treatment. And, of course, such a graph should be accompanied by plenty of positive reinforcement for a job well done.

- *Reinforce the concept of control.* Personal control is one of the most powerful counseling tools in reinforcing long-term adherence to a diet and drug regimen. While individuals cannot change their family history, they can control what they eat and how faithfully they take prescribed medication. The most successful patients are those who translate the challenges of adherence into the challenge of controlling their risk of heart disease. The positive connection between the two can make the patient feel more in control. Feeling in control can be the driving force for patients to "stick with it" day in and day out for a healthier lifetime.

TOWARD THE FUTURE: THE COMPLIANCE CHALLENGE

What is the prognosis for compliance to our collective efforts in reducing heart disease by lowering high blood cholesterol levels? Will the successes and failures in cholesterol intervention parallel that of hypertension treatment? Is it possible to do better? Can the consciousness about cholesterol be translated into the type of sustained behavioral change that can make a real difference in reducing the incidence of heart disease?

The answers are uncertain. On the positive side, patients who are beginning cholesterol treatment do so in a social environment which has become increasingly sensitive to cholesterol issues. Surveys show that consumers believe that reducing cholesterol will have an important effect on heart disease. This consumer consciousness is making an impact in doctors' offices, in restaurants, on grocery shelves and in Congress. Individuals with hypercholesterolemia and their physicians can now benefit from the NCEP. Through the efforts of the NCEP we now have standards for the laboratory measurement of cholesterol as well as guidelines for the detection and treatment of elevated blood cholesterol levels in adults and children.

Nevertheless, all the attention paid to cholesterol screening and initiating treatment of hypercholesterolemia is moot if there is limited success at lowering cholesterol *and* keeping it down. And, keeping cholesterol levels down is only accomplished by helping patients "stick with it," i.e., following the heart-healthy diet and taking their medication regularly — which as this chapter illustrates, is not an easy task.

What can be done to increase patient success with cholesterol-lowering treatment? First, practitioners must make compliance counseling an integral part of every office visit. Second, an environment must be created that supports healthy eating and adherence to a cholesterol-lowering regimen. Finally, more research must be conducted in order to better understand the fascinating but elusive area of patient compliance.

REFERENCES

1. Bartlett J. Familiar Quotations. Boston, Ma: Little Brown and Co.;1989:307.
2. Becker MH. The Health Belief Model and Personal Health Behavior. Thorofare, NJ: Charles B. Slack; 1974.
3. Cummings KM, Becker MH, Maile MC. Bringing the models together: an empirical approach to combining variables used to explain health actions. J Behav Med. 1980;3:123-145.
4. Rosenstock IM. Why people use health services. Milbank Mem Fund Q. 1966;44:94-124.
5. Becker MH. The health belief model and illness behavior. Health Educ Monogr. 1974;2:409-419.
6. Kirscht JP. The health belief model and illness behavior. Health Educ Monogr. 1974;2:387-408.
7. Becker MH, Brachman RH, Kirscht JP. A new approach to explaining sick-role behavior in low-income populations. Am J Public Health. 1974;64:205-216.
8. Levanthal H, Meyer D, Gutmann M. The role of theory in the study of compliance to high blood pressure regimens. In: Haynes RB, Mattson ME, Engebretson TO, eds. Patient Compliance to Prescribed Antihypertensive Medication Regimens. Washington, DC: National Heart, Lung and Blood Institute; 1980:9-15. U.S. Department of Health and Human Services publication NIH 81-2102.
9. Kirscht JP, Haefner DP, Kegeles SS, et al. A national study of health beliefs. J Health Hum Behav. 1966;7:248-254.
10. Becker MH, Drachman RH, Kirscht JP. Predicting mothers compliance with pediatric medical regimens. J Pediatr. 1972;81:843-854.
11. Becker MH, Maiman LA. Sociobehavioral determinants of compliance with health and medical care recommendations. Med Care. 1977;15(suppl 5):27-46.
12. Becker MH, Haefner DP, Kasl SY, et al. Selected psychosocial models and correlates of individual health behaviors. Med Care. 1977;15(suppl 5):27-46.
13. Bandura A. Self-efficacy: Toward a unifying theory of behavior change. Psychological Review. 1977;84:191-215.

14. Weinstein MC, Fineberg HY, eds. Clinical Decision Analysis. Philadelphia, Pa: WB Saunders Co; 1980.
15. McNeil BJ, Keller E, Adelstein SJ. Primer on certain elements of medical decision making. N Engl J Med. 1975;293:211-215.
16. Zimmerman RS, Connor C. Health promotion in context: the effects of significant others on health behavior changes. Health Educ Q. 1989;16:57-75.
17. Ajzen I, Fishbein M. Understanding Attitudes and Predicting Social Behavior. Englewood Cliffs, NJ: Prentice-Hall; 1980.
18. Osterweis N, Bush P, Zucherman A. Family context as a predictor of individual medicine use. Soc Sci and Med. 1979;13:287-291.
19. Earp JC, Ory MG, Strogatz DS. The effects of family involvement and practitioner home visits on the control of hypertension. Am J Public Health. 1982;72:1146-1154.
20. Morisky DE, DeMuth NM, Field-Fass M, et al. Evaluation of family health education to build social support for long-term control of high blood pressure. Health Educ Q. 1985;12:35-50.
21. Israel BA, McLeroy KR. Social networks and social support: implications for health education. Health Educ Q. 1985;12(special issue):1-112.
22. Marston MU. Compliance with medical regimens: a review of the literature. Nurs Res. 1970;19:312-322.
23. Haynes RB. A critical review of the determinants of patient compliance with therapeutic regimens. In: Sacket DL, Haynes RB, eds. Compliance with Therapeutic Regimens. Baltimore, Md: Johns Hopkins University Press; 1976:26-39.
24. Kasl SV. Socio-psychological characteristics associated with behavior which reduce cardiovascular risk. In: Enelow AJ, Henderson JB, eds. Applying Behavioral Science to Cardiovascular Risk. New York, NY: American Heart Association; 1975.
25. Crammer JA, Collins JF, Mattson RH. Can categorization of patient background probels be used to determine early termination in a clinical trial? Controlled Clin Trials. 1988;9:47-63.
26. Blackwell B. Drug therapy: patient compliance. N Engl J Med. 1973;289:249-253.
27. Porter AMW. Drug defaulting in a general practice. Br Med J. 1969;1:218-222.
28. Becker MH, Green LW. A family approach to compliance with medical treatment: a selective review of the literature. Int J Health Educ. 1975;18:173-182.
29. Francis V, Korsch BM, Morris MJ. Gaps in doctor-patient communication: patients response to medical advice. N Engl J Med. 1969;280:535-550.
30. Waitzkin H, Stowkle JB. The communication of information about illness. Adv Psychosom Med. 1972;8:180-215.
31. Elling R. Patient participation in a pediatric program. J Health Human Behav. 1960;1:183.
32. Davis N. Variations in patient compliance with doctors advice: an empirical analysis of patterns of communication. Am J Public Health. 1968;58:274.
33. Korsch B, et al. Gaps in doctor/patient communication I. Doctor/patient interaction and patient satisfaction. Pediatrics. 1968;42:855.
34. Rosenstock IM. Patient-physician communications and adherence. In: Pankey GA, Kalish GH, eds. Outpatient Antimicrobial Therapy: Recent Advances. Clifton, NJ: Health Care Communications, Inc.; 1989:18.
35. Schulman BA. Active patient orientation and outcomes in hypertensive treatment: application of a socio-organizational perspective. Med Care. 1979;17:267-280.
36. Coleman VR. Physicians behavior and compliance. J Hypertens. 1985;3(suppl 1):69-71.

37. Matthews D, Hingson R. Improving patient compliance: a guide for physicians. Med Clin North Am. 1977;61:879-889.

38. Cramer JA, Mattson RH, Prevey ML, et al. How often is medication taken as prescribed? JAMA. 1989;267:3273-3277.

39. Eraker SA, Kirscht JP, Becker MH. Understanding and improving patient compliance. Ann Intern Med. 1984;100:258-268.

40. Smickilas-Wright H, Krondl MM. Dietary counseling and the behavioral sciences. J Can Diet Assoc. 1974;40:99.

41. Zifferblatt SM, Wilbur CS. Dietary counseling: some realistic expectations and guidelines. J Am Diet Assoc. 1977;70:591.

42. Contento IR, Murphy BM. Psychosocial factors differentiating people who reported making desirable changes in their diets from those who did not. J Nutr Educ. 1990;22:6-13.

43. Berry MW, Banish SJ, Rinke W, et al. Worksite health promotion: the effects of a goal-setting program on nutrition-related behaviors. J Amer Diet Assoc. 1989;89:914.

44. Sackett DL. The magnitude of compliance and noncompliance. In: Sackett DL, Haynes RB, eds. Compliance with Therapeutic Regimens. Baltimore, Md: Johns Hopkins University Press; 1966:8-25.

45. Hulka BS, Cassal JC, Kupper LL, et al. Communication, compliance, and concordance between physicians and patients with prescribed medications. Am J Public Health. 1976;66:847-853.

46. Dunbar JM. Predictors of patient adherence: patient characteristics. In: Shumaker A, Schron ED, Ockene JK, eds. The Handbook of Health Behavior Changes. New York, NY: Springer; 1980:348-360.

47. Stoy, DB. Controlling cholesterol with drugs. Am J Nurs. 1989;89:1631-1634.